Mr Jor

The Man Who Knew Too Much

The Life and Death of Gareth Jones

Martin Shipton

Jones (front centre) with the Trinity Madrigal Society at the London Coliseum, circa 1927. (© The Gareth Vaughan Jones Estate)

Mr Jones

The Man Who Knew Too Much

The Life and Death of Gareth Jones

Martin Shipton

welsh academic press

Cardiff

Published in Wales by Welsh Academic Press, an imprint of

Ashley Drake Publishing Ltd
PO Box 733
Cardiff
CF14 7ZY

www.welsh-academic-press.wales

First Impression – 2022

ISBN
Paperback: 978-1-86057-143-5
Ebook: 978-1-86057-156-5

British Library Cataloguing-in-Publication Data.
A CIP catalogue for this book is available from the British Library.

Typeset by Prepress Plus, India (www.prepressplus.in)
Cover design by Welsh Books Council, Aberystwyth, Wales

Contents

For my father Roy Shipton 1927-2021.

A fine son of Pembrokeshire who when I was a primary schoolboy in London taught me the meaning of the phrase 'Cymru am byth'.

Introduction

It's time that Gareth Jones was elevated to the status of authentic Welsh hero that he undoubtedly deserves.

Long recognised in Ukraine for his exposure of the man-made famine known as the *Holodomor* that killed millions of the nation's citizens in the early 1930s, it took 85 years after his shocking murder on the eve of his 30th birthday in 1935 for him to become better known in his own country thanks to the release of a film.

Now, with heightened interest in Ukraine following the Russian invasion in February 2022 and the war that followed, growing attention is being given to the historic dynamic between the two countries that helps explain the circumstances in which so many died.

Having worked on this biography for the best part of three years, I've got to know him reasonably well, thanks to a large archive of his correspondence held by the National Library of Wales at Aberystwyth and a database of his articles uploaded to a website by two devoted members of his family – his niece Margaret Siriol Colley and her son Nigel Colley, both now sadly deceased.

Jones was a frequent traveller overseas from his teenage years and would write home to his parents extremely frequently from wherever he was, often several times a week. The original notebooks he used to record his observations when speaking to people in Russia and Ukraine who had been affected by the *Holodomor* are also available. There is therefore an extensive record of Jones' written output in three forms – his published articles, his notebooks and his private correspondence.

We can tell from his articles and notebooks that he was an admirable and diligent seeker after the truth, but it is the letters he wrote to close family members that give the greatest insight into his personality. They provide powerful testimony of his self-confidence, his gregariousness, his inexhaustible exuberance, his erudition, his love of Wales and the Welsh language and his tendency to gravitate towards people from different countries and with highly-placed connections, whose views he would seek on everything. They also show him to be an intellectually inquisitive livewire as well as a character happy to throw himself into the social side of life. As well as exposing one of the neglected tragedies of the 20th Century, he was a raconteur who had a brilliant ability to entertain his audience.

As one of his successors at the *Western Mail*, I can imagine him as a congenial colleague in the newsroom who would always be coming and going, but would equally have time to talk to the youngest and least experienced member of staff. He'd left the paper shortly before embarking on the final tour that cost him his life, but when he died the grief of his ex-colleagues was, by all accounts, overwhelming.

Jones achieved a lot in his short life, working successively for the greatest statesman of the day – David Lloyd George – and for the American founder of public relations, Ivy Lee. His contacts book would have been the envy of any reporter, and through his association with Lloyd George he was able to gain access to the most important politicians of the day in the most significant countries. He also managed to hold his own with the likes of Randolph Hearst, an arrogant newspaper tycoon whose commitment to truth and justice was in no way comparable to his own. Jones' internationalism was admirable at a time when the tendency was for countries to become more isolationist.

The book is primarily a chronological overview, rather than thematic study, but one important theme – concerning anti-Semitism – that emerged during my research deserves, in my view, to be considered in its own right. In addition, the growing global acknowledgement of the role played by Jones in exposing the *Holodomor* in Soviet Ukraine has also sparked accusations from pro-Russian voices that he harboured Nazi sympathies. These are two distinct matters that I have addressed in Chapter 15, which is entitled

INTRODUCTION

'A Flawed Hero? Anti-Semitism and Allegations of Nazi Sympathies'. The exploration of Jones' prejudicial comments concerning Jews is based on private correspondence in which, in a small, but important, number of instances, Jones' references to and attitude towards Jews contain anti-Semitic comments and phrases. For whatever reason, this issue has not been highlighted by earlier researchers, so in this book they are presented to a wider audience for the first time. As I state in Chapter 15, the comments do not suggest that Jones was a conscious anti-Semite, but the fact that, primarily during his student days, he occasionally employed anti-Semitic phraseology when noting his dealings with Jews makes it clear that, even though he recognised and noted it as a negative trait in others, he didn't recognise the inherent anti-Semitism of that time in himself.

I have no doubt that Gareth Jones would have been as appalled as any other right-thinking person by the ultimate fate of the Jews under the Nazi regime. He didn't, of course, live to witness the horror of the Holocaust, or to benefit from the hindsight that so many of his contemporaries reflected upon after the Second World War. In retrospect, we can see the direction of travel that Jones and his generation didn't, but ensuring that we learn from history so that all intolerance and prejudice is challenged, and does not lead to history repeating itself, is a duty we all owe to those who didn't survive.

Regarding the allegations of pro-Nazi sentiments, I suspect that what he witnessed in the Soviet Union led him to focus on the crimes of that state, and that his love of Germany, the close friendships he enjoyed with many Germans (some with clear Nazi sympathies) and his abiding faith in what he saw as the integrity and decency of German culture and society clouded his judgement as to the existential threat to Germany posed by the Nazis. Jones can be accused of naivety, but equating that with support for Nazi ideology is a completely different matter.

There has been much speculation about whether Jones was a British spy, although no evidence has ever emerged that he was. Nevertheless, he was friendly with Sir Bernard Pares, a man with an intelligence background who put him in touch with important contacts when he went travelling. While he may not have been on the payroll, it is highly likely that the secret service would have been interested in what he learnt while travelling abroad. A high proportion of intelligence information, after all, amounts to well-informed briefing, and Jones would have been a very useful contact for the intelligence services to nurture.

The circumstances of Jones' death are unclear and probably always will be. Given the fact that he unwittingly went into a danger zone with one Soviet agent, and that the car he was travelling in was supplied by another, it would be fanciful to believe these were mere coincidences. Stalin's propensity for vengeance had no geographical boundaries.

The purpose of this book is not to lionise Gareth Jones, which is why he is referred to as 'Jones', rather than 'Gareth'. Its purpose is simply to tell Jones' fascinating life story as accurately as possible, through the use of his extensive writings, and to enable more people to understand who he was, what he achieved and to contemplate his, and his generation's, legacy.

Martin Shipton
April 2022

Acknowledgements

Writing a biography of a long-dead person is largely a solitary endeavour. There is no one around who knew the subject personally or even by repute. Yet the help of others is indispensable.

Without the courteous and efficient staff of the National Library of Wales in Aberystwyth, where a substantial Gareth Jones archive is lodged, I would have been lost.

Like anyone who researches the life of Gareth Jones, I am hugely indebted to his niece, Margaret Siriol Colley, and her son Nigel Colley, who between them ensured that the history of their distinguished family member was not lost. Sadly they are both now deceased. Their excellent website *GarethJones.org* contains a huge amount of interesting material, including Gareth Jones' eclectic variety of articles. Margaret Siriol Colley also wrote two books about her uncle – *More Than a Grain of Truth* and *Gareth Jones: A Manchukuo Incident* – which I found invaluable.

Other books that I found helpful were *Gareth Jones: Eyewitness to the Holodomor* and *Gareth Jones:On Assignment in Nazi Germany*, both by Ray Gamache, and *Red Famine: Stalin's War on Ukraine* by Anne Applebaum, which gave me an understanding of the historical background to Gareth Jones' best-known scoop. I am grateful to Naomi Field, the partner of Nigel Colley, who very kindly gave me a copy of the wonderful facsimile edition of Gareth Jones' *1933 Famine Diaries*, as well as a copy of *Gareth Jones: A Manchukuo Incident*.

Louise Walsh has exemplary research skills from which I have benefitted greatly. Once again. I am very grateful to her. I thank Alun Gibbard, an author who has written a book about Gareth Jones in the Welsh language, for a conversation in which he offered me great encouragement.

Mick Antoniw MS has been very supportive of my project and made me realise the extent of the admiration for Gareth Jones in Ukraine. I am also extremely grateful to him for the moving Foreword he has contributed to this book.

Professor Jasmine Donahaye offered me great insights that assisted me greatly with Chapter 15, the most controversial and difficult-to-write section of this book.

My publisher, Ashley Drake, who commissioned me to write this book and waited patiently as I struggled, for various reasons, to complete the manuscript, not least a serious illness. He has again been a pleasure to work with and without his vision, guidance and assistance this book would never have been published.

My wife Kay and daughter Rhiannon have both indulged me as I spent an inordinate amount of time on my laptop writing this book. Rhiannon helped me frequently with the inevitable technical difficulties and Kay encouraged me to stay with my vision.

I have done my best to ensure that the book is factually accurate. Any inadvertent errors are my responsibility alone.

Martin Shipton
April 2022

Foreword

As a child, I grew up as part of a community of Ukrainian refugees who were part of the tragic legacy of the Second World War. Many had been taken by the Germans for forced labour while others were forced to flee the persecution of Nazi and Soviet occupations. Among my close childhood friends were those whose parents had lived through and survived the *Holodomor*, the artificial famine caused by Stalin's forced collectivisation of agriculture and his determination to eliminate the national and political consciousness of the Ukrainian people.

Information was scarce. Those who had lived through it were reluctant to talk about their experiences and now most are long gone. What remains, however, are the recordings of interviews and remembrances of survivors, and documents that are gradually being released from former Soviet archives. It is only since the relatively recent independence of Ukraine, and the collapse of the Soviet Union, that the *Holodomor* has now taken centre stage of national remembrance in Ukraine and, increasingly, internationally.

As I child I had never heard of Gareth Jones. It is a failure of the writing of modern Welsh history that, alongside many other compatriots, he is better known outside Wales than within. In the Ukrainian capital, Kyiv, the city council has named a street after him in his honour but in Wales, apart from a plaque at Aberystwyth University, he is largely unrecognised.

My hope is that this will change, and that his story and the contribution he made, as a proud Welshman with a global perspective, will be understood and recognised. Martin Shipton's biography of Jones is an important step in this direction.

Jones was murdered the day before his 30th birthday. In the last decade of his short life he witnessed the maelstrom of political upheaval in Europe, economic depression, poverty, famine, the growth of fascism and the emergence of the Soviet Union as a world power. All these factors, and more, combined to erupt into the horrors of the Second World War. Jones was often at the centre of some of these key events.

In the USA he met President Roosevelt. In New York he witnessed the poverty and desperation of the depression; in Germany he met with some of the leading figures in the growth of Nazism; in Moscow he was part of an international corps of journalists reporting on the emergence of Soviet communism under the leadership of Josef Stalin, and in Ukraine he broke ranks and went by foot to witness the famine for himself.

At a time of limited means of communication, the function and responsibility of the newspaper journalist in the dissemination of knowledge and information was at its peak. As a *de facto* envoy for the former Prime Minister of the British Empire, fellow Welshman and Welsh speaker, David Lloyd George, doors opened to Jones that allowed him unique access to key politicians and the political and social circles of many of those leaders who were subsequently to determine the political history and direction of Europe and the world. Some we now know for their notoriety and infamous roles in the Holocaust and in the persecution and repression of millions. These are all events whose legacy continues to impact on our world today. This is what makes this biography such an important personal and intimate insight to understanding those events and how they were perceived by many.

Shipton has incorporated into his book much detail of the notes, comments and writings of Jones which have previously not been published. Jones writes about his flight with Hitler and other members of the Nazi party on the Richthofen: 'Behind Hitler sits a little man who laughs all the time. He has a narrow Iberian head and brown eyes which twinkle with wit and intelligence. He looks like the dark small headed sharp Welsh type so often found in the Glamorgan valleys ... His is a name to remember for he will play a big part in the future ...' This was his description of Dr Joseph Goebbels, Nazi deputy leader and architect to be of what would become the greatest crime in modern human history, the persecution and genocide of six million Jews which we now know as the Holocaust.

His notes reveal the concerns of Lloyd George, with whom he would converse in Welsh. The former British Prime Minister, like many of the international figures Jones met, was fearful of the impending cataclysm of war. Lloyd George seems to have been quite an admirer of Stalin, certainly for a while, and appears from Jones' notes to share some of Stalin's contempt for the peasantry. Jones also describes the paramilitary forces of the Nazi party as 'being bound by no legalistic scruples and scorning constitutionalism'.

The rule of law in those decades had little place in the world. The Ludlow Massacre in the US where striking miners were machine gunned, the persecution of trade unions in Poland and instability in Ireland were all features of Jones' writings and discussions during the last decade of his short but full life.

Martin Shipton's biography is a much needed and welcome contribution to our understanding of Jones' experiences and his life, to his intimate and revealing conversations at a time of world-wide political instability and ideological conflict; a world where injustice, poverty, racism and rampant anti-Semitism influenced the lives of everyone, including Jones, and it is appropriate that the biography includes those parts of the notes which reflect on some of Jones' own thoughts at the time.

In Ukraine, and increasingly in Wales and internationally, he is recognised for his reporting of Stalin's famine and the *Holodomor*. As a journalist he was amongst the first to expose the starvation and the death of millions. He broke ranks from the international corps of Moscow-based journalists and their luxuriant wining and dining with Soviet authorities, to head out into the villages of Ukraine to see for himself, and then report to the world. For his honesty and journalistic integrity he was castigated and all but called a liar by leading figures such as the Pulitzer prize-winning journalist of the *New York Times,* Walter Duranty.

Perhaps in this 21st Century we still have much to learn from Gareth Jones' example and his most important journalistic legacy; that at a time of conflict, danger and instability he adopted the highest ethical standards of journalism, he sought the facts, exposed the truth and went out and told the world.

Mick Antoniw
Member of the Senedd / Welsh Parliament
Counsel General for Wales and Minister for the Constitution
April 2022

Lithuania, Janner was a brilliant student but his parents wanted him to leave school and join the family's furniture business. Edgar Jones intervened and persuaded the boy's father that it would be a terrible mistake for him to leave the school and not continue his education. Later, once he had made his way in public life, Janner wrote: 'I know none of my contemporaries as students at the school who do not experience a thrill of pleasure when he or she meets Major Edgar Jones. Was it not he in the school and his family in the soirées and other functions who were responsible for creating the atmosphere of ease and happiness which prevailed?'

On another occasion Janner commented: 'He was 50 years ahead of his time in the scholastic profession and he had a great effect on me, as he did on the other students at the school.' Speaking in 1948, at a meeting of the Cardiff and District Council of Christians and Jews, Janner said of the Major, by then aged 80:

'The influence of that great Christian, Dr Jones, upon myself and my fellow students was of such a nature that there is none of us who does not look back upon the years of that influence with considerable pleasure, and who would not willingly go back to that man for guidance in any matter which might be perturbing them. He is a great Welshman and a man who understands what tolerance really means. He imparted to the students an understanding, which enabled us to live in harmony with each other.' Janner subsequently became President of the Board of Deputies of British Jews.

Barnett Janner – a pupil of Edgar Jones at Barry Grammar School.

When Jones retired, an appreciation published by the Welsh Secondary Schools Review concluded:

'No estimate of Mr Edgar Jones would be complete ... which did not take into account the wonderful charm of his personality. It was truly said that he has a 'genius' for friendship. His genial, inspiring presence, as well as his wisdom in counsel, have always been valuable assets to the [Welsh County Schools] Association, and his potent personality will be greatly missed.'

Upon his death in 1953, an anonymous tribute published in the same review stated:

'Edgar Jones was indeed a most enthusiastic man, keen on a vast number of matters: his Territorial soldiering, adult education, music, art, literature, our colleges and our university. He had been a keen player of association football in his younger days, and later developed a great enthusiasm for the rugby game. Was he not the man whom I asked to let me have a shortlist of really distinguished Welsh rugby players who ought to be included in a biographical dictionary? And did he not swamp me with a list of more than 120? He did his best for the encouragement of Welsh publishing, and had a good knowledge of our literature. A source of great pride to him was the presence on his staff of [the distinguished Welsh language poet] R Williams Parry, and you will find in Dr Parry's recent volume an englyn [a traditional Welsh four-line poem or quatrain written according to strict metrical rules] on his old chief.'

There can be no doubt that his father's erudition and personality both helped to define the character of Gareth Jones. His mother too had a profound influence on him.

Annie Gwen Jones, whose family name was also Jones and who was brought up in Merthyr Tydfil, met Edgar while studying at the University of Wales, Aberystwyth, where she was one of the first women students admitted by the institution. After completing her studies, she went to eastern Ukraine to work for three years as a and great friendliness, and hundreds of past pupils of the County School scattered now throughout the world can recall how ably she supported her husband in everything with his post. Former pupils visited her up to the end.'

Having two such remarkable parents gave Gareth Jones a tremendous advantage: an outlook that was fundamentally internationalist and open to ideas beyond the narrow provincialism and jingoism that was prevalent in early 20th Century Britain. He was taught at home by his mother until he was seven, at which point he began attending his father's school. In 1922 he won a scholarship to study modern languages – French, German and Russian – at the University of Wales, Aberystwyth, which both his parents as well as his elder sisters Gwyneth and Eirian had attended. He greatly enjoyed his time at Aberystwyth, studying hard but also enjoying the social side of student life, attending rugby matches with friends and playing golf. Coming from a family of devout Nonconformists, he attended the Welsh Tabernacle in the town regularly, often twice on Sundays. While at Aberystwyth he also met a young German lecturer called Reinhard Haferkorn, who was to become his closest friend and with whom he would later stay in Germany on a number of occasions.

From 1923, as part of his course, he spent two years at the University of Strasbourg and while studying in Alsace wrote a letter to his parents in which he set out what he wanted to do with his life:

'I was very interested in Dada's suggestions about a fellowship and perhaps a lectureship. But I'm sorry, it does not tempt me very much. I am much more interested in people and countries and in modern Europe especially. I would a thousand times prefer to use my knowledge of languages with an aim to obtaining a position where I could meet interesting people of all nationalities and where I could really find out the characteristics of the nations of today; why there are wars, and how they could be prevented; how national, Semitic and religious prejudices can be destroyed, and why they exist; why there are certain movements, literary or political in certain countries; why people of races have certain ideals; why certain nations have their characteristics reflected in their literature. All that – and especially learning all these things by travelling and trying to make people speak out their ideas and meet interesting men – interests me much more than study for study's sake. I would much prefer a career which comprehends a knowledge of men.'

He went on to write that he was able to judge men much better than when he first came to Strasbourg – and he was able to observe their traits, national or political, much more thoroughly. Strasbourg, with students from all nations, had been an excellent experience for him in that respect. He added:

'Also, I do not want to specialise in one language alone as I could have to do if I were a professor or something of the sort, and I would certainly not like to specialise in French, since I have very little in common with the French or with their literature. I am going to continue Russian. I find that in general I get on well with people and can usually accommodate myself to different milieus. I have succeeded quite well in getting their ideas out of the Alsatians, who usually keep their ideas to themselves.'

Listing the kind of jobs he could see himself doing, Jones wrote:

'I would much prefer ... something in the League of Nations, Foreign Office, Diplomacy (? this is too costly) or Consular Service. I want to travel, and I want to learn languages. I find the world much more interesting from the human point of view than I did two years ago.'

After graduating with a first class honours degree he continued his language studies at Trinity College, Cambridge, securing a double first in German and Russian. At Cambridge, as well as joining the Trinity Madrigals as a tenor, he became chief secretary of the Cambridge League of Nations, and to further his international understanding would on a weekly basis host a meeting at which a foreign student diplomacy and with the consular service. Therefore I would be very keen on whichever service I was destined to enter.

Chairman: "Have you any questions to ask, Sir Hubert?"

Sir Hubert X: "Would you be interested in the commercial side of the consular service?"

Jones: "Yes, having studied economics etc but that besides the commercial side I would take a great interest in the culture of the country I might be sent to."

Chairman: "Have you any questions to ask, Mr Q?

Mr Q: "I see that you took an interest in athletics in school. Do you still continue that interest?"

Jones: "Yes sir." I mentioned Hares and Hounds, tennis etc.'

He wrote that the interview wound down with pleasantries. Jones said it was disappointing because it was over in no time and both he and Jasper had a feeling of 'having been done in'. He considered himself ruled out completely for the Diplomatic side of the Foreign Office but thought he might still have a chance at the Consular. Jones concluded his letter: 'It is worth seizing the opportunity and even worth going up to London for a day (car ride made a cheap sensation)'.

He resolved to write to a number of people including Sir Bernard Pares to ask for help. He enjoyed London and popped into the Ritz Hotel, but was keen to get back to work. So far as Jones was concerned, 'the Consular is just the thing for me'.

'When the diplomatic relations with Russia are renewed', he wrote to his parents, 'I might then be transferred for a short time. Look up the 'Foreign Office list' in the Cardiff library. It would interest you very much. It gives the places where various members of the Consular Service have been. I am very keen on the Consular now.'

Pares quickly responded to Jones' letter, thanking him for it and saying he would be only too glad to help him where he could. He would soon be visiting his son at Jesus College, Cambridge, but also invited Jones to meet him in London if he'd prefer. He concluded: 'I wonder if by any chance we are connections (sic), as your name unites those of two families of my cousins, the Vaughans of Leicester, and the Jones' of Waterloo near Liverpool.'

Meanwhile Jones had a letter from the university's appointments board asking him to see the careers officer Mr Roberts. Roberts suggested a job for him that the board had just been notified of – Foreign Correspondent with *The Times* – but Jones doubted he would get the post.

As things turned out, the Foreign Office job did not immediately materialise. He did, however, get a month's trial at *The Times*, which gave him his first experience of working for a newspaper, but it didn't lead to a full-time employment. He was advised to spend a year on a provincial paper.

Then, within quick succession, he was offered work as an academic coach at Trinity College and a job with the Consular Service he had applied for. He accepted the Trinity College role, but turned down the Consular job, saying he'd found work elsewhere. Then a more interesting opportunity presented itself which Jones seized with both hands: working in the private office of former Prime Minister David Lloyd George.

Jones enjoyed all aspects of student life at Cambridge. (© The Gareth Vaughan Jones Estate)

2

European Visits

The Well Travelled Student

'I had the impression this time that Germany has nearly entirely recovered and that she will soon be in a much better position than France. I believe that poor old France is in for a rough time.'

From his late teenage years, Gareth Jones made regular trips to other European countries, usually travelling by train. He developed a particular love for Germany, visiting it every year from 1923, and his letters home show him to have had a consuming interest in politics, economics, music and literature.

The punitive measures imposed on Germany at the Treaty of Versailles led to runaway inflation and the collapse of the currency under the Weimar Republic. In the summer of 1923, sitting in a Weimar café, Jones wrote:

'My dearest Everybody, [his usual opening]
I got away today with Herbert Held [a friend] in spite of a lot of trouble in the bank. Yesterday there was a run on the bank and after 11 o'clock no one could get money. So I had to wait till this morning to change some more money. It was quite an experience yesterday to see the run on the bank. Nobody however was very excited & everybody took it very calmly. This morning I got 3,400,000 for the £1.

... I am going on to Eisenach in 45 mins. I had to change here. Last night's Wilhelm Tell was very fine. I have bought a lot of good books (25) for 12/6, including 5 French books.'

He then travelled to Hamburg, where he wrote:

'I had a very interesting journey and arrived in Hamburg about a quarter past six yesterday evening. As I have to make conversation now and then with two German Frauleins I am sorry I can't write a long letter before the post goes ... By the way, do not be afraid of a Revolution or anything of the sort in Germany yet. I am told by all I have spoken to that Germany will not become Communist.

Friday morning we went to the Kunsthalle, a fine picture gallery,' he wrote to his parents a few days later. 'I saw Rembrandt, Van Dyck, Ruisdael & a lot of old Masters, also heaps of modern jazz things. Then to the History museum, also very interesting.'

While studying in Strasbourg, he wrote:

'Last night I was invited to dance in the Students' Hostel by the English girls. I had quite a nice time, danced with Russian, Tunisian, English, American, Ukrainian, Serbian, Polish, Yugoslavian & French girls!! I didn't get back till very late, and did not awake till 10.30 this morning ... Thursday I invited Mons Winckler, a law student from Nancy, who invited me to tea (9 o'clock) in his flat last week, to tea in a tea-room. He is a very good sort.'

Having seen party placards for the 1924 German election, Jones explained to his parents how proportional representation worked. Then, while attending a lecture given by one of the period's best-known medieval scholars Gustave Cohen, Jones wrote:

'I performed a lot in M[onsieur] Cohen's lecture on the Middle Ages. He was doing Tristan-Iseult (Esyllt) and I had already told him

The University of Strasbourg, circa 1920.

I was Welsh. So throughout the lecture he was asking me how to pronounce Welsh words – he was talking about Welsh influences on French literature – like Tallwch father of Trystan, march (ceffyl) etc. They thought the ll & Tallwch very funny. A few lectures ago he referred to Caerleon ar Wysg, Mabinogion, Branwen, Esyllt etc.'

He also wrote with some good news about his exam results: 'Hurray! I am top out of the 20 candidates for the Certificate,' quickly adding: 'Financial. Don't you think I deserve something for the exam? In school or in Aber I always used to have something for the exam!'

Sometimes he had a direct and entertaining way of expressing his frustrations with daily life: 'I have never met duller people than the people in the Bureau de Voyage in Strasbourg,' he wrote. 'They did not know anything. In one bureau, the clerk did not know where the Vallee de la Bruche was!! Exactly as if a clerk in a Travel Office in Cardiff did not know where the Rhymney Valley was.'

Reflecting on the forthcoming German Presidential election in 1925, Jones noted: 'Hindenburg to stand for Presidency. Not a party man.'

Contrasting what he saw as the prospects for Germany with the prospects for France, he wrote:

'I had the impression this time that Germany has nearly entirely recovered and that she will soon be in a much better position than France. I believe that poor old France is in for a rough time. The population remains the same, the countryside is being abandoned. The peasants are going to the town, Polish and Italian workmen everywhere, the Franc in a bad position.

In Germany, on the other hand, the national debt cleared, the population increasing rapidly, the mark stabilised, but nevertheless badly paid workmen and reparations to be paid – if they ever will be all paid. Then during the inflation, the industrialists who had foreign money bought good machinery & built new buildings.'

While at no stage did Jones write about any romantic attachments he may have formed, it is certainly the case that he was able to inspire affection in others towards him. Although the vast majority of correspondence in his extensive archive at the National Library of Wales consists of letters from Jones to his own family members, one undated and incomplete letter in the archive written to him by an unnamed student friend who lived in Strasbourg at the same time as him provides evidence of an emotional connection, if nothing more.

The reference to Baldwin preventing a miners' strike dates the letter to shortly after 'Red Friday', 31 July 1925, when the Prime Minister of the Conservative-led government Stanley Baldwin agreed to the demands of the Miners' Federation to provide a temporary subsidy to the mining industry to maintain miners' wages. He was buying time – the following year, when miners' wages were cut, led to the General Strike. The letter reads:

'Dear Gareth,
As you can see I have changed my decision. Instead of going to Grenoble, I have come to Paris. External circumstances have forced

3

Westminster

Working for Lloyd George

'I have come to the conclusion that the only life I can live with interest and in which I can really be of use is one connected with foreign affairs and with men and women of today; not with the writers of 2 centuries ago.'

When Gareth Jones went to work as a researcher for David Lloyd George in January 1930, Britain's last Liberal Prime Minister – and the politician who could legitimately claim to have launched the welfare state – had been out of office for seven years.

Nevertheless he remained an MP, was leading the Liberal Party and continued to be a listened-to voice, which concerned his political opponents who were worried that he might make a comeback. Lloyd George continued to run a staffed political office and was looking for a researcher to brief him on foreign affairs, especially political developments in Europe.

Jones had been introduced to Lloyd George by a family neighbour and friend in Barry, Dr Thomas Jones, who had worked as deputy cabinet secretary for him during the war. After impressing Lloyd George with a briefing on the current political situation in Germany, he was offered a contract. 'Mr Lloyd George has offered me either a 12 month or a 6 month trial and said he wouldn't think of giving me less than £400 per year', Jones explained in a letter to his parents:

'I am to decide before next Weds and I feel tempted to take it for 6 months for the following reasons:

1. Experience
2. Salary
3. Exactly the subject I am interested in.
4. Diplomatic Service. [It will not debar me at all from trying the Diplomatic Service of the Foreign Office], if I get another interview.
5. Research. I shall be in London. I shall be able to join London University for my PhD. Otherwise it is difficult to get a PhD. There are numerous difficulties in the way of a PhD unless I reside in London.
6. At the end of 6 months, I shall leave and have had a varied experience of everything and shall be free to drop the post or not.
7. I am not really keen on academic work permanently.
8. Research again. I shall not need to stay in London in vacs to work at the British Museum or the Russian Press.'

Sir Bernard Pares, the enigmatic figure who had befriended him, suggested to Jones that he write a PhD thesis on the Russian Press during the Revolution. When his father expressed concern about his inclination to work for Lloyd George, Jones wrote:

'Thank you very much for setting down so clearly the pros and cons. I see your point of view – but I am only 24! It isn't as if I wanted to marry and settle down and really I have absolutely no desire for an academic career.'

In response to further concerns that he might be labelled, politically, Jones noted:

'I have definitely decided to accept Lloyd George's offer. Everybody in Cambridge is absolutely unanimous in advising me to accept it. I am going to accept a 6 month trial, beginning on Jan 1. I shall enjoy it. Please don't worry about it. Think of Sir Edward Grigg. He was LG's secretary up to a few years ago. He is now Governor of Kenya. He is not labelled politically.'

Days later Jones sent a further letter to his parents, which said:

> 'I am delighted with the news. Mr Lloyd George offers me £500 a year. I accepted last night. I wrote to say that I would accept. I laid before Mr Sylvester [AJ Silvester, Lloyd George's private secretary and *de facto* chief of staff] my financial position in Cambridge (he asked for it) and said that I should leave Mr Lloyd George to decide the salary. Tonight, (about 6.30) I got a telegram saying £500.'

Jones' duties involved being based in London and preparing briefing notes for debates, articles and speeches, as well as some overseas travel. 'It is funny to think so, but I would have an influence on Foreign Affairs through Lloyd George,' he told his family. He very quickly found himself immersed in the world of high-level diplomacy, meeting well-placed individuals whose views he sought on the issues that Lloyd George wanted to be briefed on: the growing calls for Indian independence, the 'betrayal' of Arabs inherent in the Balfour Declaration, which supported the establishment of a Jewish homeland in Palestine, and the prospects of an international conference about naval power, for example.

Nevertheless Jones' parents remained concerned about the direction he was taking, prompting him to write in more direct terms than before a statement of intent for his life. While Major Jones and his wife would have preferred him to settle down to a safe life of academic teaching, Gareth Jones saw his future as 'connected with foreign affairs' rather than with journalism

David Lloyd George.

per se. As things turned out, of course, he became best known for bringing journalism and one particularly scandalous foreign affair together.

On 3 February 1930, after asking his family to send him a copy of a book on the Cheka (the Soviet secret police), he wrote:

'I should consider myself a flabby little coward if ever I gave up the chance of a good, interesting and useful career for the mere thought of safety. I have no respect for any man whose acceptance or judgement of a post depends on the question: Will it give me a pension? Is it safe? And I have not the slightest desire to be a lecturer for all the safety and security in the world.

'No man ever got on or did the slightest bit of good by putting the LSD [pounds, shillings and pence] he will receive at the age of 60 before considerations of public good, love of work, overwhelming interest; and to think of myself spending my life talking about German literature in which I have not the slightest interest, saying the same thing every week, every year, makes me far prefer any kind of adventure with a little excitement and with an insight into how the world moves.

'A term in one of the greatest universities in the world was quite enough for me – although I enjoyed the experience. What would it be like in some provincial university like Manchester, where I should be finally stuck?

'I have come to the conclusion that the only life I can live with interest and in which I can really be of use is one connected with foreign affairs and with men and women of today; not with the writers of 2 centuries ago.

'You talk of anxiety about my future. If I got drunk, you would be justified. If I ran from one stage-door to another, these would be cause for your anxiety. If I had been sent down from Cambridge, if

I'd had a Third, if I had no testimonials, if people disliked me and if I could get on nowhere, if I were easily depressed and always unhappy, if I'd stolen something, then I should quite understand your position. If there were no hope for the future, if I were earning about £3 - £4 per week as many Cambridge men are, if I were out of work – and millions of people can get no work – then you'd be right in being unhappy.

'Tell me why you have no confidence in my future. Why do you want a son of yours to have no courage and just stick in the mud, for the feeling of security?

'Security? Wasn't I offered a post in the consular service? Then immediately after, wasn't I made a supervisor in TRINITY COLLEGE, CAMBRIDGE? And then a couple of weeks later I was offered a post of really great responsibility at £500 per year. How many people in Cambridge got £500 a year straight after leaving? You may not think much of my job, but in the view of people in Cambridge and in the RIIA [Royal Institute of International Affairs] it is most important. It brings me into touch with people of international repute.'

On 19 March 1930, he wrote to his family, giving a flavour of a day working for Lloyd George in Westminster. He was clearly greatly enthused by it:

'Yesterday was an exciting day. At 5 to 1 the phone went and Sylvester's voice came through very excitedly. "Come to the 6th floor at once! Mr Lloyd George wants to know something about Intermediate Education in Wales!" I dashed up to the room next to LG's room on the 6th floor. "Get your hat & coat, quick!" said Sylvester. "You're going in the car!"

I got my hat & coat from my room & put some cuttings on education in my pocket & got upstairs just in time to enter the lift with LG in a dark blue coat & black hat. We went out & got into the beautiful Rolls

Royce. Smith, the man at the door, put the rug over LG's and my legs. "Where to, Sir?" said the chauffeur. "11 Downing Street!" said LG.

Then as we were gliding past the Board of Trade, down Parliament Street, LG told me what he wanted. He asked me to get him figures for the number of pupils in secondary schools in Wales, the percentage to the population & a comparison to the numbers in England, Scotland and Germany. Finally the car drove up to 11 Downing Street, LG went out and entered [Chancellor of the Exchequer Philip] Snowden's house and the chauffeur drove me back in great style near the Houses of Parliament & Westminster Abbey to 25 Old Queen Street. I got the information ready by the evening. So everything was OK.

Tell Jacques that I've gone up one. From rushing through the streets of London in a taxi, I've been gliding in a Rolls Royce with LG!! Last night I went to see the Italian Exhibition; then to the RIIA; then home. Today I am going to lunch at Craig's Court. This evening RIIA again, 6 o'clock Prince Mirsky [a Russian political and literary historian]. So life is very thrilling and interesting.'

Having been asked by Lloyd George to write an evaluation of the Soviet Union's Five Year Plan, Jones met an official from the Soviet Embassy called Nicolai Yemshikov, who told him the standard of life in Russia was being reduced in order to get money to buy exports; that there was great suffering; only children were allowed milk; a grown-up was allowed two eggs per week. A peasant revolt was possible, but the Soviet government had aeroplanes, troops and guns; everything to crush it.

Later, strolling through St James' Park so as not to be overheard, Yemshikov, who was concerned he might lose his job because he was not a member of the Communist Party, told Jones Britain was encouraging a separatist movement in Ukraine, as well as others in Turkestan and the Caucasus. Quoting Yemshikov, Jones recorded in his diary: 'There will be civil war in Russia if this continues. There is a rumour that the Foreign Secretary is giving money to Ukraine and

great force in American public life. He is Vice-Pres of the American League of Nations Union etc etc. His special interest is Russia.'

He added: 'In the morning I had a most interesting hour with Sir Bernard who feels very strongly the wickedness of the Soviet Union towards the peasants & religion.' Later he wrote: 'I feel like taking the American job for the fun and the experience.'

Ivy Lee was a legendary figure in American business circles, seen as one of the fathers of modern public relations. In 1906 he had written what would now be described as a mission statement. Lee's *Declaration of Principles* asserted that public relations practitioners have a public responsibility that extends beyond obligations to the client. In the same year, after the Atlantic City train disaster in which 53 people drowned after a train came off a bridge. Lee issued what is often considered to be the first press release, after persuading the company to disclose information to journalists before they heard it elsewhere.

Eight years later Lee was retained by John D Rockefeller Jr to represent his family and Standard Oil after 20 were killed when striking miners and their families were machine-gunned by the National Guard in Colorado in an outrage that became known as the Ludlow Massacre. The miners' homes were also burned. Lee advised Rockefeller to try to repair relations by meeting the miners and their families, inspecting the conditions of the homes and the factories, attending social events, and listening to the community's grievances. It was one of the first examples of crisis management and helped the Rockefellers repair their image.

Jones didn't go to work for Lee immediately, but it was a good connection to have made because only a few months later he was made redundant by Lloyd George. Meanwhile, however, he went on another trip to Germany.

On 4 January 1931, Jones wrote to his family from Waldheim in Saxony, stating:

'Had interview with the Foreign Minister of Germany, Dr [Julius] Curtius, in the villa of the Foreign Ministry. He spoke very, very openly. You can see that his patience is over. He received me very kindly. He seemed a sound, reasonable, business-like man, but without the spark of an LG [Lloyd George] or a Winston [Churchill].

There will be fireworks in Geneva [headquarters of the League of Nations] if he says openly against the Poles one tenth of what he told me.[Curtius engaged in anti-Polish invective which suggested the German minority in Poland was being oppressed by the Poles and were the victims of atrocities. Later, such a narrative would be deployed by Hitler to justify Germany's invasion of Poland that triggered World War Two].

The interview lasted 40 minutes and I have sent a report on it to Mr Lloyd George. After the interview the Foreign Minister Hans von Haeften (who was at Trinity) and myself walked through the private park to the Foreign Office in the Wilhelmstrasse. I had heaps of interviews – with the two Ministerial Directors of the FO [Foreign Office]. On Friday also I had a long interview with Count Harry Kessler, a very well-known ex-diplomat, writer and gentleman. All are exceedingly pessimistic about the state of Europe.

I lunched with Dr Wolfers, who is Principal of the College for Politics. He was very interesting. Then Friday night I went to Wannsee (equivalent of Richmond or Windsor) and dined with the family of Kurt Hahn, who was Secretary of Prince Max of Baden, the last Imperial Chancellor of Germany. They had a huge, beautiful house near the lake. Their car took me back to Berlin about 11 o'clock.'

Jones travelled on to Poland, where he received a letter from AJ Silvester, Lloyd George's chief of staff, which said: 'I am dictating this letter over the telephone from Criccieth and want it to reach you at the earliest possible moment. A reorganisation of staff has been decided upon which affects you and I am acquainting you at the earliest possible moment in case you may decide to postpone your trip and return to London.'

In a letter to his family written from the British Consulate in Warsaw, Jones said:

'It is entirely a matter of economy, because the reorganisation of the staff was being discussed before Christmas and Miss Edwards was exceedingly nervous about it. With the same post I received a letter from Miss Edwards saying that she was leaving the office last Thursday. And there has been talk of economising all along the line. So I should be one of the first to go, considering that I spend nearly all my time reading up about subjects.

Please don't worry. I am quite all right because I can go straight away to Ivy Lee. I am very sorry for the others though. I am not hurrying back to London, but am going on with my trip and shall go to the office a week next Monday. It's a pity Miss Edwards has to go. She has been there for years and years. I wonder who else will have to leave. Malcolm Thomson has been nervous about it too, but I don't think he'll go, because he is such an all-round man.'

He continued that he was having one of the most interesting trips he'd ever had, then concluded: 'Please don't worry. If you had a tenth of the misery which there is here & Germany and if you'd been one of the people shouting "Bread! Bread!" in Kottowitz [Katowice], you would have something to worry about. This is purely a matter of economy. They've been cutting down every little thing, books, papers, even writing paper etc.' The previous day, Jones had written about the lack of food in Katowice, where he had stayed: 'Last night there were hunger demonstrations here. Large numbers of unemployed crowded through the streets – I with them – and shouted "Bread! Bread! Hleba! Hleba!" Then the mounted police came and scattered the crowd.'

Back in London, he wrote a briefing paper for Lloyd George on the Soviet Union and the Caucasus. He interviewed Akaki Chenkeli, the Prime Minister and Foreign Minister of the Georgian Republic, who told him: 'I am sure that the countries off Trans-Caucasia will become free. This will happen not by a war against Russia but by a great crisis within the Soviet Union'. Mr Chenkeli was right – but 60 years ahead of time.

Lloyd George compensated Jones for the termination of his employment by providing a reference in glowing terms. It read: 'He is sharp, keen, reliable, and works rapidly with zest and good humour. I notice a spark of venturesomeness in him combined with solid study and the gift of getting on with people. I feel confident in predicting a brilliant future for this young man.'

Another reference from his old tutor Professor Briel was also highly complimentary: 'He is exceptionally well informed about modern German life and thought, political, social and educational questions and conditions, and has for several years been in intimate touch with the 'Youth Movement' in Germany and with other continental movements.'

Before leaving for the United States, Jones – who by now was contributing occasional articles to newspapers – wrote a series for the *Western Mail* about the Soviet Union's Five Year Plan; a subject that just two years later would make a huge impact on his life:

'The Five Year Plan begins the third act in the thrilling drama of the Bolshevik Revolution.

The first act opened with the thunder of the guns and the blood of November, 1917, when the Revolution broke out. It was the period of military Communism. There was war on all sides – against the Whites, against the Allies, against the Poles. Ruthless terror sent thousands to their death. The Communists put their principles into practice by abolishing banks, money, private trading, and by preventing the peasants from selling their grain except to the State. The curtain of the first act goes down upon the bodies of millions of Russians dead or dying in the terrible famine of 1921.

Then came the second act, the recovery, 1921-1927. Lenin, the realist, made a compromise with Capitalism and allowed peasants and shopkeepers to sell their goods openly and make a profit. This is called the New Economic Policy. In the middle of this act there was a poignant scene when the great Lenin died in January 1924.

The third act began in 1928, and was the period of reconstruction or the Act of the Five Year Plan. This plan is in reality a new revolution, a revolution lasting over a period of five years.'

Explaining the purpose of the Five Year Plan, Jones wrote:

'In 1927 the Communist Party considered that the general level of production was about the same as in 1913. But, to the horror of the Bolsheviks, Capitalism was growing in the country. Private trade, as opposed to the Stalin and co-operative shops, was still powerful. Worst of all, the Revolution had turned the peasants into capitalistic small-holders. The big estates which had produced millions of tons of grain for export had been divided into innumerable tiny patches. The vast stretches of land which used to supply whole towns and the Army with food had been split up. The Communist Revolution had led to the increase of Capitalism! It had led to a shortage of grain, for it is difficult to collect from 26,000,000 different small proprietors. It had led to the increasing of the capitalist class of richer peasants, the kulaks, who hated Communism.

The cry went round among the communists: "The time has come for change! Forward to pure Communism! No more compromise with Capitalism. We must try to introduce Communism within five years.

'We will keep out kulaks from the collective farms' – a Soviet propaganda poster bought by Jones in 1930.
(© The Gareth Vaughan Jones Estate)

51

We must build a strong industrial State and turn the millions of peasants patches into vast Socialist [collective] farms".'

But the Five Year Plan was also about rapidly industrialising a country that remained largely agricultural. To achieve such an end, desperate measures were necessary. Jones wrote: 'The State deprives the population of most commodities in order to get money to invest in industry and to buy machinery from abroad. Foreign trade is a Government monopoly. Thus no luxuries are imported, and butter, eggs, grain, and bacon, badly needed at home, are exported to get currency wherewith to buy tractors, textile-making machinery, and engines necessary to carry out the Plan.'

He concluded his *Western Mail* series with a prophesy:

'The Soviet Union has become one vast centralised business concern controlling 158,000,000 people with a miserable standard of living. So far the Five-Year Plan has been a mixture of successes and failures. It is increasing the production of Russia, but at the expense of quality and human happiness. Difficulties galore lie in its path, but if these difficulties are overcome, then Soviet Russia will be a powerful competitor.

The success of the Plan would strengthen the hands of the Communists throughout the world. It might make the twentieth century a century of struggle between Capitalism and Communism.'

As Jones himself came to realise only too well, if in any sense the Plan could be considered a success, it came at an appalling price.

4

United States of America

Ivy Lee and the Art of Public Relations

'This is a wonderful opportunity for me to study the world situation from all the best experts in world trade'

In April 1931 Jones travelled to New York to work for Ivy Lee. Describing his departure from London, he wrote: 'I was driven past the lights of Shaftesbury Avenue to the Carlton Hotel. There some of Mr Ivy Lee's boys were waiting for me. Then the taxi took me to the Reform [Club], in case there were any letters by the 9.30 post. I said goodbye to the hall porter and to the Reform and drove off to Paddington, past a lot of my haunts such as Grosvenor House, Grosvenor Square where the Soviet Embassy had been.'

He travelled to New York on the *Ile de France*, one of the most luxurious liners of the time. Lee, who was also on the ship, told Jones he wanted him to undertake research for a book he was planning to write called *What of Russia Now?* Jones' role was to provide background material on the history of the Russian Revolution and the policies of Lenin. Some work would be undertaken in New York libraries, but Jones would also follow the Russian press.

Ironically, given the way his study of Russia turned out, it later became clear to Jones that Lee intended a book that was sympathetic to the Communists. He represented Standard Oil, which was anxious for the US and the Soviet Union to have good relations. Standard Oil bought a lot of Soviet petrol and sold it in Asia.

Arriving in America, Jones was enraptured by the sight that awaited him:

'My interview with the Immigration Officer went off most rapidly & successfully. As soon as that was over I went up on deck and saw the wonderful sight of New York in the distance. It was just as I had expected from photos. It was a beautifully clear day and Mr Lee who showed me all the sights on the upper deck said that it was impossible to have a better day than to have my first glimpse of New York.'

Ivy Lee's son and Terence O'Brien, who is on Mr Lee's staff, came and greeted me on the pier. There was no trouble at all about the customs and before long I was speeding in a yellow taxi towards the North to Mr Lee's apartment. Looking out at the shops I noticed that there were Sales everywhere and 'Giving up after 40 years business' or notices saying that the business was being liquidated.'

Writing to his family from Standard Oil's headquarters high up in a Manhattan skyscraper, he stated:

Ivy Lee – the guru of Public Relations.

'Events are moving very quickly and I am just waiting to know whether I shall be leaving in a few hours for Washington or Cuba!!

Here I am sitting in Ivy Lee's luxurious offices overlooking all New York. We are 34 storeys high here. Imagine walking upstairs from the kitchen to Auntie's room 34 times. Luckily the lift takes us up in a few seconds. We are right in the heart of skyscraper land –

When he does business he does it for business' sake; when he is a philanthropist he does it for the sake of philanthropy. He would never camouflage a gift as a loan."'

The Minister then appealed to Jones as though he had some influence and then left as humbly as he had arrived, then Lee outlined to Jones what he expected of him: to write about the current situation in and prospects for Russia. In response, Jones set out what his research work on Russia would consist of:

'1 Lenin in Germany in 1917. The myth of Lenin as a German agent.
2 Russian repudiation of debts
3 Private property in Russia
4 The Terror and Soviet Justice
5 Religion
6 Social code
Anti-Bolshevik propaganda eg Zinoviev letter
The Communist International
Relations of Soviet Russia with the world'

At the end of May 1931 Jones wrote to his parents about the 'great time' he had on Decoration Day, a public holiday, spending nearly the whole of it reading in the park a few yards from his rooms, and of one particular conversation he'd enjoyed:

'A Negro preacher, very black and shiny, old with a thin kind of clergyman's collar, came and sat next to me. We entered into a conversation. I never knew how primitive negros could be.

"I seed de devil dis morning" he said; "de devil was a thousand year in hell, but now they let him out and now he's roamin' over New York. He's going to Chicago in a few days. He's perhaps in dis park. He goes into people. I can always tell him. I ain't afraid of him and he knows it. Dis morning I was in bed and he comes down de chimney. He came in the body of a woman what died in my house. I sees de

woman come down de chimney with a dog. And de dog growl and
bark. And de woman snarl at me and her teeth was two inches long.
And I knew it was the devil inside he. So I tries to clutch at him...De
devil he go away...A long time ago God he floated onde matraculous
air. I have also floated on the matracolous air. Elojim he float on de
matraculous air and he said Ethimkaloujapol apoolothima. Den he
go to de mon-transitorial kingdom,where it is sejimethopythro" (He
muttered a lot of strange words stringed together. I'm not joking).'

When Jones asked the man what happens to dead people, the
preacher said: "They stay here. Dey wander about here in de park".
Jones was thoroughly entertained by the conversation and said it
was one of his most enjoyable days.

On 14 June 1931, while travelling on a ship from Boston to New
York, he wrote to his family:

'America is in a mood of self-criticism. People here are a thousand
times more depressed and are attacking their weak points much
more than in England. And they have heaps of weak points. It must
be awful to be an unemployed worker here – no dole, no health
insurance, nothing.'

A week later he was more upbeat because Lloyd George had referred
to him in a speech he had made, writing to his family:

'Oh, LG referred to me in his Free Trade Speech (not by name, of
course). I wrote to LG and had a reply from Sylvester, saying that
LG had used my stuff. He enclosed a cutting. LG referred to me as "a
friend of mine in America; an able man in touch with some of the
leading industrialists in America".'

On 29 June he was able to announce in a letter to his family:

'Hurray! Hurray! Everything fixed up. Am going to London & Russia
with the son of Mr Heinz (57 varieties) & to get information for Mr Lee.

'Rothermere and Beaverbrook have been speculating very heavily on sterling and that is why the *Express* and *Mail* have been publishing such false news ... LG's book will probably come out in the spring.'

At the end of 1932 Jones was offered a job with the BBC, but was unsure about it and turned it down. He wrote to his parents stating:

'LG headed a deputation to the BBC this morning and was violent in his attack on the BBC's policy towards Wales. He lost his temper and was furious. He attacked [ER] Appleton [the BBC's director of regional affairs] bitterly. There is a possibility that they might have had me in mind as a future head of the BBC in Cardiff – a job I which I wouldn't like for the whole world.

Today I saw the head of Reuters and the editor of the *Sunday Times*. They all said that provincial experience is essential and thought that the BBC would be rotten ... The BBC rather strikes me as a prison.'

Jones took their advice and secured a staff job with the *Western Mail* in Cardiff, where he was due to start work at the beginning of April 1933. Meanwhile, after leaving Lloyd George's employment again, he planned to spend two months investigating the situations in Germany and Russia.

He had dinner in the Marlborough Club with Francis Butler-Thwing, whom he had known in New York, and a Soviet specialist from Harvard called Bruce Hopper, who had just returned from Russia.

Afterwards, Jones wrote to Ivy Lee, relaying what Hopper had told him:

'The Soviet Government is facing the worst crisis since 1921. The harvest is a failure, and there will be millions facing starvation this winter.

There is at the present moment a famine in the Ukraine. Collective farms have been a complete failure, and there is now a migration

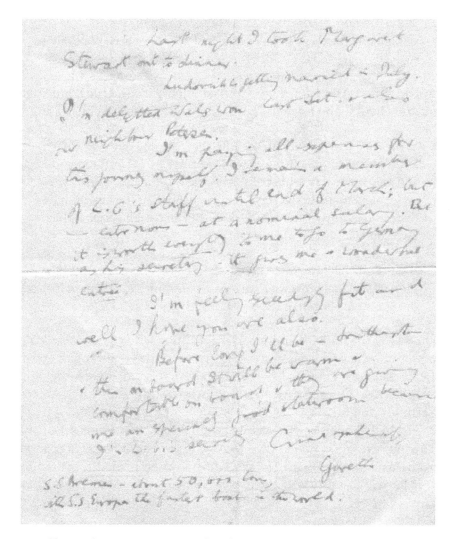

Jones' letter of January 1933 notes how his forthcoming trip to Germany and the Soviet Union as Lloyd George's 'secretary' would be a 'wonderful entreè' into the world of journalism. (© The Gareth Vaughan Jones Estate)

from the farms. There is simply nothing left in many collectives, and numbers of people from as far south as the Bessarabian frontier have wandered up to Moscow for bread. Even the army is short of food and there is grave discontent in it. Disillusion is spreading through the ranks of the party. There is no open opposition and the silence is dangerous.'

Early in the New Year, Jones wrote:

'On Wednesday, I had caviar and a long talk alone for one hour with the Soviet Ambassador, His Excellency M Maisky, a funny little chap, half-Tartar, half-Jew.'

He was confident after the meeting that the Ambassador would issue him with a visa, which he did, and in late January 1933 he set off for Germany, writing a note from Southampton commenting, 'Sir Bernard Pares has received confirmation [of the famine] from many sources,' again raising questions about the nature of his locus in the matter.

Jones wrote Lloyd George a letter while passing Dover that thanked him for employing him. It said:

May I first thank you for the wonderful experience I have had on your staff. I very much regret leaving the office now and leaving the staff at the end of March. The next month I shall spend investigating the situation in Germany and going also to Danzig and Czechoslovakia. During March I shall be in Russia, visiting Moscow and the Ukraine. I shall send you reports on what I see. In future I shall be delighted to be of any help and since I shall be especially following the Welsh, the industrial and the foreign situation for the *Western Mail*, I hope I may be of some service to you.

Yesterday I saw the Soviet Ambassador, who has been remarkably kind in obtaining material for you in Moscow. He is looking forward to having you to lunch or dinner and will be glad to hear from you at any time.

In preparing for my visit to Moscow, he said that two problems have confronted the Soviet Union; the first that of <u>construction;</u> that has been solved by the Five Year Plan, which he claims has been carried out 94%. The second problem remains unsolved – namely <u>the use of machinery.</u> That will be solved, he hoped, through the Second Five Year Plan.

Two important decisions had been taken this month: (he said); a) The food tax for the peasants. Once the peasant has paid the food tax, he is to be free to sell his surplus in the private market; b) There is to be attached to each Machine Tractor Station a special political section of the Party, which will enlighten the peasants on policy, work in the collective farms and combat hostile and kulak elements in the village.

These measures, the Ambassador claims, together with the increased production of the light industries, will lead to a brighter happier life in Russia. "In a year or two everything will be all right". (Exactly the same words as I was told two years and a year ago).

The Second Five Year Plan will aim at quality; at stabilising the situation; <u>not</u> at increasing the sowing area. Its main stress will be laid on consumption and agriculture. It will be intensive.

I am not so optimistic as the Ambassador. March will be an interesting month to judge and I shall let you know my findings in Russia.'

Jones told Lloyd George that Sir Herbert Lewis, with whom he had stayed the previous weekend, was enquiring 'most warmly' after him. Sir Harry Brittain, whom he had met that week, also sent his 'sincerest congratulations' on Lloyd George's birthday. Sir Herbert Lewis had previously represented Flintshire, and the University of taking place in Germany. The links he had nurtured, as well as the introductions from Lloyd George and his journalistic contacts, enabled him to secure access and glean the thoughts of many of the protagonists.

In an article published in the *Western Mail* on February 9 1933, headlined 'Hitler is There, But will he Stay?' Jones describes the moment, when he was staying with a friend in Leipzig, that Hitler became Chancellor:

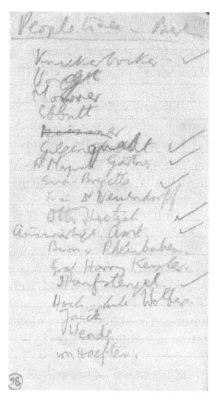

'My Saxon host came rushing into my room, slammed the door and shouted: "Hitler is Chancellor!" Even the Alsatian wolfhound in the corner barked with excitement. The Saxon continued: "Hindenburg has appointed Hitler [Chancellor]. It's a coalition between the National Socialists and the

'People to see - Berlin' – Jones' notebook of February 1933. (© The Gareth Vaughan Jones Estate)

German Nationalist party. Papen is Vice-Chancellor. At last Germany has a National Government such as you have in Britain."

I went out into the streets to see if anything were happening. All was calm. I overheard snippets of conversation: "Adolf Hitler is a second Napoleon." ... "Will there be a General Strike?"... "There'll be some murders in Berlin to-night."... "It's an attack on the working classes." ... "Hitler has gone over to the capitalists".'

Jones then described how someone thrust a leaflet produced by the Central Committee of the Communist Party of Germany into his hand. Headed, 'General Strike Against The Fascist Terror! Hitler is Chancellor', Jones noted that the leaflet stated:

> 'This new Cabinet of open Fascist Dictatorship is a most brutal declaration of war against the German working class. Instead of Schleicher we have against us bayonets of the Army and the revolvers of the Hitler bandits. It means limitless terror, the smashing of the last rights of the workers. The barbaric régime of Fascism is to be set up over Germany ... Come out onto the streets!? Lay down your tools! Down with Hitler, Papen and Hugenberg! [leader of the German National People's Party which supported Hitler's accession as Chancellor, as well as being Germany's leading media proprietor in the inter-war years] Long live the General Strike! Long live the struggle for a Workers and Peasant Republic!'

Jones continued by contrasting the message of the leaflet with the actual atmosphere in the city:

> 'In the streets all was normal. I went to the station to look for any signs of revolt or of general strike. Nothing happened I asked for a Communist newspaper. "It's banned today," said the girl. "We've just been told that it is illegal to sell it any more".'

'Will there be a general strike now that Hitler is in power?' Jones ponders, and reports the response of a friend when asked whether the Communists and Socialists would lay down their tools and join the strike. The friend replied: 'Not a bit of it. The unions have got no money; and no man would be fool enough to lose his job these days.' Jones then comments:

> 'The advent of Hitler has, therefore, been disappointingly calm. It is true that thousands upon thousands surged through the Berlin streets to greet the new Chancellor. It is true that the Hitler newspaper

handsome young boy in a Nazi uniform I read: "The father of this Storm Troop man, Gerhard Schiemminger, was one of the two million who fell for Germany. The wife he left behind bravely went along her path of duty and educated her son to be a sincere, honourable German citizen in the decadent post-war days of confusion and vice. But Gerhard, who gave all his energy for the freeing of Germany, was yesterday struck dead by a murderous Bolshevik bullet."

This throws a light upon the political passions in Germany. I look again at Hitler. He and his followers feel that the hundreds of Nazis, such as this young boy, who have died in street battles must be avenged, and they will be ruthless in crushing Communist opposition.

Hitler is now turning and smiling to his adjutant. He looks mild. Can this be the ruthless enemy of Bolshevism? It puzzles me.

We are now descending, however. Frankfurt is beneath us. A crowd is gathered below. Thousands of faces look up at us. We make a smooth landing. Nazi leaders, some in brown, some in black and silver, all with a red swastika armband, await their chief. Hitler steps out of the aeroplane. But he is now a man spiritually transformed. His eyes have a certain fixed purpose. Here is a different Hitler.

There are two Hitlers - the natural boyish Hitler, and the Hitler who is inspired by a tremendous national force, a great Hitler. It is the second Hitler who has stirred Germany to an awakening.'

With the benefit that hindsight offers us today, the fact the article fails to comment or reflect on the ominous significance of a demagogue who had repeatedly made clear what his intentions were with regard to the Jews is startling. His writing of the period clearly shows that he held no sympathies for Nazi ideology but had his close friendships with a number of supporters of the Nazi Party clouded his judgement? It can also be argued that, in common with other foreign journalists of the period, Jones was focused on reporting

Jones' photograph of Hitler speaking at the Frankfurt rally. (© The Gareth Vaughan Jones Estate)

Germany's biggest hall was packed as 25,000 people flocked to hear Hitler speak. (© The Gareth Vaughan Jones Estate)

what he was witnessing and did not foresee the Holocaust that began six years after his death.

In a further article for the *Western Mail* he described vividly the atmosphere at the Frankfurt rally to which Hitler had been flying:

'For eight hours the biggest hall in Germany has been packed with 25,000 people for whom Hitler is the saviour of his nation. They have waited, tense with national fervour.

… Wherever we go resounds the shout "Heil Hitler!" and hundreds of outstretched hands greet us as we entered the auditorium. We dash up the steps after Hitler and enter the ante-chamber. From within we hear roar upon roar of applause and the thumping, and the blare of a military band and the thud of marching feet.'

Describing the Nazi leader's oratory, Jones states:

'He begins in a calm, deep voice, which gets louder and louder, higher and higher. He loses his calmness and trembles in his excitement. In the beginning of his speech, his arms are folded and he seems hunched up, but when he is carried away he stretches out his arms and he seems to grow in stature. He attacks the rulers of Germany in the past 14 years. The applause is tremendous. He accuses them of corruption.

Another round of enthusiasm. He whips the Socialists for having vilified German culture. He appeals for the union of Nationalism with Socialism. He calls for the end of class warfare. When he shouts, "the future belongs to the young Germany which has arisen," the 25,000 hearers leap to their feet, stretch out their right hands and roar, "Heil Hitler!".'

Jones (centre) and Delmer with Hitler at the Frankfurt rally (© Sefton Delmer archive)

Thanks to their invitations as guests of the Nazi regime, Jones and Delmer were given seats in the front row of the rally. A photograph records the occasion.

A week before flying on Hitler's aircraft, Jones, who was gleaning economic as well as political information, had written to his parents about Germany's labour camps:

> 'My visit to Dresden was a great success and I learnt a tremendous amount about the Voluntary Labour Camps. The President of the Labour Service for all Saxony took me round in his car to inspect camps. Baron von Oppeln was exceedingly kind. He is a friend of a fellow member of the Reform Club. He was a typical Music Hall Baron – with eye glass, astrakhan collar etc but a remarkably [illegible word] man and we got on very well together.'

Mass unemployment, and its consequences, was of great interest to Jones and he was fascinated by the Weimar Republic's Voluntary Labour Service through which 30,000 young men were provided with work, food and basic healthcare. He was also aware of Mussolini's labour camps in Italy and Roosevelt's Civilian Conservation Corps in the United States. Thinking of the plight of the unemployed of industrial Wales, Jones welcomed the opportunity to see the camps for himself, the camps that Hitler wished to 'improve', and wrote to his parents:

> 'The camps may be set up by the private initiative of clubs, such as the YMCA, by political groups or by societies. There are Hitler camps, there are Protestant camps, Socialist camps, and other kinds but in general the neutral camp, where men of all parties and sects come together is preferred. Now, however, that Hitler is in power, the Nazis will be favoured. In each camp there is a leader who has been especially trained and put to a severe test, and who is usually over 25 years of age. His influence upon the young workers can be very great.

94

... [Many] thousands abandoned the Trade Unions in order to be able to volunteer for the camps. Contractors also fight against the Labour Service and accuse it of stealing their trade. In spite of the opposition, and in spite of financial difficulties, the movement is growing. Indeed the Hitler government wishes to make it compulsory and turn it into a kind of national conscription scheme.

Germany led the way in unemployment and health insurance. Perhaps by these labour camps Germany may be leading the way to a method of rescuing the youth of Europe from the effects of unemployment. The German authorities are still groping in the dark, and have great difficulties to face. But their experiments may be of great value to areas such as South Wales which have the same unemployment problem to tackle.'

The Weimar Republic's Voluntary Labour Service that so impressed Jones was, however, quickly changed into a compulsory programme in which the participants were indoctrinated in Nazi ideology.

The day after Jones' article about his flight with Hitler appeared in the *Western Mail*, a piece of his appeared in the *Financial Times* which appeared to accept with equanimity the arrival of a Nazi dictatorship:

'Since January 30, when Herr Hitler became Chancellor of the Reich, Germany has made rapid strides towards a Fascist Dictatorship. The National Socialists have lost no time in digging themselves in, and they are determined to cling to power, whatever obstacles may be put in their way. Hitler is in an exceedingly strong position. He has a personality which can arouse vast audiences to a frenzy of nationalist passion and the support of thirteen to fourteen million voters.

More important still than the votes of far more than one-third of Germany is the force of Defence Troops (S.S. men) and of the Storm Troops (SA men) numbering many hundreds of thousands of men, well trained in street fighting and moved by a profound devotion to their leader and to the national cause. Bound by no legalistic scruples and scorning constitutionalism, these men will form a strong barrier to any opposition movement from the Left.

Such is the basis of the National-Socialist power. It has been broadened and deepened by the grip which Herr Goering, as Reichs Commissar for Prussia, has gained over this state, which forms two thirds of the Reich. A thorough cleansing – the word itself is reminiscent of another land ruled by a dictatorship [Italy] – has removed from the police ranks those police presidents whose views smacked of Marxism, and their place has been taken by men whose devotion to country and to party is greater than their respect for the minutiae of the law. The police force, which was once considered a stronghold of Social Democracy, has thus become a powerful National-Socialist weapon, which Herr Hitler will not relinquish easily.

The National-Socialist propaganda has been masterful in its simple emotional appeal. Shortly it will have a new mouthpiece, for a Ministry is to be formed under the brilliant Dr Goebbels, which is to control the Press, the wireless and the films. Control over these organs means, with a docile people like the Germans, who are accustomed to obey authority, control over a great portion of public life.'

Inexplicably, after referring to the banning of opposition newspapers as part of the drive towards totalitarianism, Jones made it clear that he liked Goebbels very much:

'A dictator of public opinion is to be appointed – if opinion can be dictated to – and he is going to be the vivacious little man who sat behind Hitler in the aeroplane, and whose dark, narrow head and sharp brown eyes looked like those of a Glamorgan miner – Dr Goebbels. With the "Herr Doktor," as he is called, I have spent several hours. He has a remarkably appealing personality, with a sense of humour and a keen brain. One feels at home with him immediately, for he is amusing and likeable.'

On the evening of the flight from Berlin to Frankfurt and the rally which followed, Jones dined alone with Goebbels at a hotel. An entry in Goebbels' diary for that evening read:

> 'In the hotel Hitler takes his leave. He is very nice. Flies to Munich. Long conversation with Lloyd George's Secretary. Is in Germany for study purposes. An intelligent young man. Tells me terrible things about Soviet Union.'

The reference to Jones was spotted in Goebbels' diary by Professor Toby Thacker, an academic historian at Cardiff University, who passed the information on to Nigel Colley, the great nephew of Jones who did so much to preserve and promote the journalist's legacy. Jones' own diary entry for the meeting is more extensive:

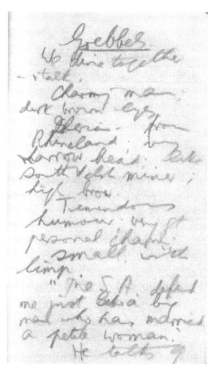

'Charming man' – Jones' notes following his meeting with Goebbels. (© The Gareth Vaughan Jones Estate)

> 'We dine together and talk. Charming man; dark brown eyes. Iberian from Rhineland; very narrow head; like South Wales Miner; high brow. Tremendous humour; very great personal charm; small; with limp. "The SA defend me just like a big man who has married a petite woman." He talks of past days as the days of idealism.'

Under the heading 'Autarchy' – meaning economic self-sufficiency – Jones quoted Goebbels, who had said:

'We don't want to lay stress on exports, of course we export to pay for raw materials; but we want to stretch towards the East. We want to take the people away from the towns and settle them on the land. To do this we must control the Baltic. That's why we have the *Danzstreuzer* [Danzig Corridor]. We must have a strong Baltic fleet. It would be in Britain's interest to allow us to spread to the East. We hope ... that Poland will realise that it will be better to give back the Corridor.

If Europe had not been exploited, we'd have had 10 wars. Europe is like a powder-barrel. Unless the causes are removed it will blow up. We are not so keen on colonies. The mistake of the past. Germany has two alternatives: Land or Sea. Army or fleet. East or West. Europe or World. Cannot do both. Mistake of pre-war days was to try and do both. It was a vital mistake to build up the fleet. We should have concentrated on the land. Great mistake to concentrate on export. The days of export are over. Our expansion to the East need not mean a conflict with Russia. Poland will be the sufferer.'

Under the further heading 'Propaganda', Jones quoted Goebbels saying:

'During the war the German propaganda was abominable; it was in the heads of people who were bourgeois and had no connection with the people. A good propagandist must know the roots. But now the Germans have become the best propagandists in the world. You watch next week, we'll flood Berlin with propaganda.'

'I wonder if Goebbels takes things serious; or is it more self-expressionism; love of fights, arguments,' noted Jones. 'Argumentation. Can imagine him in discussions in South Wales.' He further quotes Goebbels: 'It is too late to build up an international society. The chance is lost and will never come again ... It seems that the best will be to stick out of Europe ... The League of Nations is dead. Hitler has killed it.' Jones continued: 'Goebbels and I drive to the station. He says: 'We'll stick to power. Nothing will get us out. From now on there'll only be Nazi Ministers.'

Under the heading 'Speeches', Jones wrote:

> 'Hitler and Goebbels only have a few striking words (*Stichworte*) and practically never prepare. Goebbels said it took him 10 minutes to prepare a speech. Feel at home with Goebbels ... Hitler hunches himself up a little.'

Within a short space of time, Jones had established a level of intimacy with Goebbels, who confided in him after a short acquaintance in a way that can be considered unusual.

Jones made it clear that he considered Goebbels a charming and convivial companion, yet Goebbels was one of Hitler's most devoted associates, well-known for his virulent anti-Semitism. He favoured progressively harsher measures against Jews and in due course was an enthusiastic advocate of their extermination.

In 1921, at the age of 24, he wrote a semi-autobiographical novel called Michael. It is believed that he may have added anti-Semitic content as well as material about a charismatic leader to it before it was published in 1929 by Eher-Verlag, the publishing house of the Nazi party. In 1922 he began a love affair with a teacher called Else Janke, but after she told him she was half-Jewish he stated 'the enchantment was ruined', but continued to see her off and on until 1927.

Hitler appointed Goebbels the party Gauleiter (district leader) of Berlin in 1926. He encouraged violence at party meetings and demonstrations as a means of attracting attention to the Nazi party. In May 1927 the Berlin police banned the party from the city, leading to further violent incidents with thugs randomly attacking Jews in the streets.

Also in 1927 Goebbels founded the newspaper *Der Angriff* (The Attack) which published material that was highly anti-Communist and anti-Semitic. One of the paper's favourite targets was the Jewish deputy chief of the Berlin police, Bernhard Weiss. Goebbels subjected him to a relentless campaign of Jew-baiting aimed at provoking a crackdown which the Nazis could exploit.

As the Nazi party grew, Goebbels became its propaganda chief, characterising the opposition as 'November criminals' (based on the myth that Germany had not been defeated on the battlefield in the First World War, but by treacherous, backstabbing politicians), 'Jewish wire-pullers' and the Communist threat.

After Hitler's accession to power in January 1933, Goebbels became the primary mover of measures aimed at excluding Jews from public life in Germany. He wrote the text of Hitler's decree authorising the Nazi boycott of Jewish businesses, which began on 1 April 1933.

Jones could not claim to be unaware of Goebbels and his newspaper. As a fluent German speaker with several Nazi-supporting friends, he would have known of and read *Der Angriff*, as was confirmed by the American scholar, author, and Gareth Jones expert, Ray Gamache, who comments that Jones' liking of Goebbels was a 'moral blind spot'.

In another letter to his parents, Jones wrote:

'Please send me my articles. I always like to see them, as soon as possible; because I do not know what I have written. Please also state whether 'leader page' or which. They are absolutely essential in helping me to write the next one.'

Once in Berlin, he wrote:

'I went to see the Nazis on Friday at the Kaiserhof. I had 2¼ hours with Hitler's secretary – one of the funniest interviews I have ever had – he played marches on the piano and I sang nearly all the time. But must do a little more writing. I am thoroughly enjoying Germany this time. I always feel happy here.

My trip in Germany was wonderful. What a coup it was to be invited to fly with Hitler! I thoroughly enjoyed that ... The Hitler meeting [the rally in Frankfurt] was the most thrilling thing I have ever seen in my life, absolutely primitive.'

PS Don't send the Hitler articles to Russia.'

Why would Jones not have wanted his articles to be sent to Moscow? We simply don't know but the Soviet authorities would almost certainly have inspected closely any correspondence sent to him. Could it be that Jones feared the articles illustrated he had gained access to and the trust of senior Nazis, and that would hinder his chances of nurturing high-level contacts with the Soviets and prevent him from gleaning information from them?

We do know he was pleased with the way the articles were received by German officials.

Before setting off for Russia, Jones wrote a letter home in which he expressed pleasure at the positive reception of his article about flying on Hitler's plane in London's German Embassy:

'The German Embassy was very impressed with my article. It was read to the German Ambassador and considered "very balanced and reasonable and unbiased".'

By this time, of course, the Embassy was representing the Nazi regime.

An audience in Berlin giving the Nazi salute to Hitler, Goebbels, Göring and other Nazi Party leaders. (© Shutterstock)

7

Soviet Union

Eyewitness to Famine in Ukraine

'There's no food here ... In the South, 30% of the population have died of hunger, and in some parts 50%. They're murdering us.'

Gareth Jones had signalled his intention to visit Russia and Ukraine to investigate reports other journalists had picked up of serious food shortages. He arrived in Moscow on 5 March and the day after met the English journalist Malcolm Muggeridge.

In his diary Jones wrote a brief report of their conversation in note form:

> 'Collapse of Bolshevism. Returned from villages – terrible – dying. No seed for sowing. Practically no winter sowing. Outlook for next year disastrous. End of party absolutely inevitable. Stalin hated by party, but party cannot do anything. 95% of party opposed to Stalin's policy, but there is no discussion. Any opposition & man is removed.'

Two other journalists who had heard of food shortages in the northern Caucasus – William Stoneman of the *Chicago Daily News* and Ralph Barnes of the *New York Herald Tribune* – had tried to travel to the region but were arrested by the Soviet secret police and sent back to Moscow.

A ban that barred journalists from travelling far beyond Moscow had been introduced on 23 February. Jones initially took a local train to Kaluga, 93 miles to the south west, for which no permit was required. He then caught another train, alighting at a small station and continuing by foot.

His 1933 diaries include the raw notes he made after talking to people in the streets and elsewhere. Covering just a few days in early March, they provided him with the basic testimony he needed to expose the extent of the famine. They also included the notes he took after talking to Soviet officials and others about the state of the economy, how the collectivisation of the farms was going and other related matters.

They were not in themselves intended for publication, and they provide us with an insight into Jones' method of gathering information at the primary stage, before he developed the material into articles that conformed with the stylistic and sometimes ideological requirements of the newspapers in which they would appear.

On 5 March, while in Moscow, Gareth Jones wrote:

'Outside Torgsin [a hard currency store]. A beggar woman: "Want bread for my child." She was selling flowers. 1 ruble 25 a bunch. Went into Torgsin, plenty of everything. Came out & another beggar, a peasant with boy: "Please give me something to get bread for my son. We've come all the way from Ukraine. It's terrible there. No bread. They are starving. So we came up north to get bread in the town."'

Also on 5 March, *Pravda* and *Izvestia* – official newspapers whose names mean respectively Truth and News – published a statement from OGPU (the secret police) which said members of a group dedicated to opposing the collectivisation of farms had been arrested. Jones quoted the statement:

'Recently the organs of OGPU have discovered & liquidated a wrecking organisation in the People's Agricultural Commissariat or State Farm Commissariat, mainly in the agricultural districts of Ukraine, North Caucasus & White Russia.

Most of the guilty ones were civil servants from bourgeois & landowning families.

Most of the arrested men confessed their guilt. Their actions were as follows:

    1 smashing of tractors.

    2 burning of tractor stations and of flax factories.

    3 stealing of grain reserves.

    4 disorganisation of sowing.

    5 destruction of cattle.

The evidence showed that the activities of arrested men had as their aim the ruining of agriculture or the creation of famine in the country.'

Below the underlined word <u>Visits</u>, Jones wrote:

'Very great distress. Worse & worse. In villages terrible – there famine. Prices ever higher. Young Communists getting disillusioned. 1lb black bread & 1lb white bread a day. There are unemployed. Eggs have become a luxury. Practically no meat.'

Against the underlined word <u>Passports</u>, Jones wrote:

'We're terribly afraid. What if they send us out of Moscow? They say 1 ½ million have been sent out.'

Jones wrote, presumably from a conversation with an unidentified individual:

'Children get good meals in school. Terrible. Famine in the villages. There is TYPHUS in Moscow; 150 people a day going into the hospitals.'

He spoke to peasants in the street:

'Peasant from Kharkovskaya Gubernia [in Ukraine] with boy: "Give, give bread. There's famine where I live."'

The day after, March 6, he met another Ukrainian peasant boy with a sack, who came up to him and said: 'Please give me something to buy bread.' He was also from Kharkovskaya Gubernia and said: 'There's no bread. There's famine.' Asked by Jones how the spring sowing would be, he said: 'Bad. There's no seed. They took away too much last year for the [five year] plan.'

After leaving the theatre, Jones spoke, for the third time, with a Ukrainian peasant, who said: 'They are dying in the Ukraine, just like cattle, I left my village with money & came here for bread. I shall send it by post. I shall stand in a queue where I can get bread for 2 rubles a kilo. In my village there are 54 households. We used to have 80 horses. Now there are 18. We used to have one cow each dvor [farmyard] and most dvors had 2. Now there are only 6 cows left in the whole village.'

Jones then described a scene he had witnessed:

'Two private traders, one a Jew about 40 & the other a boy about 20, blood running from nose. "Citizens, he hit me. This is my place." Blood was running down & dripping on to the sweets or the toffee ... Crowd gathered. They were claiming the place. Sad feeling. Leather coats. "He hit me first". "Yes. Bully." Crowd joins in. Private traders, scum, still exist, v[ery] expensive.'

Jones meticulously noted the cost of food items. He encountered a man with a horse, who told him: 'Religion is still alive. We still believe in God. And many children still believe. It was terrible when they took down the Temple of Christ the Saviour. It was a wonderful church [the original Cathedral of Christ the Saviour in Moscow was demolished on Stalin's orders in 1931. It was supposed to make way for a colossal Palace of the Soviets to house the country's legislature, the Supreme Soviet of the USSR. Construction began in 1937 but was halted in 1941 when Germany invaded the Soviet Union. Its steel frame was disassembled in 1942 and the Palace was never built. Following the dissolution of the Soviet Union, a new cathedral with the same name was built on the same site]. They're killing the peasants. How much longer can it go on? Now a lot of peasants come up from the South, with all the money they can get. They collect the gold & silver & send a man to Moscow. Then they post the bread back home.

'I used to have 4 horses in the village & 4 cows & 2 pigs. Now I only have one horse. Our cattle is more important to us than a new factory. Only a tenth of the horses and the cattle in our village is left to us. In Moscow it is not so bad. But go into the provinces. And there's not enough seed.'

As it tends to in difficult times, black humour thrived. Jones took note of two jokes:

'There is an animal trainer. He trained animals in circus. Said: "All of you must now go out except members of the party." All animals go out except donkey. Trainer was arrested.'

The other joke had a peasant asking Soviet General Kalinin:

'"Why have we so few clothes, so little to eat?" Kalinin responded: "That's nothing. In Africa the people don't wear anything at all." To which the peasant retorted: "Well they must have had Socialism a long time".'

Jones noted:

'There is typhus in Moscow. There is black plague in the Caucasus. The politodel [political department/ secret police] means only that the GPU will be introduced into the villages more severely. They've destroyed all the best peasants. In the South, the power of the Party is disappearing. The GPU & the Army is all powerful. Party is losing its power. The Party dare say nothing. Dread of passportisation [preventing Ukrainians leaving their republic in search of food], being turned out to starve. Religious revival now in Russia; there have been passionate religious scenes. New sects. Scenes when in special religious ceremonial there is cry: "only the Virgin Mary can save us". Soviet statistics all lies. 96% against the regime.'

Describing a street scene, Jones wrote:

> 'Peasant, with 3 children, taken away by police, children yelling, shrieking, dragging on to sheepskin coat of father. Arrested for begging. Commandeered a droshke [four-wheeled open horse-drawn carriage] & driven off.'

Yet there were still pockets of prosperity in Moscow, as another entry shows:

> 'More motor cars, large number. Great increase; some good ones.'

A conversation with a boy (described as *Bachgen*, the Welsh for boy) provided Jones with further testimony about real life under Stalin's regime: 'In school a girl 15 years old said something against Stalin. GPU took her & she was condemned to 10 years imprisonment. She cried so much that her shoulders got disjointed. A lot of boys believe in God, go to church. But majority do not believe. It is bad but in school they give us good meals, meat, milk.' Jones thought he looked healthy.

'They teach us about the crisis,' said the boy. 'There is going to be a world revolution.

'It's going to be much better ... It is terrible in the villages. The people find all the gold & silver & brass they can & bring it to the Torgsin.'

Jones quoted Ralph W Barnes of the New York *Herald Tribune*, who said: 'They've had to send a lot of grain South. From Central Reserves.' Jones then met a Crimean peasant girl, selling scented white spring flowers in the street for one ruble. She told him: 'We've come up from the Crimea, my mother & I. There it's warm, not like cold Moscow. There is no bread. But there is meat there & there will be fruit. Only now there is no bread & the people are dying.'

Occasionally, Jones interspersed descriptions of what people told him with short analytical passages from which one gets the sense he was pulling ideas together to help him understand what was happening. Underlining the name of American journalist <u>Eugene Lyons</u>, he wrote:

> 'Electricity: the figures are of potential capacity. In Kiev, there is the electric light plant, but no fuel has arrived.'

Underlining the word <u>Peasants</u>, Jones wrote about the high quantity of grain extracted from peasants in taxation:

> 'New tax average 2 ½ centners of grain per hectare (about 15 poods). A centner is a Russian measurement of weight equivalent to 50 kilograms, while a pood is equivalent to 16.3807 kilograms. Average from production would not [be] much more than twice that. It's a stiff tax. After paying that & other taxes, they'll be lucky if they have enough to live on. Free market after tax is paid is academic. New name for old system.'

Under the heading 'Last 6 months', Jones listed a series of measures that introduced more authoritarianism in grain-growing districts:

> '1. Politotdel [political department]; nearly 7000 new GPU stationed in villages.
> 2 Passport system.
> 3 Extraordinary Commissars in grain regions with punitive powers & right to enforce labour.
> 4 Disciplinary measures in factories, depriving workers of cards [without which they could not work] for one day's absence.
> 5 Death penalties for stealing. Measures for defence of Socialist property.
> 6 Extension of police power in state; extension of use of whip.
> New political policy of force.'

Under the heading 'Party', Jones wrote:

'The fiction that the Party is not the Government has disappeared. Force has come out into the open. Formerly the Government & the Party issued decree separately. Division has disappeared.'

Jones went on to quote a worker: 'I earn 120 rubles a month. I get 2lbs of bread a day. No meat, no eggs, no butter. Before the war I used to get a lot of meat. Bread I can get cheaply. It's bad. I haven't had meat for a year. I get a little soup but it is not enough to work on.'

On 8 March Jones reported meeting a peasant woman on the street, who was selling milk for three rubles a litre. She told him: 'I live 50 versts [about 33 miles] from Moscow and there we have no bread. We come to Moscow and bring bread back. Moscow is feeding us. If it were not for Moscow, we should die.'

Reporting on a conversation he had with Karl Radek, the editor of *Izvestia*, Jones noted:

'War v Japan. What would be the use? Japan afraid a) that we will organise China. b) that Soviets will triumph in China and that we will chase Japan from Manchukuo/ Manchuria. c) that we will have alliance with America & that we can lend aeroplanes to US.'

Jones went on to express his own view:

'That's all rot. We are on the crossways of 2 conflicts: France v Germany. Japan v China & we wish to remain neutral. We want to remain neutral and have no alliances with other nations. We're afraid that both parties will try to bring us in. If the crisis goes on we've enough machinery to continue & we'll be able to improve standard of living.'

These comments of Jones have a particular poignancy given the fate that was to befall him two years later in China. Further reporting the views of Radek, he wrote:

'Next war will create such hatred among the population of enemy. We will never be the first to shoot. Lloyd George is the last genius whom the bourgeoisie has produced.'

Referring to the League of Nations, to which the USSR did not belong, Radek told Jones: 'We won't enter an organisation in which a majority of votes will govern ours & where there are all capitalists. Not without use. Is a clearing house of political interests where representatives of different countries can meet. But if the terms are taken by majority of votes, why should they tell us what we should do? We are ready to help the League of Nations [on] every occasion where it helps world peace. Have you ever seen a government which has been thrown out by peasants?'

Reporting the comments of a Soviet official named Andreychi, Jones wrote:

'Unemployment according to plan. We are ejecting people from the office in order to make the others work better. The decree by which labour discipline is enforced is essential. Passportisation. It is intended to force out about 2,800,000 from Moscow. That will mean that about 700,000 roughly will have to go. But these will be kulaks, officers, Nepmen [people who took advantage of business opportunities, in line with Lenin's New Economic Policy], speculators & crooks. The honest to God worker will remain, need not fear. No, the lack of food was not according to the plan. We are creating unemployment on purpose & the people understand.'

Speaking to a Soviet official identified in his diary only as L (widely believed to be the writer VG Lidin), Jones quoted him saying: 'Give us books for new readers, true books, with living truth.' When Jones asked him whether he would describe famine in villages, L responded: 'Well, there is no famine ... The present hunger is temporary. In writing books, you must have a longer view. It would be difficult to describe hunger.'

SOVIET UNION

Jones interrupted the last sentence of L's comments in the diary with the single word 'Prevarication', adding 'See Hamlet' – a reference to the greatest prevaricator in literature. Jones' great-nephew Nigel Colley, who designed and co-curated the website *garethjones.org*, stated: 'In researching the possible significance of Gareth's *Hamlet* reference, it has been discovered that *Hamlet* was the only Shakespeare play to have been effectively banned, and banned personally by Stalin. Though *Hamlet* was indeed a tyrant, his tyranny paled insignificantly in comparison to the 'unbanned' *Macbeth*. Indeed, the last Soviet performance for over 30 years (until after Stalin's death) was in 1932, which coincided with the height of the *Holodomor*. Is there a possible connection? Well quite possibly.'

Colley went on to cite the very first 1603 quarto edition of the 'To be or not to be' soliloquy, which includes the lines: 'the taste of hunger or a tyrant's reign, And thousand more calamities besides ...' A Shakespeare website run from the University of Texas stated: 'Stalin's regime banned *Hamlet*, claiming, "*Hamlet*'s indecisiveness and depression were incompatible with the new Soviet spirit of optimism, fortitude and clarity".'

Making notes about the shortcomings of the Soviet rural economy, Jones wrote:

'Agriculture. Terrible failure, idea collectives is not impossible, but peasant must have enough to eat. Otherwise he wouldn't *mitmachen* [German – take part]. Cattle. Lack of seed tractors. Like 1921. *Voelkerwanderung in die Stadte* [German - Population migration into the towns]. New bread shop opened. First day 4000.

Until 1945 it will be until they have same number of cattle as in 1928. If all the plans for import of cattle etc, if there is no disease, if there is fodder, then it will until 1945. Differentiation of the population. Restaurants for different classes. All cannot go into the restaurants. No equality. Worker can be dismissed & lose his bread card. Dismissal 25%, 30%, 50% of workers in factory. Factories – dismissals. Passportisation – to send people on to the land. Much more brutal than 1930 – hard. 1931 – *erleichterund* [German: relief, easement]. better; better food; clothes. After Stalin's speech more freedom, less seen of attacks on wreckers. Then with news of crisis, more exported to pay foreign debts.'

Quoting Alfred Cholerton, the Moscow-based correspondent of the *Daily Telegraph*, Jones wrote:

'There is going to be a purging of the village communists & half of them will have to go. Great dismissals from the factories. Party has lost great deal of power to GPU. Corruption in the GPU not in money but in goods. Now arrests are growing in Moscow; new clearing out, now directed against intelligentsia.'

On 10 March, Jones interviewed Finance Commissar Grigory Grinko, who explained that prices of consumer goods had been raised because there was a shortage of them.

Asked why the private market had also seen price rises, Grinko said: 'Speculation. Those social elements whom we chased out - they are the people who accumulate to speculate. Private traders creep in on the borders. We are carrying on a very cruel war against them. We raise prices in a way to get taxes, i.e. to get money for financing of plan & also to have order on the market.' Ironically Grinko was shot five years later following a show trial at which he was accused of opposing the policies of rapid industrialisation, forced collectivisation and central planning, as well as planning to eliminate the Soviet leadership.

On a train heading south from Moscow, Jones recorded how he was told by a Red Army soldier who was a member of the Communist Party: 'There ought to be a good harvest this year, because a lot of snow fell (as in 1923 when there was a lot of snow & a fine harvest). Government gave Ukraine 20 million poods. North Caucasus 12 million poods.

'Ukraine, 87% of seed is there. We fulfilled the autumn sowing plan. Of course we did & we sowed more in the autumn of 1932 than in 1931.'

SOVIET UNION

At a station, Jones wrote:

> 'Hundreds of peasants selling cakes, milk etc. But their refrain was: "There is no bread." Boy on train asking for bread. I dropped a small piece of bread on floor and put it in spittoon. Peasant came & picked it up & ate it. Peasant in train: "Kolkhoz [collective farm] bad. No bread". Peasant woman: "Many are dying. We're starving. There is little cattle left. They take all the grain away". Ukrainian peasant: "They took away my grain. Cattle [a little]. But there were a lot".'

Jones interviewed a member of Politotdel, who told him: "I've been a member of the Party for 12 years. They are now sending 2,700 from Moscow Politodel. They're the best, the strongest. It is semi-military. We'll smash the kulaks and smash opposition. We're promoting all

'Enemies of the 5-Year Plan' - Soviet propaganda poster highlighting the enemies of collectivisation (L-R): landowners, kulaks, drunks, priests, journalists, capitalists, Mensheviks, and White soldiers. (© The Gareth Vaughan Jones Estate)

men who served in the Civil War. The elite, chosen ones. 60% of us have been in higher educational schools.'

Jones described him:

> 'He clenched his fist & hit down with every word: resolute, ruthless, cruel. "We are all workers, mainly from the factories. We are going to organise. There'll be about 4 of us in each MTS [machine tractor station]. The MTS where I shall be will look after 15 kolkhozes. We'll give them strict control. The weather for the harvest is good i.e. lot of snow. The methods of the kulaks have changed. They used to murder. Now they are subtle. Now they say, 'Yes we're for the kolkhoz', but they'll steal & they won't work & they'll make difficulties. They try to wreck by mean tricks, but they are not dangerous any longer".'

A boy Komsomolet – member of the Soviet youth organisation – told Jones: 'Very strict now. They are dying in villages. In Belgorod [40 kilometres north of the border with Ukraine] there is bread, but that's a town. One woman stole 5 beets & got 10 years imprisonment. If you steal coal from the station, 10 years. Very bad & we don't know if it'll be better.'

Jones met a group of women peasants, who told him: 'We're starving. Two months we've hardly had bread. We're from the Ukraine and we're trying to go north. They're dying quietly in the villages. Kolkhozs are terrible. They won't give us any tickets. And we don't know what to do. Can't buy bread for money.'

Jones wrote:

> 'I dropped orange peel into spittoon. Peasant picked it up and ate it. Later apple core. Man speaking German, same story. "Tell them in England. Starving, Bellies extended. Hunger." Another peasant: "Belly extended".'

A party member told Jones: 'A large number of village party members have sided with the kulaks and have to be thrown out,' and a worker told Jones: 'They haven't paid wages for 3 months. A lot of factories are unable to pay wages. They've dismissed a lot of workers - 20,000

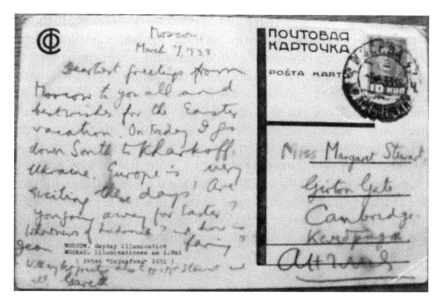

Jones' postcard to Margaret Stewart announcing his visit to Ukraine, March 1933. (© The Gareth Vaughan Jones Estate)

in Kharkov. I get 125-130 a month.' Another worker told Jones: 'They want to get the farm workers back to the farm but there is nothing to eat there.'

Some Komsomolets told him: 'Lots of Komsomolets getting dissatisfied, because no bread. I haven't had bread for a week – only potatoes. I get 60 rubles a month, but by the time they've taken away forced loans etc, I only get 20-25 rubles per half month.' They went on to tell Jones: 'Be careful in the village, because the Ukrainians are desperate. They'll grab any bread which they can see.'

The conductor on the train told Jones he was paid 67 rubles per month, and a pound of black bread per journey. 'I must work night and day,' and the Komsomolet added: 'When I left my mother & two sisters a couple of days ago, they had 2 glasses of flour left.' The Komsomolet said his brother had died of hunger.

Visiting a village school, Jones read a campaign document that was on display close to a wall newspaper displaying the life of Lenin.

It stated: 'At present moment Kolkhoz construction is going through a period of transition. We must struggle against the majority of traditions. Struggle is necessary. The preparation for the spring sowing campaign is a fight. The kulaks, opportunists, are trying to smash the plan for spring sowing but the iron muscles of the Kolkhozniki must reply to those self-seeking tendencies. The industrialisation of the country is going rapidly ahead. In agriculture, also, we must go over to the machine although this cannot be done immediately. Thus we must still pay attention to the horse. Now just look at how we treat horses in this village. Horses fall down & are dying of hunger & dirt. The Kolkhozniki of Krasny Khutor [the name of the village] must pay attention to the futile loss of horses. The horse is the first friend & helper for the spring sowing campaign.'

Jones then crossed the border into Ukraine. He wrote:

'Everywhere I talked to peasants who walked past. They all had the same story. "There is no bread. We haven't had bread for over 2 months. A lot are dying." The first village had no more potatoes left and the store of beetroot was running out. They all said: "The cattle are dying. There's nothing to feed the cattle with. We used to feed the world & now we are hungry. How can we sow when we have few horses left? How will we be able to work in the fields when we are weak from want of food?"'

Jones caught up with a bearded peasant who was walking along, who told him after Jones handed him some bread and cheese: 'You couldn't buy that anywhere for 20 rubles. There just is no food. Before the War this was all gold. We had horses and cows and pigs and chickens. Now we are ruined. We're doomed. You see that field. It was all gold, but now look at the weeds. Before the war we could have boots and meat and butter. We were the richest country in the world for grain. We fed the world. Now they have taken all away from us. Now people steal much more. Four days ago, they stole my horse. Hooligans came. There – that's where I saw the track of the horse.'

The peasant took Jones to his cottage, where he met his daughter and three smaller children, two of whom were swollen. The peasant told Jones: 'If you had come before the Revolution, we would have given you chicken and eggs and milk and fine bread. Now we have no bread in the house. They are killing us. People are dying of hunger.'

In the hut there was a spindle and the peasant's daughter showed Jones how to make thread. Jones said the peasant showed him his shirt, which was homemade, and some fine sacking which had also been homemade. The peasant said: 'But the Bolsheviks are crushing that. They won't take it. They want the factory to make everything.'

Walking for an hour, Jones chatted to everyone he met. He wrote:

'All people say the same. There is no bread. All swollen.'

One woman told him: 'We are looking forward to death.' and in one village, all the bread had gone two months before. Potatoes had also run out and there was only beetroot that would run out in a month. Jones asked himself: 'How can they live till next harvest?'

'We are looking forward to death' – Kharkiv, August 1933. (© Alexander Wienerberger)

Jones visited an unnamed kolkhoz on 11 March, and met its president. He wrote:

'The president said that they had enough seed, but that more towards the south there was a lack of seed. The discussion was very open, the peasants saying that it had never been so bad, the president saying faint-heartedly that great sacrifices had to be made. One peasant said: "If only Lenin had lived, we'd be living fine. He knew what was going to happen. Here they've been chopping and changing policy & we don't know what's going to happen next. Lenin would not have done something violently & then said that it was a mistake".'

Two soldiers then appeared, and after telling Jones that the bourgeois were crushing the working class in England, that they had shot down demonstrations, that Communists were in prison and England was going to declare war on Russia, it became clear that they had come to arrest a peasant thief, who had allegedly gone to steal potatoes from the hut of another. The owner of the hut had come out and the peasant had stabbed her with a knife. There were, said the soldiers, many instances of that happening. A Red Army soldier who appeared the next morning said: 'Don't travel by night. There are too many wild uncultured men who want food & to steal.'

Jones slept on the floor, with the president, his wife and her sister in one bed and the child in a small bed. The leader of the next kolkhoz came over the next day and said: 'We have difficulties but they have to be overcome.' Jones wrote:

'There is seed in this village. Cattle decrease disastrous. There used to be 200 oxen, now 6. Horses & cattle are down by a tremendous amount. The new tax, the Communists think, will increase the desire of workers to work. But there have been too many wreckers, too many kulaks who have been trying to influence the other peasants.'

Jones walked along by the side of the railway track. He wrote in his diary:

'There is no bread here'. (© Alexander Wienerberger)

'Talked to all the people as I tramped along the railway track. Ravens or crows with grey cap. White expanse of snow. Moscow – Sebastopol train rattled past, with sleeping wagon – politodels, party members etc. Went into village. There is no bread here.

People told him: 'We've had no bread for 2 months. Each *dvor* had one or 2 cows. Now none. There are almost no oxen left & the horses have been dying off.' A young worker in the village told Jones: 'The unemployed are growing & they're treated like cattle. They're told to get away & they get no bread card. They're cutting down men everywhere. I worked in Kharkov. There they've dismissed thousands. How can I live? I've got a pound of bread for all my family & I've come here for a short time. There's no food here. My family is in Kharkov & I don't know how they'll live. We're all getting swollen.' The young worker said: 'In the South, 30% of the population have died of hunger, and in some parts 50%. They're murdering us.'

In Kharkov Locomotive Works, the workforce of 36,000 had been reduced to 28,000 because 8,000 had been dismissed. Another factory had seen its workforce cut back from 14,000 to 8,000. Jones wrote:

> 'Nothing for unemployed. Even no bread. Where? They go anywhere. They send them anywhere they want to. They take the bread card from the unemployed and he receives nothing. While a male worker in Kharkov, the second biggest city in Ukraine, received a ration of 600 grams a day, a woman worker got only 200. In factories, workers got one meal a day: rotten cabbage and a small spoonful of "bad kasha" – effectively boiled grass.'

A worker told Jones: 'In my village you will not find a single person - every hut is empty,' and a little girl came past wearing a home-made Ukrainian dress, with red and green designs. She hadn't had a glass of milk for a year because her family's cow had been taken away. Another peasant told Jones: 'I don't care who I work for – landowner or Communist, English, German, Austria, Polish, as long as I get enough to eat. They fought here in the Civil War. Reds, whites, shot across here. We hid in that underground cellar I showed you. We didn't care who won. That cellar used to be full of potatoes, cabbages etc. The barn used to be full of grain and the cowshed of cows. Now nothing. They said it would be all right last year to sell surplus on the private market and yet they took it all away [as tax]. We don't believe it. They say they'll only take 15 poods of grain per hectare, but they'll take everything.'

Everyone Jones met along the track told him the same. 'Lots of people dying,' he was told. 'Only beetroot. Too weak for spring sowing.' One group told him: 'There are thousands of unemployed. Their bread card is taken away & they have nothing. On April 1 there'll be another cut. Go down to the Poltava district & there you'll see hundreds of cottages empty. In a village of 300 huts, only about 100 will have people living in them. The others have died or gone away, but most died.'

A group of children along the track said to Jones: 'There is no bread. There is no God. It seems that there is no God.' While a worker

'Lots of people dying'. (© Alexander Wienerberger)

from Kharkov said: 'I only get 100 grams of bread per day for wife & self.' Jones asked one peasant: 'What kind of crop will you have?' The peasant replied: 'A splendid crop – of weeds.'

A group of workers told Jones: 'Down South it's ten times worse. They're dying off, empty villages. We are too weak for the sowing. In this village, they've sent seed, but we've few horses.' Jones wrote:

> 'Resigned to fate. One village practically no seed. It is significant that the peasants eat horse flesh, for only the Tatars ate horse flesh. Against religion & peasants always religious. Many people would not buy meat on the market some years ago, because rumour that it was horse.'

In Kharkov, censors were much stricter than in Moscow. Jones wrote:

> 'Here various plays ... on bread, forbidden. Population longing for foreign films,'

Describing the living conditions in Kharkov, Jones wrote:

'Heating very bad; lack of coal. Opera house in winter so cold that artists freezing often joined the audience in order to have heat.'

Referring to a friend who worked in the German consulate in the city, Jones wrote:

'Erika and I walked alongside about a hundred ragged pale hungry people. Militiaman came out of shop, whose windows had been battered in & were covered with wood & said, "There is no bread and there will be no bread today." Shouts, angry peasants also there: "But, citizens, there is no bread."

"How long here?", I asked a man. "Two days."'

There were homeless boys on the street. Jones wrote:

'They would not go away but remained. Sometimes a cart might come up with bread, waiting with forlorn hope. Streets in terrible condition, houses rotten, ice thawing, wet, dirty.'

Comparing the situation to 12 years before in Germany, Jones wrote:

'1921. Germany. Now much worse. Much worse than war years also. Then there was no food in the towns but the peasants had food. Now neither peasants nor towns have food.'

Hundreds of thousands were unemployed, Jones was told: 'Thousands upon thousands of peasants have been transported. I've seen them on the station ... lots of German colonists, 6-7 millions sent to Siberia. Recently. Prisons crowded; 200 grams of bread a day, epidemics spreading rapidly: thousands dying.'

In *Pravda* it was reported that a number of workers, some of whom were Communist Party members, had been sentenced for organising 'counter-revolutionary wrecking' at a machine tractor station and in kolkhozes in Ukraine and North Caucasus: 35 were to be shot. Some of those sentenced were from *Narkomzen* (People's Commissariat for Agriculture) and *Narkomsovkhoz* (People's Commissariat for Soviet State Farms). Many members of the Communist Party were among those shot. Jones wrote:

> 'The GPU is getting more and more powerful. Stalin & GPU now ruling Russia. There is a struggle between the *Narkomindel* [People's Commissariat for Foreign Affairs] and GPU – an old conflict but *Narkomindel* has nothing to say.'

Among those shot was Feodar Konar, the Vice Commissar of Agriculture. Jones noted:

> 'Feeling of terror has spread through Moscow, in ranks of Party etc.'

Jones then alluded to the Soviet assault on the Ukrainian dimension:

> 'New Ukrainian policy. In last few weeks there has been a beginning of Russification appointments. Muscovites have been placed in leading positions in Kharkoff & now Russian is to be taught in the schools.'

The Commissar of Education in the Ukraine SSR, Mykola Skrypnik, who was in favour of Ukrainian rights, was accused of 'over-Ukrainisation', removed from office at the beginning of March, put on trial and committed suicide on July 7 1933.

Addressing the rising level of unemployment, Jones cited three causes. Firstly, there was the lack of raw material:

> 'The supply of coal, timber, oil etc fails. If one factory fails and [there is] no supply, it leads to trouble all along the line.'

Secondly, there was the need for financial prudence:

'Factory must make balance. Financial difficulties. Very high operating costs. Deficits caused. Also in Russian factories about 6 men are equivalent to 1 man in British or German factory. Thus, to balance, dismissals.'

The third cause was food supply:

'The factory has been made responsible for the feeding of the workers. A factory is given a certain agricultural district from which to draw supplies. A Directorium is made responsible. Now it is most hard to get food. So workers are dismissed. This also features control of factory over the country. About 20,000 out of work in Kharkoff. More dismissals to come on April 1.'

In the waiting room at Kharkov station, 300 children were being taken away. Jones wrote:

'They have been turned out by the peasants to fend for themselves. Looked in through window. One with red face & open mouth had typhus. Another half-naked had nothing but dried skin – looked like thin bones. Depressed faces. Another pale white thin face.'

While on the train, the conductor came to draw the blinds in Jones' carriage. When he tried to keep the blinds open, the conductor said they had to be shut because boys and peasants threw stones at the train in protest.

In *Izvestia*, Jones read that civil servants were held responsible by the GPU for any sabotage or burning etc that took place in their institutions – a development that he believed increased the power of the GPU tremendously. So far as Jones was concerned, forcing peasants to join collective farms represented a return of serfdom. He wrote of decrees that obliged collective farms to exclude those who 'of their own free will and without an agreement with the economic organs registered in the direction of the kolkhoz' left their *kolkhoz* household holdings. Such peasants also had their earnings confiscated.

Singled out for criticism were those kolkhoziniki who left at the time of sowing 'and then at the time of harvest & threshing return to the kolkhoz in order to misappropriate the kolkhoz goods.' This decree was signed by three high-ranking party officials: Mikhail Kalinin, Vyacheslav Molotov and Yukhym Medvedev.

Jones was angered by a report in *Pravda* on March 19 which told how metal needed for agricultural machinery factories was being held up. He wrote:

'Disgraceful work of Administrator of Southern Railway. In the storehouses of Almaznyanskii [Ukraine] Metal factory, 13,000 tons of metal lying idle, intended mainly for the agricultural machinery factories. 550 tons are waiting to be sent to Rostov Selmarsh [agricultural machinery]; 1,500 tons to Kharkov, etc; 2,000 to Stalingrad; 2,000 to [Stalin automobile factory]; 550 tons to Nizhni Autostroy. Southern Railway is only sending 12-15 wagons of iron per day instead of 35. On some days absolutely no wagons dispatched. The Director of Southern Railway, Livchin, should stop this outrage & immediately see to it that iron should be loaded immediately. Absolutely essential for the carrying out of spring sowing orders.'

Jones quoted Alexander Lukashevsky, deputy chairman of the League of the Militant Godless, who typified the Soviet view, seeing atheism as a weapon for class warfare and that anti-religious propaganda was connected with industrialised & technical progress & with food harvest. Lukashevsky told him: 'Now class warfare is going on. The dying classes are not dying without struggle & they are using religion as a weapon of wrecking. The religious have fought against collectivisation, e.g. the religious people wrote letters, said that these letters came from Heaven. "I, God, tell you that the kolkhoz is Satanic." Or: "If you go into kolkhoz, you will go to Hell." The religious peasants said in Asia that woman should not have place in the kolkhozys. Tell Lloyd George that his brother Baptist also did the

Maxim Litvinov.

same. Sectant (Baptist) killed his wife because she started to work in the communal work. He said the kulaks had said the kolkhoz system was the Devil's work. When a man entered a kolkhoz & died a few days later, a kulak got hold of the coat of the dead man & went around as a ghost, saying, "God won't let me into Heaven." Why fight against religion? Because religion upholds the old capitalist world, the kulaks etc. Take the spring sowing – in the old time they sowed on certain feast days, whether the weather was good or not. kulaks now agitate. They are against scientific methods. They stop the peasants from becoming rich ... kulak is harm to workers. Religion is enemy of science.'

On 19 March Jones met Maxim Litvinov, the People's Commissar of Foreign Affairs, and Walter Duranty, head of the *New York Times'* Moscow Bureau. Jones wrote in his diary:

'I don't trust Duranty. He still believes in collectivisation. Said, "Save face. Third International down and out".'

What Duranty meant by this cryptic remark – and what Jones thought he meant – is unclear. The Third International, founded in Moscow by Lenin in 1919, was composed of representatives of communist parties in more than 50 countries. In 1933 it was in its so-called Third Period. The organisation had proclaimed that the capitalist system was entering the period of final collapse and therefore all communist parties were to adopt an aggressive and militant ultra-left line.

Meeting some women in a Moscow courtyard, Jones was told by one of them: 'They are cruelly strict now in the factories, If you are absent one day, you are sacked, get your bread card taken away and cannot get a passport. Life is a nightmare. I cannot go in the tram, it kills my nerves. It is more terrible than ever. If you say a word now in the factory, you are dismissed. There is no freedom. They are dismissing people everywhere & taking away their bread card.' A pale and hungry mother said hysterically: 'I cannot get milk for my child.'

Another family told Jones: 'Plague, black death is coming from Central Asia & from North Caucasia. It will come here. There are thousands of people dying of typhus. Two doctors came here & stripped us naked. Shame. To examine us for typhus. In a few weeks' time we will only get bread at commercial prices. We are terrified that we will get no passports. Where can we go? Everywhere persecution. Everywhere terror. One man we know said, 'My brother died, but he still lies there & we don't know when we'll bury him, for there are queues for the burial.' There is no hope for the future.'

On 21 March Jones went out in a horse-drawn carriage. A diary entry noted:

'Suburbs of Moscow in disgraceful condition. The wonderful houses so much admired 2 or 3 years ago now shabby & look broken down. Very pale & ill crowds of people. New factories going up, Went past Neftgas [oil gas] factory. Stopped to talk.'

A peasant told him: 'Terrible. We have no bread. We have to go all the way to Moscow to get bread & then they only give us 2 kilos & we have to pay 3 rubles a kilo. How can a poor man do that? We have no potatoes left. The cattle have nearly all died. The horses also. I joined the kolkhozy 3 weeks ago. They made me pay so many taxes that life became a burden.'

A woman appeared and stated crying. She said: 'They're killing us. In my village there used to be 300 cows & now only 30. The horses have gone, died. How can I feed us all?'

A man said: 'I have a family of 10 people. How can they live?' Another woman said: 'And the kulaks! Look at what they call kulaks. Just ordinary peasants who have a cow or two. They're murdering the peasants, sending them away. Oppression, oppression, oppression.' They said: 'How can the harvest be good? We haven't enough horses & they don't give us enough to eat.'

Jones went on further and spoke to a young woman and a young man, both aged 19, who told him: 'We have nothing. If it were not for Moscow we should starve. No potatoes left. A hundred versts from Moscow it is terrible. We live here because we are near Moscow. In Chelyabinsk [Russia] it is terrible. Disease is carrying away numbers of people & the food is uneatable. I have travelled throughout Russia as a skilled worker. I get 300 rubles a month, but it is almost impossible to live. Take education. If you are not a Komsomolets [member of the Soviet youth organisation] you have little chance of getting on.'

The mother told how her little son had told her to take down an icon, which he said was of no use. She said she would keep it up because it was for her, but she asked him whether he wanted to put up a photograph of Lenin. He said: 'No, because Lenin took the bread away from us.'

The worker said he had been in 'Nijni' [a colloquial name for Nizhny Novgorod, a large city on the Volga river in Russia], where the little daughter of a friend was very ill. Two doctors had said she would die in a few hours, but the peasant's friend took her to a priest, who rubbed her head with sacred oil, which made her go to sleep and get better.

The son was a Komsomolets and there was a violent argument between him and the father.

When the son said there had been terrible conditions before the revolution, the father replied: 'Nonsense, we lived splendidly.' When the son said the people had to work for an employer, the father responded: 'But we work for a far greater slave driver now. Now it's absolute slavery. And they've ruined the peasantry,' When the son referred to 'our gigants', meaning the political giants of the day, the father said: 'Gigants indeed, when they've robbed the whole country of bread, when people are dying of hunger everywhere, when the next crop will be worse still. The workers will be too hungry to work. These Gigants – they've cleared the country of horses.'

The peasant showed Jones the cow which the woman in the house had bought from the kolkhozy for 1,500 rubles. He said it had been spoilt by the kolkhozy, because the kolkhoz had not enough fodder to feed it.

Jones' photograph of an orphanage he had visited. (© The Gareth Vaughan Jones Estate)

Jones quotes an unidentified worker saying, 'Proletarians of the World Unite is Jewish. Only Jews are the source throughout the world.' While someone else present said: 'It's slavery.' And another: 'Construction indeed, when you've destroyed all that's best in Russia.'

Jones referred in his diary to statements made to him by an unnamed senior Soviet official. The official spoke about industrialising Soviet Central Asia and the Caucasus: 'We are changing these areas from colonies into industrial areas. Result of national policy. Formerly terrible national enmity. Built huge factories in Central Asia. Think of nothing but factories. Woollen factories everywhere going up. Production cost higher in National areas. We give 2 million rubles to the budget. So it is rentable [profitable]. Where there is surplus labour, now we must cut down. Many directors of factories took on too many workers & that led to lowering of productivity. It's according to plan. Now we have more workers than October. But there was a lot of absenteeism. Now there is a struggle against absenteeism. Result – the surplus labourers got rid of. Now labour discipline is good.'

In an interview with Litvinov, the People's Commissar of Foreign Affairs, on 23 March, Jones was told that Germany would re-arm legitimately or illegitimately. Litvinov said the policy of the Soviet Union was unchangeable – not to belong to any group and not to have any alliances. He said: 'We want to be left in peace, to carry out our internal constructive programme. Any war, in which we are not involved also, would stop our plan.'

The Commissar told Jones of his concern about the expansion of Japan into China, the rise of Hitler and the possibility of conflict with Poland. Jones did not, however, raise with him the famine he had witnessed, doubtless realising that to do so could endanger him personally.

Litvinov sent his respects and regards to Lloyd George, stating he had always enjoyed being with him, and had always admired him, following his activities when he had been in London as an exile. He remembered writing articles with great enthusiasm about the national insurance scheme introduced by Lloyd George in 1909. Litvinov said he had always admired Lloyd George's speeches and his boldness. 'What politicians lack now is boldness,' he said.

Interestingly, Litninov confided in Jones about his distaste for the British Ambassador, Sir Esmond Ovey, saying: 'He has been too tactless, too bullying. He is seeking a quarrel and has as his aim the breaking off of diplomatic relations. He used to be friendly but ever since he had to pay for goods in foreign currency he has turned against us. He used to pay in rubles for supplies, but he used to get the rubles on the black market from Poland & other places. Indeed the diplomats were the chief source of income for the black market speculators & used to get their rubles at ridiculous prices. We said they should pay in foreign currency & he got very angry. We cannot have his bullying tactless way. He is a very unfortunate representative.'

Jones was also told by Litvinov that a group of British engineers arrested for spying would not be shot. The extraordinary degree of candour with which Litvinov spoke with Jones indicates the trust that existed – and that Litvinov knew that this was a safe means by which to convey a message indirectly to the UK government. Ovey was recalled to London very soon after and did not return to Moscow.

SOVIET UNION

A German journalist called Otto Schiller who had been in Central Asia told Jones there were corpses to be seen in Kazakhstan, where at least a million had died of hunger.

Schiller said: 'Their herds have died. No hope. They will probably nearly all die. They are nomadic and collectivisation tried to tie them to the soil. National feeling is terribly strong, hatred immense, but the peoples are too weak. Diseases spreading everywhere. I am afraid that they may arrest me for sabotage. Horrible conditions in Central Asia.'

Upon meeting some American workers on a train, Jones annotated their comments with one of his own: 'Terror, hunger.' The Americans told him: 'They took the passports away & we tried for two and a half years to get out of Russia. We sent the 2 boys to the villages where they had no bread for 6 months. They are destroying the machines at a rapid rate. The statistics are all lies. Production has declined, not increased. The Young *Komsomoltsi* [members of the Soviet youth organisation] have all the power and even more wages than the older, skilled workers. Many workers disappear for having criticised the regime. The specialists are now leaving. What'll happen to the machines, God knows! The workers are too weak. All are longing for WAR. Almost 100% against the Government. No responsibility. No one wants to work, No one cares whether machines are smashed or neglected. In some factories up to 50% have been dismissed.'

Jones wrote:

'New laws & decrees changing all the time, bewildered people & administrators create a feeling of insecurity & illegality.'

Jones' notes then quote from Oliver Goldsmith's *The Deserted Village*:

> *Princes and lords may flourish or may fade, -*
> *A breath can make them, as a breath has made;*
> *But a bold peasantry, their country's pride,*
> *When once destroy'd, can never be supplied.*

8

Making Headlines

Breaking News of the *Holodomor*

'If it is grave now and if millions are dying in the villages, as they are, for I did not visit a single village where many had not died, what will it be like in a month's time?'

On 17 March 1933, having returned to Moscow from his unauthorised trip to Ukraine, Jones wrote a guarded letter to his parents. To avoid being censored, the letter did not include an account of the starvation he had witnessed. He stated:

'I have arrived from Kharkoff after a most interesting journey ... In Kharkoff the people in the German Consulate were most kind to me. Tonight I am dining with the German Ambassador [Herbert von Dirksen]. This afternoon I had a talk with our Ambassador, Sir Esmond Ovey.'

He then detailed his travel arrangements, intending to arrive in London on 30 March, where he had been invited to speak at the Royal Institute that evening.

When safely in Danzig, at the home of his friends the Haferkorns, Jones wrote a much more candid letter to his parents:

'The Russian situation is absolutely terrible, famine almost everywhere, and millions are dying of starvation. I tramped for several days through villages in Ukraine, and there was no bread.

Jones' letter briefs Lloyd George on the famine in the Soviet Union.
(© The Gareth Vaughan Jones Estate)

Many children had swollen stomachs, nearly all the horses and cows had died and the people were dying. The terror has increased tremendously and the GPU has almost full control. It was a disgrace to arrest the six engineers, two of whom I know.'

The following day, Jones was back in Berlin and sent a letter to Lloyd George which stated:

'The situation in [the Soviet Union] is so much worse than in 1921 that I am amazed at your admiration for Stalin. I discussed the situation with almost every British, German and American expert. I had interviews with the following: Litvinoff, Karl Radek, the Commissar for Finance, [GT] Grinko, the Vice Commissar for Education; the President of the Atheists who has given me a special message to you as a Baptist!, the British and the German Ambassadors ... I had a long conversation with Goebbels and other Nazis, with Breitscheid, von Schleicher and others. Therefore I have much material on which you may want to question me.'

By this stage, Jones must have realised he would have to justify the testimony he was about to release about the famine. Immediately on reaching Berlin he contacted HR Knickerbocker, the German correspondent of the *New York Post*, and it is likely that with his assistance he set up a press conference to which international correspondents were invited.

Hosting a press conference rather than simply writing and publishing articles is an extremely unusual thing for a journalist to do. In this instance, it suggests that Jones was intent on ensuring that news of the famine was disseminated as quickly and as widely as possible.

Jones deserves to be praised for his selflessness, but it's also likely to be the case that he hadn't developed the hunger for exclusivity that most reporters have. Apart from a month's trial at *The Times*, he hadn't previously worked as a staff journalist – and wasn't due to start such a role with the *Western Mail* until 1 April – several days after the press conference.

Knickerbocker cabled a summary of Jones' statements at the press conference to his paper in New York: 'Mr Jones, who spoke Russian fluently, was the first foreigner to visit the Russian [sic] countryside since the Moscow authorities forbade foreign correspondents to leave the city. Famine on a colossal scale, impending death of millions from hunger, murderous terror and the beginnings of serious unemployment in a land that had hitherto prided itself on the fact that every man had a job.'

Knickerbocker's report was carried on his paper's front page under the headline 'Famine Grips Russia, Millions Dying, Idle on Rise, Says Briton', and Jones was described as 'foreign affairs secretary to former Prime Minister David Lloyd George of Great Britain'. The cachet he acquired through his association with Lloyd George was another good reason for releasing the information at a press conference.

Interestingly, the famine was described by Jones as haunting every district of the Soviet Union:

'Famine Grips Russia' – New York Evening Post, 29 March 1933.
(© The Gareth Vaughan Jones Estate)

'Everywhere was the cry, "There is no bread. We are starving." This cry came from every part of Russia, from the Volga, Siberia, White Russia, the North Caucasus, Central Asia. I tramped through the Black Earth region because that was once the richest farmland in Russia and because the correspondents have been forbidden to go there to see for themselves what is happening.'

Arriving at a village, Jones wrote that 'We are waiting for death' was his welcome from the peasants living there, who added: 'But see, we still have our cattle fodder. Go further south. There they have nothing. Many houses are empty of people already dead.'

Commenting on the suggestion by a 'foreign expert' that a million people had died in Kazakhstan from starvation, Jones told the press conference: 'I can believe it. After Stalin, the most hated man in Russia is Bernard Shaw, among those who read his glowing descriptions of plentiful food in their starving land.'

Knickerbocker wrote: 'In short, Mr Jones concluded, the collectivisation policy of the Government and the resistance of the peasants to it has brought Russia to the worst catastrophe since the famine of 1921 and has swept away the population of whole districts.'

Back in London the following day, Jones repeated his general thesis during his talk at the Royal Institute of International Affairs, Chatham House (RIIA), but also made an outspoken attack on the western media for their poor coverage of the crisis in the Soviet Union. He told his audience:

'The noose is getting tighter and tighter around the neck of the Russian peasant and exile, starvation and serfdom hover round him. May I say, as a Liberal in this regard, how disgusted I am by liberal opinion in this country. The attitude of the Liberal press has been cowardly and hypocritical. The *Manchester Guardian* gets red in the face when there are disgraceful events in Eastern Galicia, but when a hundred million peasants are condemned to hunger and serfdom the *Manchester Guardian* is quiet.

The Eastern Galicia oppression is a fleabite compared to the events in Russia. There is no excuse, for the *Manchester Guardian* has an excellent correspondent in Moscow [Malcolm Muggeridge]. I hold that that paper has betrayed the reliance upon which liberal people in the world have in it. The *News Chronicle* is not much better. It has an admirable source of information, but it has remained cowardly in its attitude of tolerating any kind of tyranny in Russia, while getting violent about any form of oppression in Germany or Italy.'

The day after his talk at Chatham House, the first of 21 articles by Jones about the famine over a three-week period appeared in the *London Evening Standard*. Reading his output at the time, it quickly becomes clear how Jones had weaved the powerful testimony he had gained from speaking to peasants about their direct experience into an overview of the famine's causes and consequences.

The first piece began with Jones telling how a few days previously he had stood in a worker's cottage outside Moscow where a father and son were glaring at each other: the father was a skilled worker in a Moscow factory, the son a member of the Young Communist League. The father saw his son as a tangible representative of the Soviet regime. Jones wrote:

'The father, trembling with excitement, lost control of himself and shouted at his Communist son: "It is terrible now. We workers are starving. Look at Chelyabinsk where I once worked. Disease there is carrying away numbers of us workers and the little food there is uneatable. That is what you have done to our Mother Russia."

The son cried back: "But look at the giants of industry which we have built. Look at the new tractor works. Look at the Dniepostroy [hydroelectric power station]. That has construction which has been worth suffering for." "Construction indeed!" was the father's reply: "What's the use of construction when you have destroyed all that's best in Russia?"'

Jones commented:

'What that worker said at least 96% of the people of Russia are thinking. There has been construction, but, in the act of building, all that was best in Russia has disappeared. The main result of the Five Year Plan has been the tragic ruin of Russian agriculture. This ruin I saw in its grim reality. I tramped through a number of villages in the snow of March. I saw children with swollen bellies. I slept in peasants' huts, sometimes nine of us in one room. I talked to every

Friday, March 31, 1933   THE EVENING

FAMINE RULES RUSSIA

The 5-year Plan Has Killed the Bread Supply

By GARETH JONES

Mr. Jones is one of Mr. Lloyd George's private secretaries. He has just returned from an extensive tour on foot in Soviet Russia. He speaks Russian fluently—and here is the terrible story the peasants told him.

A FEW days ago I stood in a worker's cottage outside Moscow. A father and a son, the father a Russian skilled worker in a Moscow factory, and the son a member of the Young Communist League, stood glaring at one another.

The father, trembling with excitement, lost control of himself and shouted at his Communist son : " It's terrible now. We workers are starving. Look at Chelyabinsk, where I once worked. Disease there is carrying away numbers of us workers and the little food there is is uneatable. That is what you have done to our Mother Russia."

The son cried back : " But look at the giants of industry which we have built. Look at the new tractor works. Look at the Dnieprostroy. That construction has been worth suffering for."

" Construction indeed ! " was the father's reply. " What's the use of construction when

MR. GARETH JONES.

" The cattle have nearly all died. How can we feed the cattle when we have only fodder to eat ourselves ? "

" And your horses ? " was the question I asked in every village I visited. The horse is now a question of life and death, for without a horse how can one plough ? And if one cannot plough, how can one sow for the next harvest ? And if one cannot sow for the next harvest, then death is the only prospect in the future.

The reply spelled doom for most of the villages. The peasants said : " Most of our horses have died and we have so little fodder that the remaining ones are scraggy and ill."

If it is grave now and if millions are dying in the villages, as they are, for I did not visit a single village where many had not died, what will it be like in a month's time? The potatoes left are being counted one by one, but in so many homes the potatoes have long run out. The beet, once used as cattle fodder, may run out in many huts before the new food comes in June, July and August, and many have not even beet.

The situation is graver than in 1921, as all peasants stated emphatically. In that year

Jones' story makes the front page of London's Evening Standard, 31 March 1933 – his first byline. (© The Gareth Vaughan Jones Estate)

peasant I met, and the general conclusion I draw is that the present state of Russian agriculture is already catastrophic but that in a year's time its condition will have worsened tenfold.

What did the peasants say? There was one cry which resounded everywhere I went and that was: "There is no bread." The other sentence, which as the *leitmotif* of my Russian visit was: "All are swollen." Even within a few miles of Moscow there is no bread left. As I was going through the countryside in that district I chatted to several women who were trudging with empty sacks towards Moscow. They all said: "It is terrible. We have no bread. We have to go all the way to Moscow to get bread and then they will only give us four pounds, which costs three roubles (six shillings nominally). How can a poor man live?"

"Have you potatoes?" I asked. Every peasant I asked nodded negatively with sadness. "What about your cows?" was the next question. To the Russian peasant the cow means wealth, food and happiness. It is almost the centre-point upon which his life gravitates. "The cattle have nearly all died. How can we feed the cattle when we have only fodder to eat ourselves?"

"And your horses?" was the question I asked in every village I visited. The horse is now a question of life and death, for without a horse how can one plough? And if one cannot plough, how can one sow for the next harvest? And if one cannot sow for the next harvest, then death is the only prospect in the future. The reply spelled doom for most of the villages. The peasants said: "Most of our horses have died and we have so little fodder that the remaining ones are all scraggy and ill."

If it is grave now and if millions are dying in the villages, as they are, for I did not visit a single village where many had not died, what will it be like in a month's time? The potatoes left are being counted one by one, but in so many homes the potatoes have long run out. The beet, once used as cattle fodder may run out in many huts before the

139

new food comes in June, July and August, and many have not even beet.

The situation is graver than in 1921, as all peasants stated emphatically. In that year there was famine in several great regions but in most parts the peasants could live. It was a localised famine, which had many millions of victims, especially along Volga. But today the famine is everywhere, in the formerly rich Ukraine, in Russia, in Central Asia, in North Caucasia - everywhere.

What of the towns? Moscow as yet does not look so stricken, and no one staying in Moscow would have an inkling of what is going on in the countryside, unless he could talk to the peasants who have come hundreds and hundreds of miles to the capital to look for bread. The people in Moscow are warmly clad, and many of the skilled workers, who have their warm meal every day at the factory, are well fed. Some of those who earn very good salaries, or who have special privileges, look even well-dressed, but the vast majority of the unskilled workers are feeling the pinch.

I talked to a worker who was hauling a heavy wooden trunk. "It is terrible now" he said. "I get two pounds of bread a day and it is rotten bread. I get no meat, no eggs, no butter. Before the War I used to get a lot of meat and it was cheap. But I haven't had meat for a year. Eggs were only a kopeck each before the war, but now they are a great luxury. I get a little soup, but it is not enough to live on."

And now a new dread visits the Russian worker. That is unemployment. In the last few months very many thousands have been dismissed from factories in many parts of the Soviet Union. I asked one unemployed man what happened to him. He replied: "We are treated like cattle. We are told to get away, and we get no bread card. How can I live? I used to get a pound of bread a day for all my family, but now there is no bread card. I have to leave the city and make my way out into the countryside where there is also no bread."

Hungersnot in Russland?

LONDON, 31. März

(Telephonat unseres Korrespondenten)

Der bisherige politische Sekretär Lloyd Georges, Gareth-Jones, hat über das Bestehen einer den grössten Teil des europäischen Russlands umfassenden Hungersnot, die sich in den nächsten Monaten weiter verschärfen werde und der Katastrophe von 1921 bereits gleichstehe, schlimmstiges Material aus Russland mitgebracht, dessen Publikation bevorsteht. Nur Moskau und Leningrad seien davon ausgenommen.

Jones hat u. a. Teile der Ukraine zu Fuss durchwandert und hat in Moskau flüchtende Bauern aus allen Teilen Russlands gefragt. Er hat aus Quellen, an deren Zuverlässigkeit er nicht zweifelt, die Nachricht bekommen, dass bereits

ein Fünftel der Bevölkerung von Kasakstan an Hunger zugrunde gegangen sei.

Der Schrei, „es gibt kein Brot, wir müssen sterben", sei ihm überall auf seinen Reisen entgegengeklungen, auch in Kollektiven,

deren er eine grosse Anzahl besucht hat. Vor den Augen eines Kommunisten, der das Bestehen von Hunger in Russland bestritt, habe ein Bauer, der im gleichen Eisenbahnwagen sass, ein Stück Brot aus einem Spucknapf herausgeholt, das Jones aus der Hand gefallen war.

Gareth-Jones ist eine sehr bekannte und angesehene Persönlichkeit in London, besonders in politischen und publizistischen Kreisen. Seine früheren Artikel über Russland, die er regelmässig auf seinen jährlichen Reisen dorthin veröffentlicht, sind allseits stets als objektiv und ausserordentlich gut informiert anerkannt worden. Dass die Sowjetunion mit allen Mitteln die Wahrheit über den fürchterlichen Ausgang des Kollektivierungsversuchs von 100 Millionen russischen Bauern seit langem unterdrückt, war bekannt. Gareth-Jones weist darauf hin, dass die ausländischen Korrespondenten in Moskau mit geraumer Zeit nicht mehr in das Innere Russlands hineindürften. Im übrigen ist es auch bekannt, dass Korrespondenten in Moskau durch die Zensur und andere Mittel, besonders durch Druck in der Aufenthaltsbewilligung behindert werden, die Wahrheit zu schreiben. Als im Jahre 1929 der Kampf gegen die Kulaken zugleich mit der Kollektivierung begann, war es schon offenbar, dass sich das gleiche Unglück wiederholen werde, das schon 1920 und 1921 das russische Volk betroffen hat.

'Hunger in Russia' – Berliner Tageblatt, 31 March 1933. (© The Gareth Vaughan Jones Estate)

> The Five Year Plan has built many fine factories. But it is bread that makes factory wheels go round, and the Five Year Plan has destroyed the bread-supplier of Russia.'

Jones also wrote a series of articles for the *Daily Express*, at the time the best-selling daily paper in the world. The articles were announced in an advance front-page plug which made it clear that their subject matter was wider than the famine alone:

> 'This is the first of a remarkable series which will reveal the truth about Russia today – the truth about the villages, the factories, the towns and the Kremlin itself.
>
> For some time past Mr Gareth Jones has been Research Adviser on Foreign Affairs to Mr. Lloyd George. He speaks and writes Russian fluently.
>
> He went there in 1930 and doubted.
> He went there in 1931 and wondered.
> He went there a few weeks ago – and has come back with a story that will startle the world.

The Soviet Union will not admit the representatives of British newspapers into Russia. Mr. Gareth Jones' articles will break the silence which the Soviet Union has tried to impose upon the newspapers of Great Britain.'

The first article focused on the case of six British engineers, working for the company Metropolitan-Vickers, who had been arrested by the secret service OGPU and accused of 'espionage, wrecking and bribery' in the electricity industry. Jones had previously met one of the accused, Alan Monkhouse, on an earlier trip to Russia. Indignant at the arrests, Jones considered what might be the motivating factor for such trumped-up charges. Looking across the Moscow river, he wrote:

'Within that citadel, the Kremlin, lives Stalin. There the whole policy has been framed which has changed the life of every man, woman, and child in Russia in the last five years. There Ivan the Terrible, many hundreds of years ago, held sway and indulged in an orgy of terror and torture. Was the clue to be found in the traditions of the Kremlin, which has no respect for the life or rights of any human individual?

The Kremlin gave me one clue to the arrest. Half an hour later I walked past another building. It was of ugly grey and yellow brick, and was formerly an insurance office. Outside, on the pavement, a few Red sentries marched up and down with fixed bayonets. This building gave me another clue. It was the Lubyanka, the headquarters of the OGPU. Then I realised that the cause for the arrests was to be found in the Kremlin and in the OGPU.

The Kremlin is now panic-stricken, for a catastrophe has come over that rich country of Russia. The people are seething with discontent. Among the ranks of the young Communists there is an ominous rumble of wrath at the crashing of their ideals. The worker, having been promised a paradise, has had his fine dream shattered.

Fear, which has so often gripped the Kremlin in centuries past, has returned to haunt its dwellers. That passion which has stamped its mark upon all who lived there, from the early Muscovite princes to Ivan the Terrible, has now attacked the proletarian Communists who reign within its portals. Once, hundreds of years ago, the rulers dreaded the coming of Tatar hordes. Now they dread the wrath of a starving peasantry. Seized with panic, they seek to find the foreigner on whom to put the blame when their promises fail.'

While it is undoubtedly the case that Jones had found widespread evidence of dissatisfaction with the Soviet regime, it was far-fetched to suggest that the starving peasantry posed a threat to the Soviet regime, which had a powerful security and military machine behind it. The tone of the article – and the hint that the regime was in peril – chimed with the stridently right wing views of the *Express*' proprietor Lord Beaverbrook, who had been Minister of Information during the latter period of the First World War and responsible for propaganda in Allied and neutral countries.

The second article in the *Express* series was more specifically based on Jones' eye-witness testimony in the Ukrainian villages. He also highlighted the contrast between the famine conditions in which peasants lived and died and the availability of luxury goods in the state-run Torgsin shops. Visiting such a shop in Moscow, he wrote:

'We see a peasant enter a shop that is crammed full with goods. Big loaves of pure white bread are piled on the counters. Vast slabs of butter stand side by side with pyramids of cheeses of every kind. Oranges, apples, figs, dates are there in plenty. Clothes of every hue hang in one department. Fur coats are being examined by inquisitive girls in another corner. Fish from the Volga and the Caspian Sea fraternise with products from the Baltic.

Can this really be Russia? Why are nearly all the other shops empty while this is brimming over with plenty? We shall follow the peasant and see. He turns round and comes up to us and says: "Please, I am from the village, and I have some gold earrings which I have kept for a long time. They tell me I can buy things for gold here." That is the solution to the mystery. In this shop one can buy with gold or silver, or with foreign currency, and this is another magnet for the peasants to come into the towns.

In many villages there was a little gold left, and so one or more peasants would come to Moscow to this so-called Torgsin shop, and in exchange for gold or silver receive bread and other objects. There has therefore been a flow of gold and silver from the villages into the towns, and a flow of bread back. But there are not many fortunate peasants who have gold or silver, and soon this supply of food will be stopped. Some of the peasants who wander into the towns in search of bread have dollars which they have received from relatives who have emigrated abroad. With these they can buy bread and post it home to their families. Some of them still have silver roubles from the days of the Tsar Nicholas. Some of them bring silver spoons. Having delved into all their treasures they have only one thought: "How can I get bread?"'

The third *Express* article focused on Jones' train trip south from Moscow. He pointed out pertinently:

'To see Russia one must travel 'hard class' and go by a slow train. Those tourists who travel 'soft class' and by express trains get only an impression, and do not see the real Russia.'

He had been warned by an unidentified diplomat before setting off that he should avoid visiting villages: 'The peasants are starving, and will steal anything they can get hold of,' he had been told.

On the train he met a member of the Communist Party who told him that in England every Communist was starving to death as a prisoner in the Tower of London. Jones wrote:

'He thinks that Scotland Yard has as firm a grip over English life as the OGPU has in Russia.'

The Communist told him: 'Scotland Yard is all powerful!', and said it was 'ruthlessly crushing the English working class,' but that Scotland Yard will not be able to 'stop the upsurge of revolutionary forces for long. The revolution will come there, and then you must have a Cheka as ruthless as ours.'

'We talk about freedom in England', replied Jones.'Freedom, indeed,' the Communist retorted. 'You have only freedom to chatter. But suppose you organised a military force to fight against the King, would you be allowed to do so? Certainly not. That is a proof that you have no freedom!'

Jones noted that two Russians were listening 'intently' to the conversation, but did not 'say a single word ... It is not safe for a Russian to argue in front of a Communist Party member.'

In another anecdote, a disillusioned young Communist had a conversation with Jones as they stood in the corridor of the train looking at a snow-covered landscape. 'A lot of us,' he said, 'are getting dissatisfied because we have no bread. I have had none for a week, although I work in a town – only potatoes. I only get sixty roubles a month but by the time they have taken a lot away I only get about forty to fifty. How can I live?'

'What do you mean when you say they take part of your wages away from you?' Jones asked. Getting angry, the young Communist replied: 'Don't you know that we are forced to give up part of our wages for loans? What do I want to subscribe to the Five Year Plan in four per cent loans for? But they take it away at the source. And that's not the only thing either. They docket lots of things ... When I left my mother and two sisters a couple of days ago they only had two glasses of flour left. My brother died of hunger. No wonder we young Communists cannot help feeling sick at things.'

Jones also described an encounter he had with a sinister official who was travelling to Ukraine to impose discipline on the peasants, writing:

'A domineering man in a khaki coat then talks with me. At the first glance one can tell that he is a party member, for most Communists in Russia have a stamp of vigour and ruthlessness which marks them as the ruling class. He tells me that he is a member of the Politodel (the Political Department), and I prick up my ears, for the Political Department is that detachment of many thousands of Communists who have been sent to the villages to make a violent drive to force the peasants to work. He looks ruthless and cruel.'

Clenching his fist, the party apparatchik continued: 'We are semi-military. We'll smash the kulaks and we'll smash all opposition. We are practically all men who served in the civil war. I was in the cavalry in the finest Red regiment. We who are now going into the villages are the chosen ones, the strongest, and we are all workers, mainly from the factories. We shall show the peasants what strict control means.'

'This man is typical of the spirit in which the villages are to be tackled,' noted Jones. 'He will not hesitate at shooting. He is filled with the doctrine of class warfare in the villages, and he is determined to carry on what he considers to be a holy war against all those who are against the Communist collective farms.'

Jones then describes how he got off the train and set off walking. He was initially still in Russia but after passing through several villages crossed the unmarked border into Ukraine.

In another article for the *Express* he described what he had observed, essentially writing in newspaper language what he had previously recorded in his notebooks:

'My stay in [an unnamed] village threw much light on what the peasants thought. There was only one Communist among the whole population. The hut in which I stayed became a Mecca to which came all those who wished to see and wonder. They all laid their griefs before me openly. They had no fear in telling me that never had it been so bad and that it was much worse than in 1921.'

The cattle decrease was disastrous, they told him: 'We used to have two hundred oxen but now, alas there are only six. Our horses and our cows have perished and we only have about one-tenth left.'

To Jones, the horses looked scraggy and diseased, as did all the horses in the countryside. Many peasants in the village had died of hunger. He wrote:

> 'Bewilderment reigned there as it did over the twelve to fourteen collective farms through which I tramped. The peasants nodded their heads at the continuous changing of policy: "We do not know where we are," one peasant said. "If only Lenin had lived we would be living splendidly. We could foresee what was going to happen. But now they have been chopping and changing their policy and we do not know what is going to happen next. Lenin would not have done something violently and then suddenly have turned round and said it was a mistake".'

One old peasant stopped Jones, pointed sadly to the fields and told him: 'In the old times, that was one pure mass of gold. Now it is all weeds. In the old times we had horses and cows and pigs and chickens. Now we are dying of hunger. In the old days we fed the world. Now they have taken all we had away from us and we have nothing. In the old days I should have bade you welcome, and given you as my guest chickens and eggs and milk and fine, white bread. Now we have no bread in the house. They are killing us.'

In one of the peasant's cottages in which Jones stayed, he slept with eight members of the family in the single room:

> 'It was pitiful to see that two out of the three children had swollen stomachs. All there was to eat in the hut was a very dirty watery soup, with a slice or two of potato, which all the family – and in the family I included myself – ate from a common bowl with wooden spoons.

> Fear of death loomed over the cottage, for they had not enough potatoes to last until the next crop. When I shared my white bread and butter and cheese one of the peasant women said, "Now I have eaten such wonderful things I can die happy." I set forth again further

towards the south and heard the villagers say, "We are waiting for death".'

Later, after arriving in the city of Kharkiv [NB: Kharkoff was an anglicised version of the Russian, Kharkov. Kharkiv is the Ukrainian spelling of the city and now it's official name], Jones noted:

'What I had seen in one small part of vast Russia was typical of conditions throughout the country, from the borders of Poland to the distant parts of Siberia.'

In a further *Express* article, Jones told how he was struck by the number of ragged, homeless boys, the so-called *bezprizorny* or street children:

'With the foulest of rags and the most depraved of faces, they hover about. In 1930 I saw few of these homeless boys. The Soviet Government had made a gallant fight to remove the swarms of ruffians who were the legacy of the civil war. In 1931 I saw still fewer, although they would sometimes shout in stations to passengers: "Give us cigarettes."

In 1933 I have seen the resurgence of the homeless boys. They wander about the streets of the towns. I have seen some being captured by the police and taken away. When I left Kharkoff it was the homeless boys who remained as the last and deepest impression.

In the station waiting-room three hundred of them were herded to be taken away. I peeped through the window. One of them near the window lay on the floor, his face red with fever and breathing heavily, with his mouth open. "Typhus," said another man, who was looking at them. Another lay in rags stretched on the ground, with part of his body uncovered, revealing dried up flesh and thin arms.

I turned away and entered the train for Moscow. In the corridor stood a little girl. She was well dressed. Her cheeks were rosy. She held a toy in one hand and a piece of cake in the other. She was probably the daughter of a Communist Party member or of an engineer.

In 1930 there were class differences. In 1931 they were as great as ever. In 1933 they are one of the most striking features of the Soviet Union. These children are not the relics of the civil war. They are the homeless children of hunger, most of them turned out from their homes to fend for themselves because the peasants have no bread.'

Back in Moscow, Jones decided to go into the back streets to see what life was like for working class people. While talking with a bedridden woman in her frugal apartment, a girl aged about 12 came in, her face around her eyes swollen with crying. Her mother followed her, whose face was also swollen with tears.

'What is the matter?' Jones asked. 'We have been refused passports,' the mother replied, 'and we have to leave Moscow by March 30. We know no one in the world except in Moscow, but we have to go beyond sixty-five miles from Moscow. Where can we go? How will we have food there?'

'But surely they will leave you your bread card?' Jones enquired.

'Not even a bread card, and we have no money,' came the reply.

The old woman said also that she was refused a visa, and would have to leave Moscow. These people, wrote Jones, were the victims of 'passportisation', adding:

'No wonder I got angry next day when a Communist, who seemed to know every statistic there was to be known, told me: "We hope that by our system of passportisation we shall be able to remove the surplus labour from the towns. About 700,000 will leave Moscow. But I can assure you that only crooks, speculators, kulaks, private traders, and ex-officers will have to go".'

That same evening Jones talked to a factory woman, who told him: 'They are cruelly strict now in the factories. If you are absent one day you are sacked, get your bread card taken away, and cannot get a passport. Life is a nightmare. I walk to my factory every day, for travelling in the crowded tram kills my nerves. It is more terrible than ever. If you say a word now in the factories you are dismissed.'

'This strictness in the factories is the result of the Government decrees on labour discipline,' observed Jones:

> 'Its main aim is to tie the good worker to the factory and to get rid of the slacker. Cursed by a continuous desertion of the factories by disgruntled workers, who left for other factories, the Soviet Government has decided to put a stop to it by a severity which is nothing else than slavery.
>
> In Moscow, in Kharkoff, in every city, thousands are being turned out of the factories. They receive no bread card, as I was told by numerous workers, or in some cases a bread-card for a fortnight. They receive no unemployment insurance. They are deprived of passports and are sent away from the towns into the countryside, where there is no bread and where they often know no one.
>
> More and more workers are leaving the factory gates to face starvation. A vigorous economy drive is cutting down staffs in many offices, and in some factories from 25% to 40%. "Why do you have so many unemployed?" was the question I asked a well-known Communist. His answer was typical of the hypocrisy of many Bolsheviks. "Our unemployment is according to plan. We are ejecting people from the offices in order to make the others work better. We are creating unemployment on purpose, and the people understand".'

Jones concluded his article condemning the system that had created such a situation:

> '"According to plan!' It does not matter to human life, as long as everything is "according to plan!" Passportisation, labour discipline and unemployment. Those are the three spectres which haunt the Russian worker.'

Jones joined the staff of the *Western Mail* on 1 April 1933, a Saturday, immediately after his return from Russia on Monday 3 April the paper published his first piece as a staff writer – an interview with Alexander Kerensky, the final non-Bolshevik Prime Minister of Russia who participated in the revolution of February 1917 but was overthrown later that year and spent the rest of his life in exile. 'Before his death in 1924,' Kerensky told Jones, 'Lenin, in his famous political testament wrote that certain features of Stalin's character were dangerous to the Communist Party. Lenin had in mind the stubbornness of Stalin (Stalin's will-power is stronger than his reason), and also the absence in Stalin of the feeling of personal fear. When Stalin is convinced of something or wishes to obtain something he pushes straight on regardless of the consequences. These two characteristics combined, stubbornness and absence of personal fear, have made Stalin into the grave-digger of the Bolshevik dictatorship.'

'On the lines of the New Economic Policy,' Kerensky continued, 'when freedom of internal trade was restored, Bolshevism could have reigned over Russia for decades. But Stalin ended the New Economic Policy and within four years completely wrecked Russian agriculture. The ruin of agriculture is the great achievement of the dictatorship of Stalin. In my opinion, during all the existence of the Bolshevik dictatorship no one has dealt so severe a blow to the Communist Party as Stalin. Events are now moving rapidly, for not only the ordinary people but also many members of the Communist Party and of the Young Communist League are against the regime.'

As we know in retrospect, Kerensky seriously underestimated the power of Stalin's monolithic state, but he added, accurately: 'You have just told me that you have seen with your own eyes the ruin of the Russian countryside, and all the evidence I receive from Russia confirms your observations. Now in Russia famine is gripping a vast area and is far greater than in 1921. The Ukraine, the Volga, West Siberia, North Caucasia, the provinces which formerly supplied all Europe with grain, have no longer bread, meat, butter nor enough potatoes. The stock of cattle has been reduced by two-thirds. The peasant has hardly any agricultural implements, and the tractors destined for the collective farms and State farms are mainly broken and are at this present moment, when the spring sowing is beginning, in the repair shops.'

Kerensky drew the general conclusion: 'Russia is mainly an agricultural country and the destruction of agriculture will have as its inevitable logical conclusion the wrecking of industry, to build which the Russian peasant was expropriated from his land. For the sake of industry all Russia was condemned to famine. The Five Year Plan is one of the greatest bluffs in history, and now the bill has to be met.'

Explaining what he thought was the way out of the 'chaos', Kerensky said: 'There is only one way out. Freedom should be given to work, and to make and to buy, and to sell. The peasant should have his land back and his right to free labour. Only thus will he able to make a proper living. In the towns freedom for the trade unions should be given back to the worker, because now the Russian is more exploited than the negroes in the colonies. Russia should return to the foundation of civil law, which it received, from the Provisional Government.

'Under Tsarism, economic conditions were undoubtedly better than today, but Tsarism was doomed to destruction because the last monarch hated political freedom. If Tsarism had gone along the path of reform and had brought in a Constitution it would be existing today. Now the present regime has destroyed those few bases of democratic rule which already existed, and has introduced a tyranny in which not only political, but also civil rights have been destroyed. Thus the present regime is doomed, like the monarchy.'

In a further article for the *Western Mail* headlined 'Starving Russians Seething with Discontent', Jones wrote about the arrest of the British engineers and related it to his own experience:

'I had narrowly escaped being arrested myself not long before at a small railway station in the Ukraine, where I had entered into conversation with some peasants. These were bewailing their hunger to me, and were gathering a crowd, all murmuring, "There is no bread," when a militiaman had appeared. "Stop that growling," he had shouted to the peasants, while to me he said, "Come along; where are your documents?" A civilian (an OGPU man) appeared from nowhere, and they both submitted me to a thorough grilling of questions. They discussed among themselves what they should do with me, and finally the OGPU man decided to accompany me on the train to the big city of Kharkoff, where at last he left me in peace. There was to be no arrest.'

Returning to the British engineers, Jones again directed his attack against the whole Soviet system:

'The fate of the other British subjects in Russia was a less fortunate one, and now they await their trial. This event is more than an isolated act of violence by the political police. It is a symbol of the panic which has come over the Soviet rulers.

Hunger, far greater than in the famine days of 1921, is condemning the Russian people to despair and making them hate the Communist Party more than ever. Even the young communists, once passionately enthusiastic, are now resentful at the disillusion which has come. The workers want food and fear loss of work.

The peasant, having lost his cow, his land, and his bread, and being doomed to starvation without a finger being raised to help him, is cursing the day that Lenin took command. A sop must be provided for the wrath of the hungry mob. The wicked foreigner must be found on whom to put the blame. Thus our British subjects have been seized. The imprisonment of the Metro-Vickers' specialists is a continuation of that hunt for victims which characterises the spring of 1933 in Russia.'

Referring to political executions, Jones commented:

'Last month the Vice Commissar for Agriculture for the whole of the Soviet Union was shot and with him specialists and 34 workers in the agricultural sphere. Many of them were in the Ministry of Agriculture, Moscow, and in the Ministry for State Farms, and during a previous visit I met one of them, Mr. Wolff, an outstanding expert on agriculture and a man respected by all who knew him.

Imagine in this country the shooting of the Parliamentary Secretary of the Ministry of Agriculture because the agricultural policy of the Government had failed! They were accused of counter-revolutionary wrecking in the machine-tractor stations and in the state farms in the Ukraine, North Caucasia, and White Russia.'

Jones reported how the agriculturists had been tortured into confessing themselves guilty of smashing tractors, burning tractor stations and factories, stealing grain reserves, and being responsible for the disorganisation of sowing and the destruction of cattle. This was, said Jones, surely a formidable task for 35 men to carry out in a country which stretched 6,000 miles:

'Just as these men were arrested because of the tragic ruin of agriculture, so the British engineers were arrested because the electrical plans failed. The Bolsheviks boasted of their magnificent Dnieperstroy [a hydroelectric power station on the Dnieper River in Ukraine, opened in October 1932], which was to flood the Ukraine with light and make the machines in a vast area throb with energy. What happened?

'In spite of the heralding of this achievement throughout the world as a super-triumph for Socialist construction, the tramways within the very area of the Dnieperstroy stopped because there was no electric current. The great cities of Kharkoff and Kiev, the leading cities of the Ukraine, were often plunged for hours on end into darkness, and men and women and children had to huddle in blackened rooms, because it was difficult to buy candles and lamp oil. In the theatres in Kharkoff the lights would suddenly go out, and hundreds of people would sit there, dreading the crush and the fight in the dark for the way out.'

MAKING HEADLINES

Pointing out that propaganda was being used by the Soviet Union to convey a message that was the opposite of the truth, Jones wrote:

'At the same time as the people not many miles away from the Dnieperstroy sat in darkness, resounding slogans of the triumph of the Soviet electrical industry were drummed into the imagination of the world's proletariat by impressive statistics and by skilfully taken photographs of electric works and of workers wreathed in smiles.'

In a further *Western Mail* article, Jones wrote of the increasingly repressive nature of the Soviet regime:

'When I was in Russia in 1931 a period of toleration had begun. The OGPU had had some of its fangs extracted and was under the control of Akuloff, a moderate man and an economist. The dangerous Yagoda had been removed. Stalin had preached the doctrine of fair-play to non-Communists and the whole country breathed a sigh of relief that the terror was over.

But now, in 1933, the terror has returned and in a form multiplied a hundredfold. Yagoda is back again at his work, slashing out left and right at all those suspected of opposition to the regime. The drive is now against all kinds of opposition. Formerly there would have been a drive against the right wing opposition, then against the Trotskyists, then against the former bourgeois.

But now the attack is on all fronts - on party members, of whom numbers have been shot; on the intelligentsia, of whom there are countless representatives in Solovki [a remote prison camp in the Arctic described by Alexsandr Solzhenitsyn as the 'mother of the Gulag']; on the peasants for merely having wished to till their soil for themselves, and on the Ukrainian, Georgian, and Central Asian nationalists who have struggled for the rights of small countries.

More and more power is being put into the bands of the OGPU and a small clique dominates the rest of the party, the members of which, although in their hearts, recognising the colossal failure of the Five Year Plan policy, do not dare to raise even one small voice in contradiction to the general line of Stalin.'

According to Jones, OGPU had made its greatest ever mistake when it arrested the six British engineers. He said it was indicative of the fact that the Soviet regime was finding it difficult to pay its international debts. The blame for economic woes was put on foreigners like the British engineers as a diversionary tactic, he argued. Jones analysed in more detail the economic difficulties caused to the Soviet Union by a trade embargo imposed by the British. He wrote:

'The main goods which the United Kingdom exports to Russia are chemicals, ferrous metals, textile machinery, electrical appliances, and iron and steel manufactures. Before the war Great Britain exported 6,998,434 tons of coal, to the value of £4,336,000, to Russia, but in 1932 only 8,800 tons were exported, to the value of £42,701. The coal industry will, therefore, be little affected by an embargo on Soviet goods.

The main exports of the Soviet Union are wheat, butter, oil, furs, timber, eggs, etc.. The export of most of these products, however, declined rapidly last year. In the first ten months of 1932 - Russia exported wheat to the value of approximately £1,200,000, compared with £6,800,000 in 1931. The export of butter declined from about £4,700,000 in 1931 to about £600,000 in 1932.

The imports of timber from Russia into Great Britain have also declined in value. In 1930 the Soviet Union exported £7,423,000 worth of soft wood (not planed or dressed). In 1932 the value was £4,522,000. In 1932 the United Kingdom imported £985,000 worth of pit-props from Russia.

The rapid decline in the value of Soviet exports made it difficult for the Soviet Union to meet its payments abroad.'

Crucially, argued Jones, writing in the *Western Mail*, the British Ambassador who had previously been sympathetic to the Soviet Union had changed his mind:

'There is no doubt that Sir Esmond Ovey has placed the facts about the whole situation before the Government. His testimony is all the more to be believed on account of his former sympathy for the Soviet Government.

When he went to Moscow from Mexico three years ago he was immediately impressed by Russia's achievements. Some of the Moscow-British colony thought that he was too pro-Bolshevik. Indeed, I often heard him accused of prejudice in favour of the Soviet Government, and of a lack of perception of their difficulties.

He has recently, however, become fully aware of the catastrophic conditions in Russia, as I gathered a fortnight ago in the Embassy in Moscow. He is often accused of being tactless, but in his firm handling of the present case he has earned the praise of the most critical journalists in Moscow.'

On the train out of Russia, Jones reported in the *Western Mail* how he had met some American workers who had arrived two and a half years before with an idealised view of the Communist regime, but were now disillusioned. They told him: 'No one wants to work. No one cares whether the machines are smashed or neglected. In the factory where I was, almost 100% of the workers are against the Government. The workers are too weak to do real work. Now they are afraid of losing their jobs because in some factories up to 50% of the workers have been dismissed.'

Jones wrote that Russia could not be considered a European country, despite its geography. Going there, he stated, was to take a journey back several centuries:

'Russia never had the Reformation, which affected so deeply the life of Wales. Russia is now in the middle of her Industrial Revolution, which Britain went through over a century ago. The effects of the French Revolution were slight. Russia only abolished serfdom in 1881. The fight for freedom which created the free British and French characters had been crushed. Thus Russia remains Asia, although territorially in Europe. It is Asiatic in the past and present poverty and in the fatalism of its peasants.'

It had, he concluded, 'tried in vain to catch up many centuries of industrialism in the brief span of five years'.

In another *Western Mail* article, Jones made it clear that the famine affected all the parts of the Soviet Union that he had visited:

'Famine, far greater than the famine of 1921, is now visiting Russia. The hunger of twelve years ago was only prevalent in the Volga and in some other regions, but today the hunger has attacked the Ukraine, the North Caucasus, the Volga district, Central Asia, Siberia - indeed, every part of Russia. I have spoken to peasants or to eye-witnesses from every one of those districts and their story is the same. There is hardly any bread left, the peasants either exist on potatoes and cattle fodder, or, if they have none of these, die off.

In the three agricultural districts which I visited, namely, the Moscow region, the Central Black Earth district, and North Ukraine, there was no bread left in any village out of the total of 20 villages to which I went. In almost every village peasants had died of hunger.'

Explaining the causes of the famine in a way a Welsh audience could relate to, he wrote:

'Last year, the weather was ideal. Climatic conditions have, in the past few years, blessed the Soviet Government. Then why the catastrophe? In the first place, the land has been taken away from 70 per cent of the peasantry, and all incentive to work has disappeared.

MAKING HEADLINES

Anyone with the blood of Welsh farmers in his veins will understand what it means to a farmer or a peasant to have his own land taken away from him.

Last year nearly all the crops of the peasants were violently seized, and the peasant was left almost nothing for himself. Under the five Year Plan the Soviet Government aimed at setting up big collective farms, where the land would be owned in common and run by tractors. But the Russian peasant in one respect is no different from the Welsh farmer. He wants his own land, and if his land is taken away from him he will not work. The passive resistance of the peasant has been a stronger factor than all the speeches of Stalin.

In the second place, the cow was taken away from the peasant. Imagine what would happen in the Vale of Glamorgan or in Cardiganshire if the county councils took away the cows of the farmers! The cattle were to be owned in common, and cared for in common by the collective farms. Many of the cattle were seized and put into vast State cattle factories.

The result of this policy was a widespread massacre of cattle by the peasants, who did not wish to sacrifice their property for nothing. Another result was that on these State cattle factories, which were entirely unprepared and had not enough sheds, innumerable live-stock died of exposure and epidemics. Horses died from lack of fodder. The livestock of the Soviet Union has now been so depleted that not until 1945 can it reach the level of 1928. And that is provided all the plans for the import of cattle succeed, provided there is no disease, and provided there is fodder. That date 1945 was given me by one of the most reliable foreign experts in Moscow.

In the third place, six or seven millions of the best farmers (ie the kulaks) in Russia have been uprooted and have been exiled with a barbarity which is not realised in Britain. Although two years ago the Soviet Government claimed that the kulak had been destroyed,

159

the savage drive against the better peasant continued with increased violence last winter. It was the aim of the Bolsheviks to destroy the kulaks as a class, because they were "the capitalists of the village".

The final reason for the famine in Soviet Russia has been the Soviet export of food stuffs. So anxious has the Soviet Government been to meet its obligations abroad that it has exported grain, butter, and eggs in order to buy machinery while the population was starving at home. In this respect the Soviet Government has followed the example of the Tsarist Government, which used to export grain even in a year of food shortage. There was never in Tsarist Russia, however, a famine which hit every part of Russia as today. To export food at such a period has aggravated the hunger, and although the Soviet Government deserves praise for its habit of paying punctually it has by its policy harmed the health and endangered the life of a considerable section of its population.

The taking of the land away from the peasant, the massacre of the cattle, the exile of the most hard-working peasants, and the export of food - those are the four main reasons why there is famine in Russia today.'

Another *Western Mail* article explained why unemployment was rising since the second Five Year Plan began at the beginning of 1933:

'The first reason is the shortage of raw materials. The supply of coal, timber or oil fails and the factories have to stand idle, waiting until the necessary fuel arrives. In Kharkoff, not many miles away from the richest coal district of Russia, there was a shortage of coal and led to long delays in factories. In Moscow there was a shortage of petrol, and this also led to stoppages. Bad transport is responsible for these delays. The railway lines get blocked, and this disorganises distribution.

The second reason for unemployment in Russia is financial. There is now a rigid economy campaign being carried on. Many factories have had large deficits. The operating costs are exceedingly high. "What do you do when factories have a deficit?" I asked an official in the Commissariat for Finance. He replied: "We apply methods to force them to economise. We even oblige them not to pay salaries and make them dismiss their staffs."

That tends to increase unemployment. The director of the factory has to make both ends meet, and thus dismisses workmen.

The third reason for the unemployment in Soviet Russia is the food shortage. Each factory has been made responsible for the feeding of its workers. A factory is given a certain agricultural district from which to draw supplies. A director is made responsible for the feeding. There is hardly ever enough food for all the workers in the factory on account of the breakdown of agriculture. In order to make the food supply go round workers are dismissed and are sent to the countryside. The food shortage is probably the main cause of unemployment.

The final cause for unemployment was given to me by a director of the Kharkoff Tractor Factory. "Why have you dismissed men?" I asked him. He replied: "We've improved our technical knowledge and so we do not need so many men." An admission that technological unemployment is not a feature of capitalism alone.

The Five Year Plan was intended to make Russia independent of the rest of the world. This aim has failed. Foreign specialists are leaving Russia. When they have gone woe betide the Soviet machines.

The lack of raw materials, financial difficulties, the food shortage, and increase in the use of machines - those are the four causes of unemployment in Russia.'

Having written that the famine was ubiquitous in the Soviet Union, Jones wrote a further *Western Mail* article in which he referred to a rising tide of nationalism in Ukraine and elsewhere:

> 'Russia will not attack because throughout her territory there are national minorities waiting for the war-drums to beat in order to gain their independence. In the Ukraine, the Home Rule movement is ever growing and the Ukrainians hate the Great Russians with increasing bitterness.
>
> The policy of Russification which the Soviet Government began about two months ago will increase the rebellious feelings of the Ukraine and will weaken Russia's military strength.
>
> In Georgia the nationalists are increasing their strength and there are many underground plots to overthrow the Soviet régime. In Central Asia national movements are ever strong and have been fanned by Moscow's tolerant policy of encouraging native languages and literature. These minorities are waiting for war in order to rise. Thus Moscow will avoid foreign conflicts.'

Again in the *Western Mail*, Jones wrote of the Bolsheviks' attack on religion in which they blamed Christians for seeking to wreck the collective farm system:

> 'Religious people, the Communists complain, are fighting against the Socialist collective farms. The priests have been writing letters which they purported to have come from God, stating, "I, God, tell you that the collective farm is the work of the Devil". According to the Communists, religious peasants have been warning the others that if they entered the collective farms they would go to hell. The Communists complain that the religious peasants have been agitating against scientific methods, and that they are still in favour of the three-field system, because, as they say, "Even God is for the

three-field system, because God is for the Trinity, and the Trinity is symbolic for the three-field system".

Thus the Bolsheviks are attempting to crush religion. Although they have stated that they wish to abandon forceful methods, thousands of preachers and priests are now half-starving in prison. How great has their success been? Among children the propaganda. and the teaching in the schools have undoubtedly had a great effect. If you ask Russian children, "Do you believe in God?" most will answer emphatically, "No".

But there are many young people who believe in God. One Russian girl told me that she believed in God, but that she was going to join the Young Communist League. "How can you join the Young Communist League when you believe in God?" I asked. She replied, "Of course I can. I shall pretend to be a Communist and make wonderful Communist speeches, but all the time I shall believe in God," and she added a phrase which impressed me deeply: "For what my lips say, my heart need not believe".

The hearts of the Russian people often remain Christian while their lips utter vilifications against God. Religion has not been crushed.'

A further *Western Mail* article revisited the arrest of the British engineers, describing it as a major blunder by OGPU. Jones wrote:

'What the OGPU did is in keeping with the Bolshevik mentality. It was motivated by a great fear of the capitalist nations. According to the Bolsheviks, the capitalists are ever plotting the overthrow of the Soviet Union and send swarms of spies to Russia. "England and America are preparing war on the Soviet Union. The Pope and the Hitlerites are allies in preparing to attack the Soviet Union."

Those are typical propaganda posters which one sees everywhere. This fear of capitalist attack is deeply impressed on the Russian mind, for the Bolsheviks credulously accept Lenin's prophecy that the war between Capitalism and Communism is bound to come.

What wonder that most British experts or observers going to Russia are suspected of being spies?'

What is clear – and undoubtedly significant – is that Jones' articles, while revealing much compelling detail based on first person testimony related to the famine, also collectively provided a searing critique of the totalitarian state that the Soviet Union had become.

In addition to his newspaper articles, Jones spoke about his experiences in the Soviet Union at public events.
(© The Gareth Vaughan Jones Estate)

9

Betrayal

The Denigration of Gareth Jones

'I don't trust Duranty'

When Gareth Jones wrote his articles exposing the famine in the Soviet Union, he realised he would provoke a backlash.

There was a group of foreign correspondents based in Moscow who enjoyed a privileged lifestyle and pulled their punches when analysing political and social developments. They understood that if they crossed a fairly tame line, they would be expelled from the country.

At the same time, Western intellectuals proved notoriously gullible when visiting the workers' paradise and wouldn't countenance any criticism of the Soviet state.

On 2 March 1933, the *Manchester Guardian* published what has become a notorious letter signed by the socialist playwright George Bernard Shaw and 20 other recent British visitors to the Soviet Union. At the time Shaw was arguably the most famous writer in the world.

It began by suggesting that increasing unemployment in the capitalist world was leading to greater interest in the progress being made by the Soviet Union. As a consequence, claimed Shaw and his co-signatories, there had been a redoubling in intensity of a 'blind and reckless' campaign to discredit the country. The letter continued:

'Particularly offensive and ridiculous is the revival of the old attempts to represent the condition of Russian workers as one of slavery and starvation, the Five-Year Plan as a failure, the new enterprises as bankrupt and the Communist regime as tottering to its fall. Although such inflammatory irresponsibility is easily laughed at, we must not forget that there are many people not sufficiently well informed politically to be proof against it, and that there are diehards among our diplomats who still dream of starting a counter-revolutionary war anywhere and anyhow, if only they can stampede public opinion into the necessary panic through the press. The seriousness of the situation is emphasized by the British Government's termination of the trade agreement with the USSR and the provocative questions and answers in the House of Commons.

'We the undersigned are recent visitors to the USSR. Some of us travelled throughout the greater part of its civilised territory. We desire to record that we saw nowhere evidence of such economic slavery, privation, unemployment and cynical despair of betterment as are accepted as inevitable and ignored by the press as having 'no news value' in our own countries. Everywhere we saw hopeful and enthusiastic working-class [people], self-respecting [and] free up to the limits imposed on them by nature and a terrible inheritance from tyranny and incompetence of their former rulers, developing public works, increasing health services, extending education, achieving the economic independence of women and the security of

George Bernard Shaw - one of the signatories of the letter criticising Jones.

the child and in spite of many grievous difficulties and mistakes which social experiments involve at first (and which they have never concealed nor denied) setting an example of industry and conduct which would greatly enrich us if our systems supplied our workers with any incentive to follow it.

'We would regard it as a calamity if the present lie campaign were to be allowed to make headway without contradiction and to damage the relationship between our country and the USSR. Accordingly we urge all men and women of goodwill to take every opportunity of informing themselves of the real facts of the situation and to support the movements which demand peace, trade and closer friendship with and understanding of the greater Workers Republic of Russia.'

Shaw had long been a supporter of the Soviet state. In fact, three years before the Revolution he had sent a letter to the editorial office of the Communist newspaper *Pravda* offering congratulations on a Russian labour organisation's anniversary. After the Revolution he participated in the Hands Off Russia campaign, which opposed the backing given by western powers to the White Army, which hoped to overthrow the Bolshevik government. At the time he referred to Lenin as 'the only really interesting statesman in Europe.'

Having said on various occasions that he didn't want to die without seeing the Soviet Union, he undertook a nine-day trip there in 1931. He was feted as one of the country's leading foreign supporters, and chauffeured around in an open-top saloon.

On the first day he visited Lenin's mausoleum in Red Square, after which he said of the late revolutionary: 'A pure intellectual type, that is the true aristocracy ... Henceforth Napoleon's tomb ranks second instead of first.'

Shaw was carefully chaperoned to numerous places in Moscow and elsewhere, but the highlight of his visit was a meeting with Stalin, at which he was accompanied by Lord and Lady Astor. They conversed for three hours, after which Shaw said: 'I expected to see a Russian worker and I found a Georgian gentleman.' He was so impressed by the trip that before leaving the Soviet Union he said: 'Tomorrow I leave this land of hope and return to our western countries - the countries of despair.'

Shaw's visit to the Soviet Union had a strong impact on the playwright. Returning to the capitalist west, he was first interviewed in Berlin where he claimed that Stalin was a 'giant', while other politicians were 'pygmies'. A few days later in London the writer made a long speech about his trip. To dispel the myth about severe hunger in the Soviet Union he said that in Russia he 'ate the most slashing dinner in my life.'

The default position for many on the left was support for the Soviet Union, and many intellectuals and labour movement activists went along with that. It also has to be remembered that in Germany the far-right was on the rise – a situation that prompted a tendency to see a binary choice between support for the USSR or acquiescence to the rise in fascism.

Gareth Jones, a self-proclaimed liberal who adhered to neither camp, quickly became the subject of a very personal attack from a high-profile member of the Moscow press group.

On 31 March 1933 – two days after Jones' press conference in Berlin – the *New York Times* published an article by its Moscow bureau chief Walter Duranty that unashamedly sought to deny Jones' claim that peasants were starving. Headlined 'Russians Hungry But Not Starving', it began:

'In the middle of the diplomatic duel between Great Britain and

Walter Duranty.

168

the Soviet Union over the accused British engineers there appears from a British source a big scare story in the American press about famine in the Soviet Union, with "thousands already dead and millions menaced by death and starvation".

'Its author is Gareth Jones, who is a former secretary to David Lloyd George and who recently spent three weeks in the Soviet Union and reached the conclusion that the country was "on the verge of a terrific smash", as he told the writer.

'Mr Jones is a man of a keen and active mind, and he has taken the trouble to learn Russian, which he speaks with considerable fluency, but the writer thought Mr Jones's judgment was somewhat hasty and asked him on what it was based. It appeared that he had made a forty-mile walk through villages in the neighborhood of Kharkov and had found conditions sad.

'I suggested that that was a rather inadequate cross-section of a big country but nothing could shake his conviction of impending doom.'

Duranty went on to allude to earlier instances where foreigners 'especially Britons' had believed false stories about the Soviet Union.

His first example was a rumour that circulated during the Versailles Peace Conference after the First World War, to the effect that the White Russian leader Admiral Kolchak had captured the city of Kazan and that Soviet power was 'on the verge of an abyss'. Neither assertion was true.

Similar false rumours about the early collapse of the Bolshevik regime were also adduced by Duranty, who added:

'A couple of years ago another British "eyewitness" reported a mutiny in the Moscow garrison and "rows of corpses neatly piled in Theatre Square", and only this week a British news agency revealed a revolt of the Soviet Fifty-fifth Regiment at Duria, on the Manchurian border. All bunk, of course.

RUSSIANS HUNGRY, BUT NOT STARVING

Deaths From Diseases Due to Malnutrition High, Yet the Soviet Is Entrenched.

LARGER CITIES HAVE FOOD

Ukraine, North Caucasus and Lower Volga Regions Suffer From Shortages.

KREMLIN'S 'DOOM' DENIED

Russians and Foreign Observers In Country See No Ground for Predictions of Disaster.

By WALTER DURANTY.
Special Cable to THE NEW YORK TIMES.
MOSCOW, March 30.—In the middle of the diplomatic duel between Great Britain and the Soviet Union over the accused British engineers there appears from a British source a big scare story in the American press about famine in the Soviet Union, with "thousands already dead and millions menaced by death from starvation."

Its author is Gareth Jones, who is a former secretary to David Lloyd George and who recently spent three weeks in the Soviet Union and reached the conclusion that the country was "on the verge of a terrific smash," as he told the writer.

Saw No One Dying.

But to return to Mr. Jones. He told me there was virtually no bread in the villages he had visited and that the adults were haggard, gaunt and discouraged, but that he had seen no dead or dying animals or human beings.

I believed him because I knew it to be correct not only of some parts of the Ukraine but of sections of the North Caucasus and lower Volga regions and, for that matter, Kazakstan, where the attempt to change the stock-raising nomads of the type and the period of Abraham and Isaac into 1933 collective grain farmers has produced the most deplorable results.

It is all too true that the novelty and mismanagement of collective farming, plus the quite efficient conspiracy of Feodor M. Konar and his associates in agricultural commissariats, have made a mess of Soviet food production. [Konar was executed for sabotage.]

But—to put it brutally—you can't make an omelette without breaking eggs, and the Bolshevist leaders are just as indifferent to the casualties that may be involved in their drive toward socialization as any General during the World War who ordered a costly attack in order to show his superiors that he and his division possessed the proper soldierly spirit. In fact, the Bolsheviki are more indifferent because they are animated by fanatical conviction.

'You can't make an omelette without breaking eggs' - Duranty's New York Times denial of famine in the Soviet Union.

'This is not to mention a more regrettable incident of three years ago when an American correspondent discovered half of Ukraine flaming with rebellion and "proved" it by authentic documents eagerly proffered by Rumanians, which documents on examination appeared to relate to events of eight or ten years earlier.'

Compiling such a list of false stories was clearly intended to get the reader to identify Gareth Jones subliminally as another purveyor of fake news. It was especially insulting to his integrity as a journalist and an eye-witness, given the explosive nature of Jones' revelations about the famine. In his article, then, Duranty had effectively branded Jones as a liar before he even addressed the substance of the Welshman's allegations.

However, in his actual discussion of Jones' claims, Duranty preferred to patronise the younger man's assessment of what he had seen. He wrote:

> 'But to return to Mr Jones. He told me there was virtually no bread in the villages he had visited and that the adults were haggard, gaunt and discouraged, but that he had seen no dead or dying animals or human beings.

> I believed him because I knew it to be correct not only of some parts of the Ukraine but of sections of the North Caucasus and lower Volga regions and, for that matter, Kazakstan, where the attempt to change the stock-raising nomads of the type and the period of Abraham and Isaac into 1933 collective grain farmers has produced the most deplorable results.

> It is all too true that the novelty and mismanagement of collective farming, plus the quite efficient conspiracy of [Vice Commissar for Agriculture] Feodor M Konar and his associates in agricultural commissariats, have made a mess of Soviet food production. [Konar was executed for sabotage.]

> But – to put it brutally – you can't make an omelette without breaking eggs, and the Bolshevist leaders are just as indifferent to the casualties that may be involved in their drive toward socialisation as any General during the World War who ordered a costly attack in order to show his superiors that he and his division possessed the proper soldierly spirit. In fact, the Bolsheviki are more indifferent because they are animated by fanatical conviction.

MR JONES – THE MAN WHO KNEW TOO MUCH

Since I talked to Mr Jones I have made exhaustive inquiries about this alleged famine situation. I have inquired in Soviet commissariats and in foreign embassies with their network of consuls, and I have tabulated information from Britons working as specialists and from my personal connections, Russian and foreign.

All of this seems to me to be more trustworthy information than I could get by a brief trip through any one area. The Soviet Union is too big to permit a hasty study, and it is the foreign correspondent's job to present a whole picture, not a part of it. And here are the facts:

There is a serious food shortage throughout the country, with occasional cases of well-managed State or collective farms. The big cities and the army are adequately supplied with food. There is no actual starvation or deaths from starvation, but there is widespread mortality from diseases due to malnutrition.

In short, conditions are definitely bad in certain sections - the Ukraine, North Caucasus and Lower Volga. The rest of the country is on short rations but nothing worse. These conditions are bad, but there is no famine.

The critical months in this country are February and March, after which a supply of eggs, milk and vegetables comes to supplement the shortage of bread - if, as now, there is a shortage of bread. In every Russian village food conditions will improve henceforth, but that will not answer one really vital question - what about the coming grain crop?

Upon that depends not the future of the Soviet power, which cannot and will not be smashed, but the future policy of the Kremlin. If through climatic conditions, as in 1921, the crop fails, then, indeed, Russia will be menaced by famine. If not, the present difficulties will be speedily forgotten.

For Duranty, then, any problems with the collectivisation of farms were not inherent to the system but the faults of individual officials. In this, he was in exact alignment with the Soviet hierarchy.

Very quickly a letter was received and published by the *New York Times* from Katherine E Schutock of Jackson Heights, New York. She wrote:

'I note the denial of the starvation of those in Ukraine, North Caucasus and Lower Volga regions by your correspondent Walter Duranty, in this morning's issue of *The Times*.

Private letters from persons in these regions indicate that thousands have already died and more are dying of starvation.

The people who write such pathetic letters are not looking for help, because it cannot reach them. Money cannot reach them, and if it does they receive only half of what they sign for. Receipt of help from America only gets them into trouble with the Cheka. Most of the letters I have seen end thus: "If you do not hear from us again, you can be sure we are not alive. We are either getting it for this letter, or we are through. The agony of living and dying of hunger is so painful and so long. What torture is it to live in hunger and know you are dying slowly of hunger".

The Soviet Government is repeating the deeds of 1921, when the famine situation was not known until it was too late to help those five millions in the Ukraine, who died of starvation just on account of false information. HH Fisher tells us of this in the book Famine in Soviet Russia 1919-1923, when he writes: "The Moscow Government failed to bring the Ukrainian situation to the knowledge of the ARA [American Relief Administration]".

Established in 1919, in the aftermath of the First World War, the ARA was an American relief mission to Europe with future President Herbert Hoover as its programme director. Unusually, it offered help to the Soviet Union. In 1921, to ease famine in Russia, the ARA's director in Europe, Walter Lyman Brown, began negotiating with Maxim Litvinov, the People's Commissar for Foreign Affairs in Riga, Latvia. An agreement was reached and the US Congress allocated $20m for relief under the Russian Famine Relief Act, a newly enacted piece of legislation.

At its peak, the ARA employed 300 Americans, more than 120,000 Russians and fed 10.5 million people daily. The medical division of the ARA functioned from November 1921 until June 1923 and helped overcome the typhus epidemic then ravaging Russia. The ARA's famine relief operations ran in parallel with much smaller Mennonite, Jewish and Quaker famine relief operations in Russia.

However, the ARA's operations in Russia were shut down on 15 June 1923, after it was discovered that Russia had renewed the export of grain.

Days after the article in which he sought to discredit Jones' famine claims, Duranty wrote a more impersonal piece for the *New York Times* that came to the Soviet Union's defence from a different angle:

'In the excitement over the Spring sowing campaign and the reports of an increased food shortage, a fact that has been almost overlooked is that the production of coal, pig iron, steel, oil, automobiles, tractors, automotive parts, locomotives and machine tools has increased by 20 to 35 per cent during recent months.

That is the most effective proof that the food shortage as a whole is less grave than was believed – or, if not, at least distribution has greatly improved, which comes to the same thing for practical purposes.

Coal production dropped before Christmas to 160,000 tons a day. Today it is averaging 195,000 tons a day. The pig iron output dropped to 14,000 tons daily in January, and steel to 12,000 tons daily. Today the production of pig iron and steel is 19,000 and 20,000 tons a day, respectively.

Moscow Province, which supplies almost half the nation's tractor parts, and Leningrad Province, which produces a quarter of the parts, both surpassed the program for the first three months of this year, So did the automotive plants at Nizhni-Novgorod, Kharkov and Moscow, and the huge new ball-bearing plant on the outskirts of Moscow.

There was also a marked reduction in first costs, especially in heavy machine production. All of which goes to show that the recent pessimism - voiced in the Soviet press as self-criticism, no less than by foreigners - was exaggerated and did not take into account the fact that Russian workers are gradually learning to handle their industrial machinery, despite delays and obstacles.

It is true, too, that, although the press insists the rate of Spring sowing in the North Caucasus, South Ukraine and Volga regions is much lower than it should be, the total sown area compares favorably with last year, when the sowing was retarded by cold weather.

This year Spring came early throughout the country and the Moscow River is bringing down ice in its Spring flood - an occurrence that is not unusual before the third week of April. While many sections of the South are foul with weeds and while there is a lack of animal traction and, in some areas, apathy and discouragement among the peasants, it is beginning to look as if the sowing prospects are better than was generally expected and the Kremlin has once more proved capable of stimulating its followers to overcome a difficult and apparently critical situation.'

Duranty's article reads like a Soviet press release.

In a response to Duranty's original article, written by Jones on 1 May 1933 and published in the *New York Times* on 13 May, the Welshman went out of his way not to attack Duranty personally, but to set out his case clearly and concisely. Privately, however, as previously referred to in Chapter 7, he had a low opinion of Duranty,

Jones' note – 'I don't trust Duranty'.
(© The Gareth Vaughan Jones Estate)

confiding to his diary after meeting him on 19 March 1933: 'I don't trust Duranty – he still believes in collectivisation.'

In his article published on 13 May, Jones wrote:

'On my return from Russia at the end of March, I stated in an interview in Berlin that everywhere I went in the Russian villages I heard the cry; "There is no bread, we are dying," and that there was famine in the Soviet Union, menacing the lives of millions of people.

Walter Duranty, whom I must thank for his continued kindness and helpfulness to hundreds of American and British visitors to Moscow, immediately cabled a denial of the famine. He suggested that my judgment was only based on a forty-mile tramp through villages. He stated that he had inquired in Soviet commissariats and in the foreign embassies and had come to the conclusion that there was no famine, but that there was a "serious food shortage throughout the country ... No actual starvation or deaths from starvation, but there is widespread mortality from diseases due to malnutrition".

While partially agreeing with my statement, he implied that my report was a "scare story" and compared it with certain fantastic prophecies of Soviet downfall. He also made the strange suggestion that I was forecasting the doom of the Soviet régime, a forecast I have never ventured.

I stand by my statement that Soviet Russia is suffering from a severe famine. It would be foolish to draw this conclusion from my tramp

through a small part of vast Russia, although I must remind Mr
Duranty that it was my third visit to Russia, that I devoted four years
of university life to the study of the Russian language and history
and that on this occasion alone I visited in all twenty villages, not
only in the Ukraine, but also in the black earth district, and in the
Moscow region, and that I slept in peasants' cottages, and did not
immediately leave for the next village.'

Enumerating the various kinds of evidence he had assembled before
drafting his articles exposing the famine, Jones wrote:

'My first evidence was gathered from foreign observers. Since Mr
Duranty introduces consuls into the discussion, a thing I am loath to
do, for they are official representatives of their countries and should
not be quoted, may I say that I discussed the Russian situation with
between twenty and thirty consuls and diplomatic representatives
of various nations and that their evidence supported my point of
view. But they are not allowed to express their views in the press, and
therefore remain silent.

Journalists, on the other hand, are allowed to write, but the
censorship has turned them into masters of euphemism and
understatement. Hence they give "famine" the polite name of
"food shortage" and "starving to death" is softened down to read as
"widespread mortality from diseases due to malnutrition". Consuls
are not so reticent in private conversation.

My second evidence was based on conversations with peasants who
had migrated into the towns from various parts of Russia. Peasants
from the richest parts of Russia coming into the towns for bread.
Their story of the deaths in their villages from starvation and of the
death of the greater part of their cattle and horses was tragic, and
each conversation corroborated the previous one.

Third, my evidence was based upon letters written by German colonists in Russia, appealing for help to their compatriots in Germany. "My brother's four children have died of hunger". "We have had no bread for six months". "If we do not get help from abroad, there is nothing left but to die of hunger". Those are typical passages from these letters.

Fourth, I gathered evidence from journalists and technical experts who had been in the countryside. In *The Manchester Guardian*, which has been exceedingly sympathetic toward the Soviet régime, there appeared on March 25, 27 and 28 an excellent series of articles on "The Soviet and the Peasantry" (which had not been submitted to the censor). The correspondent, who had visited North Caucasus and the Ukraine, states: "To say that there is famine in some of the most fertile parts of Russia is to say much less than the truth: there is not only famine, but – in the case of the North Caucasus at least – a state of war, a military occupation". Of the Ukraine, he writes: "The population is starving".

My final evidence is based on my talks with hundreds of peasants. They were not the "kulaks" – those mythical scapegoats for the hunger in Russia – but ordinary peasants. I talked with them alone in Russian and jotted down their conversations, which are an unanswerable indictment of Soviet agricultural policy. The peasants said emphatically that the famine was worse than in 1921 and that fellow-villagers had died or were dying.

Mr Duranty says that I saw in the villages no dead human beings nor animals. That is true, but one does not need a particularly nimble brain to grasp that even in the Russian famine districts the dead are buried and that there the dead animals are devoured.

May I in conclusion congratulate the Soviet Foreign Office on its skill in concealing the true situation in the USSR? Moscow is not Russia, and the sight of well fed people there tends to hide the real Russia.'

BETRAYAL

Later in the year, in October 1933, the *Manchester Guardian* published an article by its regular Moscow correspondent WH Chamberlin, in which he poured scorn on the suggestion that there had been a famine, as described by Jones.

Visiting the Ukrainian town of Poltava, Chamberlin met Mr Mezhuev, president of the local Soviet Executive Committee, who spoke in glowing terms about that year's grain harvest. Chamberlin wrote:

> 'He characterised the harvest this year as excellent, averaging over twenty bushels an acre. The area planted in the spring was 37,500 hectares, double that of last year despite the fact that the number of horses had declined from 8,000 to 4,800. Two important economic 'campaigns' one for grain deliveries to the State, the other for the autumn planting, had been finished before the end of September, whereas last year both had dragged on for a much longer period of time. "To what do you attribute the improvement?" I inquired. "Several factors have been at work," replied Mr. Mezhuev. "The establishment of a fixed and unalterable grain levy; Stalin's declaration that it is our ideal to make all collective farmers well-to-do; more concrete and practical leadership of the collective farms by the party and Soviet authorities."

'What is the truth of rumours about food shortage in the Poltava district last winter and spring?' Chamberlin asked. Weighing his words carefully, Mezhuev responded:

> 'Elements of hunger (elementi goloda) there were. There were deaths from hunger. But the stories in the émigré press about wholesale starvation are nonsense. The best refutation is our successful spring planting and our good harvest.'

Chamberlin thus reproduced without qualification the assertion of a Soviet official who had a clear vested interest in playing down the extent of food shortages.

Crucial testimony about the way the Moscow press corps closed ranks against Jones was provided by Eugene Lyons, the United Press agency's correspondent in the Soviet capital – a Communist sympathiser who had previously worked for the Soviet news agency Tass.

In his book *Assignment in Utopia*, published in 1937, two years after Jones' death, Lyons wrote in a chapter titled 'The Press Corps Conceals a Famine':

'Jones had a conscientious streak in his make-up which took him on a secret journey to the Ukraine and a brief walking tour through its countryside. That same streak was to take him a few years later into the interior of China during political disturbances, and was to cost him his life at the hands of Chinese military bandits.

'An earnest and meticulous little man, Gareth Jones was the sort who carries a notebook and unashamedly records your words as you talk. Patiently he went from one correspondent to the next, asking questions and writing down the answers.

'To protect us, and perhaps with some idea of heightening the authenticity of his reports, he emphasised his Ukrainian foray rather than our conversation as the chief source of his information.

'Throwing down Jones was as unpleasant a chore as fell to any of us in years of juggling facts to please dictatorial regimes – but throw him down we did, unanimously and in almost identical formulas of equivocation. Poor Gareth Jones must have been the most surprised human being alive when the facts he so painstakingly garnered from our mouths were snowed under by our denials.

'The scene in which the American press corps combined to repudiate Jones is fresh in my mind. It was in the evening and Comrade Umansky [a Soviet press censor], the soul of graciousness, consented to meet us in the hotel room of a correspondent. He knew that he

180

had a strategic advantage over us because of the Metro-Vickers story. He could afford to be gracious. Forced by competitive journalism to jockey for the inside track with officials, it would have been professional suicide to make an issue of the famine at this particular time. There was much bargaining in a spirit of gentlemanly give-and-take, under the effulgence of Umansky's gilded smile, before a formula of denial was worked out.

'We admitted enough to sooth our consciences, but in roundabout phrases that damned Jones as a liar. The filthy business having been disposed of, someone ordered vodka and zakuski [snacks often served with vodka], Umansky joined the celebration, and the party did not break up until the early morning hours.'

The validity of Jones' reporting of the mass starvation he witnessed while in Ukraine, purposely inflicted by Stalin's genocidal tyranny, is indisputable and globally acknowledged.

10

Nazi Germany

The Crushing of Democracy

'There is an urge, shared by almost all Germans, even by Socialists, to have a powerful army again, and this reverence for an army is typically described by Hitler in his autobiography when he writes: 'What the German people owes to the Army can be summed up in one word, namely, Everything.'

In May 1933, when Jones visited Germany once more, he wrote a series of articles for the *Western Mail* in which he set out his views on the regime's first four months and sought to explain further how it had come to power:

'The German National Revolution [as he termed it], although possessing a far narrower economic and philosophical foundation than that brought about by Lenin, has certainly been more rapid than its Russian counterpart ... The lightning pace of the National Socialist triumph makes the French Revolution appear almost like prolonged slow motion.'

Stressing the comprehensive nature of the Nazi takeover, Jones wrote:

'The Brownshirts have put one party, and one party only, into control, and that is the National Socialist party, which has become as all-powerful as the Communists in Russia and the Fascists in Italy. The Nazis have put themselves into the position of leaders in the universities, in all committees, in factories, on boards of directors, in schools, in public offices.

... They have started a ruthless campaign against the Jews. Distinguished scholars and great men, whom we in Britain would be honoured to consider as our citizens, are not allowed to enrich German scholarship or law courts or hospitals.

GERMANY *under* **HITLER.**

Mr. GARETH JONES,

who has just returned from a tour in Germany and Danzig, will write a series of articles in the *Western Mail & South Wales News* next week

on

HITLERISM.

Mr. Gareth Jones has visited Germany at least once every year since 1923, and has enjoyed special facilities for studying the country and its peoples.

He has met Hitler, Goebbels, and other Nazi leaders, and his impressions of the new movement in Germany will be read with deep interest.

The first article will appear in the *Western Mail & South Wales News* next Monday.

Order your copy from your newsagent.

The Western Mail's promotion of their young journalist's eyewitness reporting from Nazi Germany.
(© The Gareth Vaughan Jones Estate)

... They have abolished two powerful parties, the Social Democrats, who numbered about eight million voters and the Communists, who numbered almost six million, and have seized their funds, the private property of those parties. They have imprisoned many tens of thousands of men and women for their political views and hold them now captive in prisons and concentration camps. They have swept away the liberty of the press, and they come down with a heavy hand upon any editor who dares criticise the leader or his policy. They have created a secret police which will make still more nebulous any freedom of expression which may remain ... They have reorganised education on lines of narrow nationalism and intolerance. They have had midnight bonfires of some of Germany's most valuable Socialistic books.'

Having summarised the extremely negative consequences of regime change, Jones went on to place the Nazi takeover in the context of recent historical events:

'... the German democracy of 1918-33 was, in the eyes of young Germany, a regime of old men. 'Make way for youth' became the slogan of young people, and they were determined to overthrow the republic which had so little room for them.

Young Germans not only felt themselves enslaved by their system at home, but also longed to break the shackles of the Treaty of Versailles. They were not willing to admit they had been defeated in the war but attributed their debacle to a Socialist 'stab in the back' in November 1918.

The War Guilt Clause, the sending of troops into the Rhineland by the French, the refusal to admit Germany into the League of Nations until 1926, the inferiority in armaments, the need to pay £100m a year in reparations - all these forces mounted up resulting in revolution in 1933.'

Jones went on to spell out the greatest grievance, which years later was the one that precipitated the Second World War:

'What rankled most in the German mind was the taking away from Germany of lands inhabited by Germans, and placing them under peoples like the Poles, whom they despised. Millions grew up with the conviction that they would willingly die on the battlefield to win back for Germany the Polish Corridor, and other parts which they longed to see reunited with the Fatherland.'

In a further *Western Mail* article, Jones wrote about the central role of the soldier in the Nazis' vision for Germany, displaying prescience when referring to the likelihood of an expansionist war in eastern Europe:

'If you listen to the wireless in Germany today, you will hear in the intervals four notes being played time and again, and you find that it is the tune 'People to Arms! People to Arms!' which is being drummed into the ears and the minds of listeners.

... The worship of the soldier is again being implanted in the minds of young Germans, and no nobler death is presented to them than death on the battlefield. There is an urge, shared by almost all Germans, even by Socialists, to have a powerful army again, and this reverence for an army is typically described by Hitler in his autobiography when he writes: 'What the German people owes to the Army can be summed up in one word, namely, Everything.'

Towards the East! That is his policy, and to carry out that policy which means in the long run a war with Poland, he is determined to have a powerful army, a strong air force and a modern Baltic fleet. Germany must expand and carry out the policy of conquering Eastern Europe which was the Prussian policy of six centuries ago.'

In a bid to understand Hitler's antagonism to the Jews, had Jones read *Mein Kampf*. Again in the *Western Mail* – in an article headlined 'Campaign of Hatred against the Jews' – he wrote:

'This is what he [Hitler] said of England: "In this country of free democracy, the Jew is almost the unlimited dictator through the devious method of controlling public opinion." It was not the British, in Hitler's opinion, but the Jews who wished the destruction of Germany in 1914-18. Now the Jews, he says, are aiming at the destruction of Japan, for Japan is the barrier to a world Jewish dictatorship. Therefore, the Jews are now rousing the peoples of the world against Japan.'

Quoting from *Mein Kampf*, Jones highlighted Hitler's comment that, 'Everything which we see in human civilisation, in achievements of art, science and engineering, is almost exclusively the creative production of the Aryan.' Rejecting such a racist perspective outright, however, Jones stated:

WESTERN MAIL & SOUTH WALES NEWS, WEDNESDAY, JUNE 7, 1933.

Germany Under Hitler—Third Article

CAMPAIGN OF HATRED AGAINST THE JEWS

NATIONAL LOSS IN TRADE AND INITIATIVE

By GARETH JONES

One day a leading Nazi said to me: "I tremble when I think of England. You are on the verge of a precipice and nothing but ruin awaits you. Do you know why?"

I waited for the reply, and it came: "You are doomed because of the Jews, who are working your downfall."

I almost rubbed my eyes. Here was a man of influence in the government of Germany, and he was talking in the terms of the Middle Ages. He continued in strains of fantastic ignorance, and his eyes sparkled as he enumerated the sins of the Jews. As I listened to him I felt as if I had been transported back many centuries, to an age of witchcraft and black magic, so unreal was his description of the so-called machinations of the Hebrew race.

When I got cut into the streets of Berlin I almost imagined that a pogrom might take place, so burning had been the

Indeed, Hitler looks upon the Bolshevik Revolution as a Jewish scheme to conquer the world, blissfully unaware of the fact that Lenin was no Jew, that Stalin is no Jew, that the most powerful Jews in the world are allied to capitalism, and that the Jewish shopkeeper is the greatest sufferer in a proletarian revolution. But these little inconsistencies do not matter in the eyes of Nazis, for Nazis are quite capable of believing that Jewish Bolsheviks are working for the triumph of Jewish High Finance and that Jewish High Finance is subsidising a world revolution!

Even Jewish jokes are regarded by many Nazis as part of the subtle scheme of world domination by the Jews. Hitler suggests that the Jews try to depict themselves in comic newspapers as a harmless, humorous people in order to mislead public opinion into thinking that they are no danger.

Jews are largely responsible for the decline in morals and for the corruption in public life. They state that the influx of Polish Jews has been damaging to Germany.

The revolt against the Jews can finally be traced to the antagonism of the small shopkeeper to the fierce competition and unscrupulous methods of many of the larger Jewish concerns.

Thus the Nazis have dismissed Jewish doctors and lawyers, officials and professors. Even Jewish workers and employés have been thrown out to make way for men of German origin. In the realm of sport and art, science and education, the possession of Jewish blood is a barrier to progress.

What of the future? There are signs that the persecution is dying down, but the damage done to Germany by it has been tremendous. Shakespeare wrote of the Jews: "If you wrong us, shall not we revenge?" and the revenge has come.

Leipzig, the centre of the fur trade, has been dealt a severe blow. Germany's exports have suffered through a boycott of German goods. But the greatest loss to Germany, in my opinion, will be the loss in brains, in initiative, and in economic genius through which Jews enrich the countries where they live.

'Campaign of Hatred against the Jews' reports Jones in June 1933.
(© The Gareth Vaughan Jones Estate)

'With one sentence Hitler swept the Japanese art, Chinese philosophy and Jewish science, the achievements of an Einstein or the healing of Jewish doctors, into the wastepaper basket. The worship of the Germanic past led to an orgy of inventions about the history of Germany. The fact that the Germans are a people of mixed origin, and that the Slav element in the Prussian is exceedingly strong, were brushed aside scornfully, for Hitler had spoken, and Hitler was always right.'

Jones continued with the explanation that the

'Nazis launched a campaign against the Jews, because they believed that Jews were largely responsible for the decline in morals, and for the corruption in public life. They stated that the influx of Polish Jews had been damaging to Germany. The Jews were accused of the nefarious purpose of desiring the triumph of Parliamentarianism.

... But the greatest loss to Germany, in my opinion, will be the loss in brains, in initiative, and in economic genius through which Jews enrich the countries where they live.'

Herr Hitler's Breakaway—As the German Sees It . By GARETH JONES

'The New Salute' - Hitler's attitude towards the League of Nations.
(© The Gareth Vaughan Jones Estate)

In a further *Western Mail* article, headlined 'Methods of the Nazis, Fascists and Bolsheviks', Jones compared the atmosphere in Nazi Germany with that in Soviet Russia and Mussolini's Italy:

'Where had I experienced before a similar atmosphere of idealism combined with fear, of unbounded hope on one side, and of whispered despair on the other? Then I realised that it was in Soviet Russia and in Fascist Italy that same atmosphere had encircled me.

The first point of contact was the idealism of many of the leaders. The Hitlerites expect a new heaven on earth, just as the Bolsheviks are convinced that they will build up in Russia a paradise.

This idealism has led to an admirable feeling of self-sacrifice, courage and selflessness, and the Brownshirt, who in Germany is willing to lay down his life for his leader, has his counterpart in the Russian Young Communist, who will work 20 hours voluntarily for the sake of the Five Year Plan. But the idealism of the Nazis and of the Bolsheviks has its dark side of intolerance, and their faith is that of the fanatic who, driven by deep emotion, keeps his mind completely closed to another point of view. You cannot argue with a Nazi, or with a Bolshevik, any more than you could convince a fundamentalist believer in the Bible of the validity of Darwin's theories.

"Germany" has become a religion for the followers of Hitler, in the same way as Communism has become a religion for Bolsheviks. Even the worship of Hitler makes one think of the worship of Lenin in Russia, and of Mussolini in Italy. In each office his photo hangs, just as Lenin's and Stalin's adorn the Bolshevik office. The cult of the leader is the feature of every dictatorship.'

For Jones, however, there were limits to the comparison:

'However much the methods of the Nazis and the Bolsheviks may be similar, they differ profoundly in aims, for the Nazis believe in maintaining private property, whereas the Bolsheviks hold private property to be the root cause of human ills.'

As someone who had recently seen at close hand the deadly effects of the abolition of private property in the context of farming in the Soviet Union, and having a mother who had tutored the children of the Hughes family who had founded the formerly private

NAZIS RUTHLESS

But German People Kindly and Hospitable

"Hitler will probably move towards the Right and the dictatorship will become more severe. There will be an increase in the power of the secret police and of the black-uniformed Storm Troopers (the S.S.). As a result the might of Goering and of Himmler, head of the black-uniformed troops, will probably grow even greater."

These statements were made by Mr. Gareth Jones, of the *Western Mail & South Wales News*, in an address to the Cardiff Rotary Club on Monday. Mr. Fred Hooper, the new president of the club, was in the chair.

Mr. Gareth Jones foresaw in Germany an exceedingly grave economic crisis which would still further lessen public confidence in Hitler. Prices were rushing upwards and there might soon have to be food rationing.

"Travelling through Germany a few weeks ago," he said, "I was impressed by the disastrous outlook of the harvest. This forebodes evil for next winter, for Germany has little foreign currency to import foodstuffs."

In spite of ruthless methods of their rulers, he had always found the mass of Germans sentimental, kindly, and most hospitable. Travellers to Germany might rest assured that they would be excellently treated and would be as secure as in any country.

Jones spoke about his views on events in Germany to a meeting of Cardiff Rotary Club.
(© The Gareth Vaughan Jones Estate)

– then Soviet controlled – steel mill in what is now Donetsk, Jones clearly despised Bolshevik ideology. Coming from a very liberal and internationalist-minded family, Jones also rejected Nazism, but perhaps not as unequivocally.

In January 1934 Jones wrote a piece expressing surprise at the fact that Germany and Poland had signed a non-aggression pact, supposedly to last for 10 years. He stated:

'It shows that Hitler has a sense of reality and a grasp of Germany's need for peace which few people would have expected of him. It shows that Germany's foreign policy is not to be based upon the hallucinations and glaring slogans of propagandist pamphlets, but on a sincere recognition that frontiers are frontiers, and that there are other peoples in Europe than the Germans who want justice done to them.'

As the American academic Ray Gamache states in his book *Gareth Jones - On Assignment in Nazi Germany 1933-34,*

'Surprisingly, Jones believed that this sudden deviation in course meant that Hitler had abandoned his ideology of hate for a foreign policy based on acceptance of territorial sovereignty.'

Passages of this kind inevitably raise doubts about the degree to which Jones was convinced that Hitler and the Nazis were irredeemably evil. It is as if there were occasions when he could recognise the evil for what it was, but had lingering doubts about whether the worst of what he saw really reflected the reality of Nazi Germany, or whether – despite the abundance of evidence – the truth was not as bad as it seemed.

Whether this stemmed from his unconditional love for Germany, his loyalty to his Nazi-supporting friends or the misplaced sense of being 'at home' he felt in the presence of the likes of Goebbels is a matter for speculation.

MR JONES – THE MAN WHO KNEW TOO MUCH

In June 1934 Jones made a further visit to Germany, going to Berlin with two friends, during which he was captivated by an air display orchestrated by the leading Nazi Hermann Göring. He wrote:

'This afternoon Eric, Idris Morgan and I are going to the great [Berlin] Flying Gala where we shall hear Göring speak. It will be a great occasion; thousands of balloons and aeroplanes will fly; the aeroplane stormtroopers will march and will be received by Göring in his capacity as Air Minister. The aeroplane Stormtroopers look fine in a blue-grey uniform.'

Recalling a blue banner he had seen outside Berlin's main station with a message which read 'Germany Must Become A Nation of Aviators', Jones wrote:

'It was a declaration of Germany's greatest ambition of the moment – to lead the world in civil and military aviation. The Germans are air-mad; their passion for flying is being fostered by the leaders of the National Socialist Party. Hitler, when he visits a town, swoops down upon it from the air.

... The real force behind the German air plans is not Hitler, however, but Göring, who probably cares nought about the economic visions of the National Socialist Party as long as he has power to blacken the European sky with a host of German squadrons. Göring was the inspirer of the air display which I visited in Berlin, and which not only impressed, but startled me.

Through the Berlin aerodrome ground marched thousands upon thousands of strapping young men clad in the new grey-blue uniform of the German aviators. As I watched their keen, determined faces, their fine physique, and the perfection of their marching, I thought that Germany had in them the germ of a magnificent air force.'

Jones pointed out that 10,000 aeroplanes were standing on the German frontiers, ready to defend the country against attack from outside. Equally, of course, the planes could be used in an aggressive way – and indeed were.

Having travelled to Prague in the hope of meeting President Jan Masarysk, Jones learnt that the leader of Czechoslovakia had been ordered to rest in the country. Returning to Leipzig the next day, he spoke to a Stormtroop leader on the train who wanted more emphasis on the Socialist element of National Socialism. Pointing to his black, white and red swastika armband, the Stormtrooper shouted:

'That swastika is going to be the symbol of Socialism as well as of nationalism. The future lies with us people of the Left, and the day will come when we shall sweep away the accursed remnants of the capitalists, who are still ruling Germany. The revolution is not yet at an end. The money makers, the big bankers, the manufacturers who live by crushing the poor have to be mercilessly crushed. And we shall do it.'

Summing up the general mood in Germany, Jones wrote:

'The German crisis is grave, and popular disillusion is considerable. Nevertheless, Hitler has recognised many factors on his side which should not be underestimated ... It is recognised that he has restored order to public life. He has in the view of millions of Germans banished the spectre of Bolshevism. He has, through the German Youth, the Labour Camps, and the Stormtroops contributed to the health, sturdiness, and discipline of the nation.

Moreover, even the discontented Germans realise that the only alternatives to Hitlerism are a dictatorship based upon the bayonets of Reichswehr [the military organisation of Germany, united with the new Wehrmacht in 1935] or a civil war.'

Despite the brutal suppression that was taking place, and getting worse, Jones made it clear that he saw the Nazi regime as the only realistic option for the country at the time.

Nevertheless, Jones was soon to suffer a huge shock. Just five days after the article, suggesting there was no alternative to a Nazi regime, was published, came the infamous Night of the Long Knives, in which Hitler displayed his ruthlessness towards those who had been his most loyal and trusted supporters. Jones wrote:

'These Stormtroopers (Brownshirts), known also as the 'SA' men (not for their 'sex appeal' but because SA stood for 'Storm Department') were composed of the lower middle class and unemployed supporters of Hitler. Recently, there has been a wave of discontent among their ranks, because the Socialist era to which they had been looking forward has seemed farther away than ever, and because the big capitalists, the financiers, the proprietors of the large stores, and the aristocratic landowners are as firmly in the saddle as they were before Hitler came. The Communistically inclined Brownshirts well deserved their nickname of "Beefsteaks" (brown outside but red within).

... The event began with Hitler entering Röhm's house [Ernst Röhm was a close friend and early ally of Hitler's, as well as a co-founder of the SA] early on Saturday morning and arresting the startled plotter. Röhm was a military adventurer of low moral standard, but a brilliant organiser. He and a number of other Brownshirt leaders were shot on June 30. Röhm had allied himself with left wing men, including General Schleicher, who was murdered with his wife at the same time in the coup.

This General Schleicher, Chancellor prior to Hitler [and previously seen by Jones as shrewder than Hitler] was not the reactionary he is sometimes reputed to have been. He was definitely a left wing man, who during his Chancellorship flirted with the trade unions. Had a vision of a "socially ruled" empire, and was preparing to deal a smashing blow at the big landowners when he was cast out of power. Such were probably the three ingredients in the plot which has failed: the baulked ambitions of Stormtroop leaders, the bitter disillusion of the "National Bolsheviks" and the left wing intrigue of the "Socialist General".

The plotters are dead. Röhm's place has been taken by Victor Lutze, a man with whom I lunched a year ago on the train between Berlin and Hanover. I have rarely met a man who impressed me so much by his ruthlessness, grimness, lack of humour and fanaticism.'

Here, then, was the other, much more realistic, side of what the Nazis represented – a world apart from the convivial idyll Jones had conjured up from his encounters with Goebbels and others.

Two days before a referendum held on 19 August 1934, on whether Hitler's role as Chancellor should be combined with that of Germany's President, with him assuming the title Führer, Jones attended a Nazi rally in Munich that was addressed by Göring. He opens his article for the *Western Mail* by acknowledging that

'A cruel, fleshy fist, ever moving, ever threatening, fascinates me and I can hardly take my eyes away from it.'

The fist belonged to Göring and for Jones symbolised the brutality and cruelty of the Nazi regime. Nevertheless, he described the rally as 'the most magnificently staged drama I have seen', adding:

'Like a priest surrounded by the chorus in a Greek play, Göring stood motionless beneath the Ionic columns of the temple, while the Storm Troop flag bearers carried their brilliant banners with the silver crests glittering beneath the searchlights.'

Seeking to distance himself from the staged hysteria, Jones wrote:

'The crowd stood with outstretched arms – I must have been the only one in that vast multitude whose right arm remained obstinately unraised.'

While it would have been considered totally inappropriate, and a serious breach of ethical conduct, for a reporter to show partiality at a political event they are covering, at a time when pressure was being exerted on foreign visitors to acknowledge the Nazi regime via the 'Sieg Heil' salute, Jones' comment provides clear evidence of his rejection of Nazism.

Jones again suggested that people in Germany were becoming disillusioned with Hitler, although his proposed constitutional change was approved overwhelmingly at the referendum (by 38.4 million votes to 4.3 million), and in a passage in which he admitted having been impressed by the fervour of the previous year, Jones stated:

> '[With] all his gifts of oratory, with all the passion which had filled his purple patches, and with all his triumphs of stage management, Göring must have left the meeting a slightly saddened man.
>
> Where was the enthusiasm which filled the assembly 18 months ago? Where was the spirit of religious fervour which once sent a shiver through the limbs and hearts of Germans?
>
> …Yes, they were lacking the old keenness which had impressed me so deeply in the first fine careless raptures of Hitler's revolution.'

Historian Ian Kershaw, in his book *Hitler 1889-1936: Hubris*, took a different view, stating that even after accounting for the manipulation of the voting process, the results 'reflected the fact that Hitler had the backing, much of it fervently enthusiastic, of the great majority of the German people' at the time.

Germany, however, was soon to be relegated in Jones' list of priorities.

11

Wales and Ireland

Celtic Culture and Nationalism

'Wales is full of citizens of the world, and I met many of them when I walked through mining villages, along mountain streams'

After his highly controversial trip to the Soviet Union, Gareth Jones started a new role on 1 April 1933 as a staff reporter for the *Western Mail*, described then, as now, as the 'National Newspaper of Wales'. Living at home with his parents in *Eryl*, the house they had bought at his urging, in a leafy and relatively prosperous part of Barry several years before, he travelled by bus to the *Western Mail's* head office in Cardiff city centre.

While he continued to analyse international political events, during the summer of 1933 he demonstrated his versatility as a journalist by writing a series of articles about rural Wales. Taken together, the articles can be read as a lament for a dying way of life, written by a journalist with enormous empathy for Wales and for what was being lost.

They also show that he had a deep love for his country as an entity in its own right, rather than as a region of Britain, and that he became intrigued by the political situation in the neighbouring Celtic nation of Ireland, which had fought for its independence when Jones was a teenager. Home rule had been granted only on condition that the Unionist-dominated north east of the country remained controlled

Jones loved his visits to rural Wales and reporting on its characters and traditions. (© The Gareth Vaughan Jones Estate)

by Britain - a proviso insisted upon by the British government led by Jones' former employer Lloyd George.

Especially notable among his articles about rural Wales was a group focusing on craftsmen and women. In one, Jones made a pilgrimage to Abergorlech in Carmarthenshire to meet hammer mill-owner Tom Rhydderch, who used a traditional technique to shrink and dye cloth. Describing his journey – presumably by car – to the mill, Jones wrote:

'Passing farms and tiny villages, which had been newly-whitewashed and looked dazzlingly clean in the July sun and leaving one mill, Felingwm, which the General Post Office disgraces by anglicising into Velingwm, I reached Brechfa, in the Cothi Valley.'

Before continuing to see Rhydderch, Jones called in to see Marged Lewis, who until recently had run another mill with her now deceased sister:

'Near the bridge at Nant-y-Ffin I found the mill and, entering it, met old Marged Lewis, a type of the Wales of yesterday. In Welsh she told the history of her factory, how her father took it on in 1844, and how after his death she and her sister managed the factory until three years ago. But her sister died two years ago, and life in the silent, empty mill, where the wheel has stopped, where there is no sound of spinning, and where the only signs of existence are the dripping of water from the mill-stream, and the clatter of Marged's feet as she potters about, is sad and lonely.

She dreams of the old days, when the mills of West Wales were working busily, when the farmers brought their wool down from the hills, exchanging not only goods and coin, but the gossip of the countryside, the points of their sheep-dogs, the text and the *"hwyl"* [joyousness] of last Sunday's sermon, and the events of the last fair.

That is the world in which Marged has lived, and it is a world fast disappearing around her. She says: "It is very lonely now. The mills are shut and we can do nothing. How much better it was in the old days when we worked at home! The fine old Welsh days are over, when we used to make everything ourselves. Now those English do it all. Is it not a shame that we allow the English to do it?".'

It's easy to imagine Jones nodding his head in agreement with her. For him, the loss of traditional Welsh crafts was to be mourned not simply for its own sake, but because it marked a retreat from the integrity of centuries-old indigenous Welsh communities and an advance for encroaching Anglicisation. More recently it's what we have come to recognise as the negative side of globalisation.

In another sketch, Jones wrote in his engaging style about how Brechfa had once been an unlikely setting for the oil industry:

'One could hardly credit the charming village of Brechfa, in Carmarthenshire, with once having been the Texas of Wales. I do not mean to say that wild cowboys cracking revolvers dashed along after Indians in the Cothi Valley, or that Carmarthenshire millionaires,

Jones with a copy of the Western Mail at the 1933 National Eisteddfod in Wrexham. (© The Gareth Vaughan Jones Estate)

puffing great cigars, drew vast fortunes from that district to spend them at Barry, the Coney Island of Wales, or in the speakeasies of Cardiff. I mean that Brechfa was once the home of the oil industry, and what Llandarcy, with its refineries near Swansea, is today, Brechfa was yesterday.

You will not see the series of high derricks of Texas nor the stirring sight of high gushers when oil is ejected into the air. In fact, you will see nothing except a collection of some of the tallest finest trees in Wales, a profusion of red and yellow plants and weeds, shrubberies of alders, the remains of a few kilns overgrown by brushwood, some heaps of lime and some traces of charcoal. That is all that is left of the once flourishing oil works of Brechfa.'

Jones went on to explain how oil and charcoal were extracted from the trees, and how the products were used in the manufacture of munitions during the First World War:

'Today the oil works of the past have an interest for the botanist, for shrubs and weeds and flowers have sprung up at a very rapid rate in the soil, which has been influenced by the products of the works.

And when you say good-bye to Brechfa and your American or Persian or Rumanian or Russian petrol makes you speed along, just think of the contrast between the world oil industry of to-day and that humble but ingenious Welsh industry of yesterday.'

By championing this short-lived example of a local oil industry, Jones was demonstrating that he wasn't a nostalgic sentimentalist who was opposed to all change.

Describing a walk he undertook through the borderland between rural Wales and industrial Wales, Jones quoted Francis Bacon, 'If a man be gracious and courteous to strangers, it shows that he is a citizen of the world', then continued:

'Bacon: If I was right, Wales is full of citizens of the world, and I met many of them when I walked through mining villages, along mountain streams, following the border of Breconshire and Carmarthenshire, across the Black Mountains to the Usk and from the Usk to the Towy.

It was a tramp in search of personalities. Before setting out I asked myself: has the 20th Century crushed the Welsh hospitality and courtesy of the past? Has our mechanical age levelled men and women until they are all alike? Is there still left in Wales the Celtic fantasy and legend which delighted our ancestors? Has Puritanism banished humour from our midst?

My answer to these questions will be to tell of the gracious welcome of people to whom I was a stranger, of "the wit which sparkles in Welsh villages, of the laughter which still resounds in Welsh cottages, and of the fairy tales still told around the kitchen fire".'

The starting point for Jones' journey was Pontardawe, but he wrote that he experienced his first strange encounter when the bus was leaving Swansea and approaching Clydach:

'Behind me I heard strains of melancholy song, monotonous and weird, yet not unlike a Welsh hymn in the minor key, sung by two men with high voices. Looking around, I saw two Indians, whom I greeted and questioned. One replied: "That was one of the songs we used to sing in our village in Lahore."

"What is it like in your village?" Their faces brightened and one of them replied in his strange broken English: "There are some rich farms there and much fruit growing. It is not like South Wales. We make everything in our own village, make our own cloth and the potter, you see him making pots out of clay in the road." I remarked that Gandhi favoured home industries and asked whether they liked Gandhi. One answered with enthusiasm: "Gandhi good man. He holy man. He fasting and can never die through fasting." The other broke in: "I can fast too. I fasted for two weeks and only had water and salt."

They continued to tell me of their adoration of Gandhi, how he wanted India to be free and how he wanted the English to go. "What do you think of us in Wales?", I asked. The Hindu with the moustache pondered and said: "Welsh treat us good. They are different from

John Buchan.

English, they are better, kinder, more friendly. My brother here and me, we learn Welsh."

"Oh, and what have you learned?"

"We know Bore da, Nos da [Good morning, Good night], but we hope that *Dim arian* will not be true in Brecon where we now go to sell ties".'

In another article, in which Jones interviewed the writer John Buchan, most famous as author of the spy novel *The 39 Steps*, the issue of Welsh nationalism cropped up. Plaid Genedlaethol Cymru (The Welsh National Party) had been formed in 1925, but was not to gain Parliamentary representation until 1966 by which time it had revised its name to the one it still uses, Plaid Cymru. Nevertheless, Jones was curious to see what Buchan had to say about the issue.

At the time Buchan was Unionist MP for the Combined Scottish Universities. During the First World War he had been Director of Information when Lloyd George was Prime Minister.

'Perhaps there is history being made to-day in Wales with the growth of nationalism,' Jones suggested to Buchan. 'What do you think of Welsh nationalism?' Reporting the writer's response, Jones noted:

> 'Col. Buchan wanted to learn more about the Welsh Nationalist movement before stating an opinion, but finally he said: "Where nationalism is concerned, as in Scotland or Wales, I think that at the present moment, when things are in the melting-pot, the deepest foundation is not political, but cultural".'

It seems likely from this exchange that Jones was what today might be termed 'indy curious' as far as the future of Wales might be concerned. While he didn't overtly express support for independence, neither did he express hostility towards it. He was a strong supporter of the Eisteddfod movement, and as a Welsh speaker would have met Welsh Nationalists for whom the Eisteddfod Genedlaethol (National Eisteddfod) was the most important event in the calendar. His diaries note that Jones attended the National Eisteddfod when it was held in Wrexham in August 1933.

During a speech Jones delivered at that year's Eisteddfod, on the subject of 'The Omnipotent State' and the three authoritarian regimes in Europe – Germany, Italy and 'Russia' – Jones was asked by a member of the audience if there was any danger that the Welsh National Party would lead Wales towards dictatorship. The Welsh language newspaper Y Cymro (The Welshman) published an article about the speech and reported Jones' response in full:

'Y mae rhaglen y Blaid Genedlaethol yn newid yn aml ac ymddengys i mi mai rhaglen yn cael ei llunio yw ei rhaglen bresennol, a byddai'n well gennyf beidio datgan barn arni hyd nes caf weled y rhaglen gyflawn. Ar hyn o bryd y mae gan y Blaid wahanol raglenni mewn gwahanol ardaloedd o weriniaeth i ddominiwn.'

'The National Party's programme changes often and it appears to me that the present programme is a programme in development, and I would prefer not to express opinion on the matter until I see the full programme. At present The National Party has various programmes in various areas relating to state and dominion.'

In her book *Plaid Cymru: The Emergence of a Political Party*, Professor Laura McAllister points out that in 1932 Plaid had launched its first English-language paper, *The Welsh Nationalist*. Two years before, JE Jones had taken over as national secretary, and was pressing for English to be given equal status with Welsh in the party's administration. In the same period, the economist and essayist DJ Davies and his wife Noëlle Davies were arguing that Plaid needed to show greater rigour in analysing Wales' economic and social position and develop a programme for the future. According to Professor McAllister, 'These were significant and radical developments in the maturing of the party, signalling a recognition of the need to broaden Plaid's base by reaching out beyond its "natural" support in order to grow.' Jones would undoubtedly have been aware of these currents, and discussed them enthusiastically with nationalistically minded friends.

In October 1933 Jones spread his wings again and organised a trip to Ireland. He had been inspired to go after meeting people in London with conflicting views about the country, which had been partitioned in 1921 into two entities – The Irish Free State and Northern Ireland – following negotiations between the British delegation led by Lloyd George and delegates from the breakaway *Dáil Éireann* [Irish Parliament] led by Michael Collins.

Jones took a ferry from Liverpool to Belfast, capital of the six northern counties that remained in the UK as Northern Ireland,

and weighed up the contrasting views he had picked up about the complicated political situation.

In Belfast he visited the headquarters of the Unionist Party, where he met a political organiser who reminded him of a New York Tammany Hall 'boss' – and who gave him a blunt *precis* of the Unionists' perspective. The organiser told Jones: 'We in the North are British to the core,' prompting the journalist to observe:

'I noted mentally that this was the first and the most important result of the religious strife. The Protestants are made more British by their antagonism to the Catholics, who usually become more Nationalistic against Protestant domination.

The Protestant versus Catholic fight becomes a British versus Irish struggle and the Protestant section (nearly two-thirds of the population) do all in their power to keep the upper hand over the Catholic minority. The memory of Carson [the Unionist leader who insisted on the creation of a Protestant-dominated Northern Ireland statelet], whose name to some sounds like a hiss and a rattle of guns, and to others like a harsh but strong British rallying cry, enflames this political rivalry. "We are two nations, North and South," said the political boss, and in that phrase I saw the second result of the religious strife, namely, the fear and trembling in Ulster at the prospect of being submerged in a United Ireland. "We would never submit to rule from Dublin," I read in one newspaper, and that sentence pointed to a vital element in Irish politics, the partition of 1921, which separated Ulster (the six counties) from the 26 counties of the Free State. We have not heard the last of that partition.

The final result of the religious strife is the growth of the Irish Republican Army in Ulster. "The boys are drilling up in the hills," was one of the first phrases I heard in Belfast, and it meant the IRA men training for the day when they will rise and attempt to destroy what they call the domination by pro-British Protestants, and to fight for a United Irish Republic.'

Jones also told a more human story that illustrated with dark humour the degree of antagonism between the two communities.

'My hostess [told me of] an English family who had come to live in Ulster and laughed at the tradition that Catholic and Protestant servants could not be mixed. They engaged a Catholic cook – fat and 40 – and a little wisp of a Protestant kitchen maid. The experiment was a great success, and the atmosphere in the kitchen was as amicable as it could be, until the family went away for a holiday, leaving the pair behind.

One day the English people received a telegram: "Come back immediately. House wrecked." They took the first train home, entered the house and found shattered furniture, broken pictures and a litter of smashed crockery. After a bout of questioning, they got to the cause of the destruction. The Catholic cook and the Protestant maid had been seated happily before the fire, when the cook said, "I wonder what William of Orange is now doing in hell." "Having a chat with the Pope, probably," replied the Orange girl, and the fury of centuries of religious strife entered their souls, gave power to their arms, and they did not rest until they lay weary amid the wreckage their fight had caused.'

Jones later wrote in the *Western Mail*, quoting a white-haired old gentleman he had met in a London club, who'd commented: "Mark my words, Ireland is heading full-speed towards the blood and terror of a civil war." Jones noted:

'I felt a keen desire to take the first train to Dublin, but thought twice of it and telephoned an Irish friend. "Civil war! Nonsense!" came his voice across the wires. "De Valera has the whole country at his command and is building up a stronger, finer Ireland, and winning the economic battle against England."

I was intrigued and, deciding to seek another view, walked into the office of an expert on the Irish Free State, who declared: "De

Valera, that half-Mexican dictator, is sending the country to wrack and ruin. Ireland is doomed. O'Duffy's Blue Shirts [a right-wing paramilitary group, some of whose members later fought on the side of Franco in the Spanish Civil War] are the only ones who can rescue the country."

What a medley of clashing views! The more I asked the more I was puzzled by the varying analyses of those, on one hand, who described a sinister Irish Republican Army, drilling in secret with smuggled rifles and machine-guns, and of those on the other – especially Welsh Nationalist friends of mine – whose picture of Ireland was a land blossoming under de Valera into a paradise of prosperous peasant proprietors; of those who bade me hasten there lest I should be too late to see de Valera declare a republic; and of those who said a republic was never to come.'

Jones moved on to Dublin, where he was given a fascinating tour of the city by Professor Michael Hayes, a former Speaker of the *Dáil*. Hayes, "an energetic Irishman with a rollicking laugh" who had been a prisoner of the British after the Easter Rising of 1916, provided Jones with an insight into the Irish point of view towards the British that enabled him to write articles that many British newspapers would refuse to publish to this day. In a brilliant piece published by the *Western Mail* in November 1933, Jones wrote:

'Imagine the bitterness that would exist in any South Wales town in which a spot could be pointed out where the enemy had shot a fellow-citizen; in which the finest buildings had been shattered by the invaders' shell; and in which each man you met could tell you tales of murder, ambushes and street fighting between Welshman and foreigner. Imagine that and you will have a glimpse of public sentiment In Ireland.'

As we drove down the main street, O'Connell Street, [Hayes] pointed out the Post Office. "That building," he told me, "brings back

205

memories of the shot and shell in 1916, when, on Easter Monday, we rose against the British and occupied the building. For almost a week this street – one of the finest in Europe – was a shambles. You could hear the thud of the British bombarding us from the river a few hundred yards away. We stuck out until the Saturday, a grim feat of determination. Just think of it, a small band of men defying an empire for the sake of freedom."

O'Connell Street was practically destroyed and new buildings now line it; but however new the buildings, their aspect cannot wipe out the memory of Easter Week, 1916, and I learned why later when I stood with Professor Hayes looking at an ugly grey building. "That is Mountjoy Prison," he said. "That is where the battle for freedom was won, for behind those walls the young leaders of the Easter Week Rising were executed." [In fact the executions of the rebel leaders took place in Kilmainham Gaol, also in Dublin].

From Mountjoy Prison we went to a structure which looked dominating and cruel and to which I took an instant dislike. "Dublin Castle," said the Professor, as we entered a cold courtyard. "There," he pointed to a bare wall in an ugly patch of ground, "is where a number of Irishmen were shot down. I myself spent some time behind prison bars here," and he smiled.

From place to place we went where once there had been ruthless war between the Sinn Féiners and the British. "Look down that side street," my guide bade me, "That is where Dick Mulcahy, who was Chief of Staff, hid in my rooms for many months in 1919, when he was on the run and when the British had a hue and cry after him. We had a narrow escape one night, when a British officer and a policeman came to raid us, but Dick just got out in time over the roof!"

No wonder there was a tone of cold bitterness in General Mulcahy's voice when, a few days later, I talked to him about Wales, and he recalled weary months of imprisonment in Frongoch camp, near Bala, after the 1916 Rising.

Further on there were streets and canal banks where occurred the conflicts with the Black and Tans – events which make young Irish people clench their fists. To the British these are vague happenings in a distant age, but to the Irish they are ever present, for in Irish politics memory of the past is the most important factor. This was impressed upon me deeply during that journey which had begun with the General Post Office battleground of 1916 and had culminated with scenes of Black and Tan skirmishes.

The Irish pass these spots every day; they still mourn friends executed in the times of trouble; they can see the bullet marks on the Bank of Ireland columns; every stone speaks of the struggle against the British. To the British, 1916 is many years ago and the Irish War of 1920 is stuff for memoirs, not for emotions; but to the Irish they both happened yesterday, and for them Cromwell lived only the day before. As a result, hatred of Britain still is the greatest rallying-cry to whip up Irish feelings.'

Jones went on to describe the additional level of bitterness caused by the civil war that occurred after the establishment of the Irish Free State, between those who supported the Free State and those who saw it as a betrayal of the cause of a united Ireland.

'Although the "Cease Fire" of 1923 ended the internecine bloodshed, memories of Civil War are green. Republicans still recall their fellow-fighters being blown to pieces by Free State bombs and Free Staters cannot forget the ambushes which destroyed some of their finest soldiers, such as Michael Collins. Desire for revenge, living on from the Civil War, explained why at a private dance at which Gen. Mulcahy [head of the Free State government] was present I saw in the ball a bodyguard watching with a revolver, and in the grounds of the house three guards armed with a machine-gun.'

However orderly and even prosperous may appear the streets of present-day Ireland, the Civil War still goes on in the hearts of a minority of irreconcilables, and is one cause of the acidity of political discussion, of the unbalanced views, of the word 'traitor' bandied about in every other sentence, and of the part played by personal animosity, which are such striking features of Irish politics.'

Jones' personal observations of the animosity had already been set out in letters to his family:

'On Sunday I went to Kilkenny to the United Ireland Party [then in opposition – better known today as *Fine Gael*] meeting and saw all the fun there. The IRA tried to interfere with the meeting and there were scuffles with the police. The soldiers (in steel helmets and gasmasks) were called out. I had a splendid view from the platform.

On Monday night I went to a thrilling dinner party given by General Dick Mulcahy, one of the most famous Irish gunmen and the

successor of Michael Collins as Commander in Chief of the Army. He is always guarded by 4 bodyguards, one of whom I saw in the garden watching.

He will be present at the dance the O'Donnells are giving tomorrow night and the 4 bodyguards will be surrounding the O'Donnells' house in case Dick Mulcahy gets shot by the IRA men.'

Despite such political bitterness, Jones also recognised the innate generosity and kindness of Irish people:

General Richard 'Dick' Mulcahy.

208

'Irish hospitality knows no national boundary, and to individuals it is gay, unselfish, and sincere. Irish friends are of unlimited kindness to visitors, whether they be Welsh or English ... A strange combination of national characteristics – humour, hospitality and hatred – may lead Ireland into dark days, for it is again splitting the country into opposing forces.'

Having had to postpone an interview with Eamon de Valera because the latter had a chill, Jones caught up with the head of government (at the time officially known as President of the Executive Council) in his Dublin office early in 1934. In an article published by the *Western Mail* in March 1934, Jones wrote:

'He was not as I had pictured him. I expected a grim, fierce, rigid type, but I found a man whose face lit up from time to time with a subtle, charming smile. After shaking hands, he bade me sit by him at the desk, and began discussing the respective positions of the native language in Wales and in Ireland. "I have always admired the way in which the people of Wales have clung to their language," he said.

"Welsh has been preserved as a spoken tongue and has been used and is being used in life and literature to a far greater extent than Irish is being used in Ireland, but we are making headway in preserving Irish as a community language and extending its use throughout the country."

Eamon de Valera.

Contrasting nationalism in Wales with that in Ireland, de Valera said that the Welsh people had paid more regard to linguistic and cultural nationalism than the Irish people, and that for a considerable period the idea of political independence had overshadowed the cultural aspects of nationality in Ireland.

He added that the more the people of Wales and other countries with their own distinctive cultures retained their national individuality, the richer would be the variety of thought and achievement in the world.'

A professional photograph of Jones taken in 1934. (© The Gareth Vaughan Jones Estate)

12

The Round the World Trip

Embarking on the Final Journey

'The editor of the local paper came rushing in to interview me, and by this time I was feeling like the Prince of Wales'

Writing to his friend Margaret Stewart – the daughter of Jones' professor at Trinity and the sister of Ludovick, one of Jones' closest acquaintances from university – who was due to visit Russia in summer 1934, Jones offered some practical advice and made a joking reference to how he was no longer welcome in the Soviet Union:

'Your summer trip to Russia sounds most exciting. The Caucasus is a thousand times more interesting than the Volga, which is grossly over-written.

It will be a job to evade Intourist [the state-owned tourism company] and do it cheaply, unless you have someone with you who knows Russian. I am afraid that unless you're very lucky Intourist will get hold of you.

One thing you might do is take your tickets through Intourist for the journey, and for the first 2 or 3 days in Russia, and then try and go off on your own. But it will be difficult and terribly expensive, unless you are wicked enough – as all the journalists and diplomats are – to buy some smuggled roubles on the Black Market (i.e. get about

250 roubles to the £ by illegal buying instead of the 7 roubles at the bank).

I do wish I could be in the region of Russia when you are about. Alas! You will be very amused to hear that inoffensive little Joneski has achieved the dignity of being a marked man on the black list of the OGPU and is barred from entering the Soviet Union. I hear that there is a long list of crimes which I have committed under my name in the secret police file in Moscow, and funnily enough espionage is said to be among them. *

So, I have not the slightest relations with any of the people I know.

*As a matter of fact Litvinoff [the People's Commissar for Foreign Affairs] sent a special cable from Moscow to the Soviet Embassy in London to tell them to make the strongest complaints to Mr Lloyd George about me.'

We know from this that Jones' articles about the famine had angered those at the highest level in the Soviet Union – but that Jones himself did not apparently consider that he could be in danger as a result.

He was intending to undertake a 'round the world fact finding tour' after leaving the *Western Mail* in the autumn of 1934. In the meantime, as he wrote to his parents:

'It is funny. Jobs seem to be showering down on me. *International News* suggest I become Berlin Correspondent. What terms, I asked Connolly in the train. "Oh, our correspondents get a couple of hundred dollars a week". (about £2,000 a year) ... *International News* suggest, also, articles on the Far East. (£40 an article).

Paul Block, a big American newspaper man, who has been staying in St Donat's, and travels up to London, says he doesn't want to take a good man from Hearst, but if I refuse Hearst, "I can offer you something good in Europe". [He's offered] me £100 and expenses if I accompany him over Europe for a fortnight. I don't think it is possible – it's Eisteddfod time.

I saw Pulvermacher of *The Telegraph*. He suggested (not a definite offer) that I go round the world for *The Telegraph* writing descriptive and political articles.

So there you are! I think I may be able to combine *Telegraph* and *International News* with Round-the-World trip; although Germany at about £2,000 a year seems also tempting.'

Jones did take up Block's invitation to travel with him in Europe, thinking he could be back in Wales in time for the National Eisteddfod in Neath, but Block was ill and there were delays, ruling out a return for the highlight of the Welsh cultural and political calendar. Jones was unimpressed with Block, telling his family:

'It's not much fun travelling about with a poor fellow whose colossal conceit at his brain power is as astounding as his real ignorance and who at the same time is cringing and subservient.'

One incident that particularly embarrassed Jones occurred when they visited the Schönbrunn Palace in Vienna. Jones wrote:

'I got absolutely furious but I said nothing. Mr Block saw a picture (a very charming one) of Marie Antoinette as a child. He turned to the guide and said: "Can I buy that"!!!! ... He asked, "Was Maria Theresa [Archduchess and ruler of Austria from 1740-1780] the wife of Franz Joseph [Emperor of Austria 1848-1916, and of the Austro-Hungarian Empire, 1867-1916]?" The guide winced.

He has insulted every Viennese he has met by his tactlessness. "What's the use of you bringing me here to see this river?", he asked when the guide took us to look at the Danube. "It's just like any other river".'

Happy days at The Knapp in Jones' hometown, Barry. (© The Gareth Vaughan Jones Estate)

If Jones had any doubts about going on a round-the-world trip rather than taking up Block's offer to work in Europe, they were surely dispelled by the bad experience he had travelling with him.

In preparation for his trip, he spoke to a number of friends including Sir Bernard Pares, the enigmatic academic with a background in the security services. Pares gave him introductions to a number of academics in the United States, which he was to visit before going on to the Far East.

He also met Hugh Hessell Tiltman, a writer and journalist who had worked in China and suggested that Jones research subjects including 'Life in Manchuria Today', and 'Japan Today: with particular reference to factory working conditions'.

Jones had already been commissioned by the *Manchester Guardian* to write eight articles while he was away – two about the United States and two about the Far East. He had written a paper entitled

THE ROUND THE WORLD TRIP

Journey Round The World in which he had laid out his travel plans and sought commissions:

> 'On October 25 I shall sail to New York on a journey round the world. The aim of the journey will be to get news on the United States under Roosevelt; the prospects of a war between Japan and Soviet Russia; the aims of Japan's foreign policy and her relations with the United States; the internal situation in Japan and trade competition with Great Britain; the situation in Manchukuo; Japanese and Soviet penetration of Mongolia; and Communist rule in southern China.
>
> I shall take the following route.
>
> End October 1934 – February 1 1935: New York across to the United States to San Francisco. A lecture tour is now being arranged by my New York lecture agent.
>
> February 1935: San Francisco to Honolulu; stay Hawaii for a fortnight.
>
> End February: Arrive in Japan. The length of my stay in Japan will depend entirely upon whether Japan is in the news.
>
> From Japan I shall go to Korea and Manchukuo. In Manchukuo I shall travel to the Soviet frontier and shall attempt a journey on horseback in that region.
>
> I intend to go northward from Peking into Inner Mongolia. From Peking I shall go to Shanghai and Nanking. Then I shall try and find out what is happening in the communist areas of southern China.
>
> From China I will go to the Philippines, Singapore, Colombo, Bombay, Egypt and home.
>
> I offer my services which will be based on years of experience of foreign affairs and on journalistic training (reporting, sub-editing, leader writing and special articles) to a newspaper organisation.'

Mr. Gareth Jones, whose brilliant articles in the "Western Mail & South Wales News" have attracted wide attention, is leaving to-day for a tour round the world.

He will visit the United States, Japan, Manchukuo, China, the Philippines, Singapore, Ceylon, India, and Egypt.

From time to time he will keep the readers of the *Western Mail & South Wales News* informed as to the situation in those parts of the world.

The " Western Mail & South Wales News " will thus maintain its tradition of supplying first-hand news and views on events throughout the world.

The Western Mail's promotion for the articles Jones was to write during his round-the-world trip.
(© The Gareth Vaughan Jones Estate)

Arriving in New York, Jones visited old friends and undertook a number of speaking engagements, including one in Worcester, Massachusetts, where he spoke to an audience of 700 at a meeting of the city's Women's Club – a reflection of the celebrity status he had acquired as a result of his exposure of the famine in Ukraine.

In a letter to his family, he wrote:

'We came to a place where literally hundreds of cars were assembled and I saw a huge building into which men and women in evening dress were pouring. I was to address the whole elegance of Worcester, which is a city of about 600,000 or more than twice the size of Cardiff.

The president took me behind the scenes and led me up a high iron staircase and brought me to a stage. I found 700 people in front all dressed to kill and I was looking down. Anyway, I began and described graphically my flight with Hitler etc and they listened with open mouths. After I'd finished and had disappeared behind the curtain, I heard the applause continuing for a long time. Afterwards, I was like the Prince of Wales, trying to bow and shake hands fractiously to the high-hats of the city. It was very funny.'

While in Worcester, Jones learnt that his former employer Ivy Lee had died of a brain tumour at the age of 57. He wrote:

'Poor Ivy Lee is dead. I saw it in the paper in Worcester. I am very sorry, because he was most kind to me. I called at his office the day after I arrived, but did not know he was so ill. I wrote from New England to Mrs Lee and Jim Lee. I think that Mr Lee had great worries in the last few years.'

During his stay in New England, Jones visited some of the academics to whom he had introductions from Sir Bernard Pares. After taking a ferry from Boston to New York, he wrote to Pares:

'I have just returned from New England where your letters of introduction opened all portals. Professor Andrews sends his warm greetings to you and is exceedingly anxious for you to come soon to the United States. Professor Fay, Professor Wilson, Professor Langer and others who met you have entrusted me with many warm messages for you.

I shall write to you about my other talks with your friends in New York and Washington. In the middle of December, I shall be in California.

With my best thanks for your splendid help.'

Before travelling to California, Jones went to visit Frank Lloyd Wright, the world famous architect of Welsh descent, at his home, Taliesin, in Spring Green, Wisconsin. Wright had attained a level of notoriety arising out of his colourful private life, and this – together with the Welsh influences on him – was reflected in an article Jones wrote for the *Western Mail*:

'Frank Lloyd Wright! When you mention his name, note the expression on the faces of those with whom you talk in America. There is hatred, there is shock, there is disapproval, there is jealousy, there is respect, worship, adoration, but one expression you will never find, and that is indifference. "He wrestled with fire, and insanity, and a hostile public opinion with an indomitable will, and his story is a saga of experience," was the verdict of an American writer.

217

Frank Lloyd Wright.

Of Frank Lloyd Wright as an architect I can say little. I can only repeat what artists say, and that is that by bursting the fetters of architecture in the 'nineties he freed it from its unnatural, imitative character and from its imprisonment in a fortress far removed from life and that he is more responsible than any other individual for the beauty of new buildings in Europe and America.

But of Frank Lloyd Wright the man I can say much. With his piercing, witty sparkling twinkle which is ever playing around his lips, with the deep sincerity of his musical voice, with the force and faith of his views, and with the charm which he radiates, he has fascinated me more than any man with the exception of Mr Lloyd George.

The story of this rebel has its roots in the Wales of the Victorian times, when there dwelt a maker of Welsh hats who, on Sunday, preached an impassioned and unpopular Unitarianism. The hatter-preacher married Mary Lloyd, and came to America, penetrating to the valley of the Wisconsin River, where they created the Lloyd-Jones family from which sprang the child who was to change the architecture of the world. And today Lloyd Wright considers himself a thorough Welshman for all the influences which have moulded him were Welsh: the chapel where his uncle Jenkin Lloyd-Jones preached in the countryside was Welsh, and his motto which has guided him in his battles against a disapproving world is Welsh – it is, '*Y Gwir yn Erbyn y Byd*'[The Truth against the World].

218

The name of his home, Taliesin, is Welsh, and carved in wood and chiselled in stone you see the Druidic symbol / | \ in different parts of the house.

From this Welsh environment arose the fighter and thinker who has so impressed me by his philosophy and by the calmness of his perfected personality, and whom I now see in grey country tweed, with a bright red jacket as he strides through the snow. Even his stride reveals a solidity and a faith which are characteristic of his work and thought and are illustrated by episodes in his troubled life.'

Jones also visited Waukesha County, Wisconsin, where many immigrants from Wales and their descendents lived. Contrasting the gangsterism of big cities like Chicago and Milwaukee with the rural tranquillity of the Welsh villages, he wrote:

'Within twenty-four hours [of leaving Milwaukee] I slept in the quiet house of the Rev, and Mrs John Pugh Jones. There was a Bible by the bedside, a religious picture on the wall, a library of philosophical works and of Welsh poetry not far away. No thought of locking a door, no thought of gangsterdom! I was in Wales, and I was in a Welsh atmosphere. Within a day I had escaped from the America of the great cities and I was back with my own countrymen.

Moreover, I was back in the spirit of Wales, for I was amazed to see how Welsh characteristics and the Welsh tongue live on in that part of America. A veneer of Americanisms in speech, it is true, is covering the surface of the Welsh people. They say "Shucks" and "Oh, boy," and their accents are often pure Middle West, but beneath it all you find the old Welsh features, of which the first is hospitality.

I was feted and dined and invited and asked to speak until I felt like a visiting Prime Minister. When I stepped into the Avalon Hotel at Waukesha and the word went round the town that a Welshman from the Old Country had arrived, the Welsh citizens came trooping in, as African natives assemble when they hear the beating of the tom-toms. There was the Rev Hugh Owen, who, although born in America, spoke Welsh with a powerful Anglesey accent ("Oh, his praying is beautiful," whispered an ardent Welsh-American to me), and there were many others. Invitations were showered upon me. The editor of the local paper came rushing in to interview me, and by this time I was feeling like the Prince of Wales. Had I stayed there much longer I believe I should be bestowing autographs.'

In December 1934, Jones took the Grand Canyon Limited train from Chicago to Los Angeles, with a brief stopover to see friends in Santa Fe, New Mexico. Thrilled to be in Hollywood, he wrote a 20-page Christmas letter to his parents which began:

'What a week! I have been chased by a Red Indian woman with a poker, have travelled 2,000 miles, have come from the snow to palm trees and June weather, have galloped on the swiftest horses I have ever been on, and had a collision with another horse, have lived in a house made of mud and have crossed a desert and have addressed the most famous and elegant audience in the West of America on a subject for which I only had 24 hours' notice, have seen oranges and lemons and strawberries ripening in December, have broadcast to 11 States of America at five minutes notice, have been in tropical floods, have talked with a man, an Indian, 109 years old and arrived in the film city of the world ...'

Jones' frenetic adventures included being driven at speed by an academic, along avenues of palm trees in a tropical rainstorm, to a radio station which broadcast from a bedroom. He was asked to speak about aviation in Russia and writing about a lecture he delivered at a 'depressing' conference run by the Institute of World Affairs, he noted:

'Hurray! It went off splendidly and the audience clapped so much that the chairman told me to get up and bow (just like an actor). I was very relieved. I brought in Russia, Hitler's foreign policy and the New Commonwealth.'

He had told the conference, held in Riverside, California:

'On a visit [to the Soviet Union] last year I found the people dying of hunger. They had no bread left. Some families were eating cattle fodder and the children had swollen stomachs through lack of food. The famine is a result of the Soviet policy of collectivisation, which takes the land from the Russian peasant and destroys his desire to work. The exile of five million kulaks was one of the most brutal crimes in European history.'

'I've never been in such a wonderful and beautiful place as this' – California 1934. (© The Gareth Vaughan Jones Estate)

Two days before Christmas Day, he wrote from Hollywood:

'I have never been in such a wonderful and beautiful place as this. It's Christmas Eve tomorrow and it's like June ... I am being feted and entertained and motored around. I have never known such kindness.'

Jones enjoyed visiting the MGM Studios, where he lunched in the same room as two of the Marx brothers. He also received a telegram from Randolph Hearst inviting him to his castle, San Simeon, on the coast between Los Angeles and San Francisco. It read: 'Glad to see you any time. Let me know when you will come. W R Hearst.'

Earlier in 1934, Hearst had visited Berlin to interview Hitler. When Hitler asked why he was so misunderstood by the American press, Hearst responded: "Because Americans believe in democracy, and are averse to dictatorship." Hearst's papers, nevertheless, ran articles, without rebuttal, by leading Nazi Hermann Göring and by Hitler himself, as well as by Mussolini and other dictators in Europe and Latin America. Hearst had also turned against President Roosevelt's New Deal policy, seeing its interventionism as a blow against the 'rugged individualism' of the American ideal.

This was not the view of Jones, who wrote in an article in the *Manchester Guardian*:

> '(While) the business men are reactionary ... there is among the mass of the people a new faith and a new confidence in the future, that the whole outlook is brighter than it was in 1932, that in spite of conservative antagonism President Roosevelt has achieved in less than two years the task of saving the banks, of abolishing child labour and the sweat shops, of giving to the workers the right to organise which they have had for many years in Great Britain, of saving many hundred thousands of farmers from foreclosure, of increasing the price of farm produces, and of introducing a new philosophy of security through social insurance for the worker which was conspicuously absent from the nomadic, unsettled United States of pre-Roosevelt day'

Jones with William Randolph Hearst.
(© The Gareth Vaughan Jones Estate)

There is no record of what Hearst and Jones discussed during the latter's visit to San Simeon, but on 5 January 1935, after Jones' departure, Hearst gave a radio address in which he launched a bitter attack on the Soviet Union. The following day, Jones wrote to inform his parents that he'd been commissioned by Hearst to write three short articles on Russia for $225.

The first article, like the others syndicated across Hearst's newspaper empire which included the *New York American* and the *Los Angeles Examiner*, set the unashamedly anti-Communist tone of the series. It took as its starting point the assassination of Sergei Kirov, the Leningrad Communist Party chief who had been a friend of Stalin, and whose death – almost certainly ordered by Stalin – was used as the pretext for the Great Purge, in which many leading officials who had lost Stalin's trust were subjected to show trials and then executed. The article began:

'The eery [sic - old-fashioned spelling] voice of the secret police agent, the crack of the firing squad and the thud of a falling victim have been heard more often in the last few weeks in Russia than for many years. For 1935 has dawned upon a period of terror following the assassination of Stalin's friend, on December 1.

But no one has yet told the true story of the wave of shootings which is terrifying Moscow. What is behind the rifle shots? Why is Stalin descending with such ruthless slaughter upon Soviet citizens at a time when he claims to have brought happiness and prosperity into their lives?

I shall attempt to give the answer by describing my adventures among the Russian people, when I wandered alone on foot through a number of Russian villages, sleeping on hard floors of peasants' huts, and speaking to the rank and file of the real folk, to the 'forgotten men' in their own language, Russian.

It was among the hungry masses that I followed the real reason for the shootings in the Russia of 1935 and it is this: that there is throughout the country a feeling of revolt and of hatred of the Communists that Stalin can only crush by terror and still more terror.'

The rest of the first article, and the whole of the second, largely retold Jones' experiences as he walked through the villages where people were starving. The third article – headlined 'Reds Let Peasants Starve' – focused on the fate of the kulaks and was more overtly political. It began:

'"The Communists came and seized our land, they stole our cattle and they tried to make us work like serfs in a farm where nearly everything was owned in common" – the eyes of the group of Ukrainian farmers flashed with anger as they spoke to me – "and do you know what they did to those who resisted? They shot them ruthlessly".'

Jones took up the narrative:

'I was listening to another famine-stricken village further down the icy railroad track which I was tramping and the story I now heard was one of real warfare in the villages.

The peasants told me how in each village the group of the hardest-working men – the kulaks they called them – had been captured and their land, livestock and houses confiscated, and they themselves herded into cattle trucks and sent for a thousand or two thousand miles or more with almost no food on a journey to the forests of the north where they were to cut timber as political prisoners.

In one village which was inhabited by German colonists – and what a spotlessly clean and well-kept place it was! – they told me trainloads had left the district packed full of wailing farmers and their families.

Torn [a]way from their homes, prisoners of the heartless secret police and the hated land army, which exists to drive the peasants to work, these formerly well-to-do farmers had as their only crime the fact that they had worked all day and into the night, had had a little more land and had accumulated one or two more cows than others.

Some months later the news arrived in the district about the exiled colonists, and it was this: NINETY CHILDREN HAD DIED OF HUNGER

224

AND DISEASE ON THE WAY TO SIBERIA. The Communists I spoke to did not deny that they had ruthlessly exiled the hardest working farmers.

On the contrary they were proud of it and boasted that they would show no mercy to those who wanted to own their own land. "We must be strong and crush the accursed enemies of the working class," the Communists would say to me. "Let them suffer now. We have no place for them in our society".

Nor did they deny the shootings that had gone on in the villages. "If any man, woman or child goes out into the field at night in the Summer and picks a single ear of wheat, then the punishment according to law is death by shooting," the Communists explained to me, and the peasants assured me that this was true.

The greatest crime in Russia is the taking of socialised property and murder is regarded as a mere relic of capitalist upbringing and comparatively unimportant compared with the sin of the mother who goes out to the field at night to gather ears of grain in order to feed her children.'

After describing the severe impact of bread shortages in the city of Kharkov, Jones wrote:

'The most terrible sight ... was the homeless boys, who wandered about the street in filthy rags, who were covered with the sores of diseases, and whose features were depraved and criminal.

Three hundred of them had been rounded up and were homed in the station, where I glanced at them through a window and noticed some lying on the bare ground in a severe state of typhus.

Those have been some of the results of the Soviet regime which I witnessed MYSELF. Can it be wondered at that there has been a feeling of revolt among the population and that there have been plots within the Communist Party itself?

The opposition is too weak to overthrow the regime which is powerfully entrenched, but nevertheless the disillusion and the despair of the masses of the Russian people, typified by the scenes which I have described in the Ukraine, are the real reasons why Stalin was forced this Christmas and New Year to inaugurate a new reign of terror in the land of the Soviets.'

Already a pariah in the Soviet Union for what he had written in 1933, the syndication of such strident articles may have turned Jones into a marked man.

Hearst published further anti-Soviet articles as well as comment pieces, leading to protests by pro-Stalin activists, and on 26 February 1935 as many as 15,000 demonstrators gathered in New York's Madison Square Garden to protest with the Friends of the Soviet Union against the collapse of debt negotiations between the US and the USSR. Hearst was singled out for blame for the failed talks because of his papers' strong opposition to a deal.

On 18 January 1935, Jones took the SS Munroe from San Francisco to Hawaii. It was a stormy voyage and, finding his fellow passengers uncongenial, spent most of his time reading a best-selling book called *One's Company: A Journey to China* by Peter Fleming, a correspondent of *The Times* of London. The book describes the author's journey from London to Moscow, eastwards on the Trans-Siberian Railway, through Japanese-run Manchukuo and on to Nanking, the capital of China in the 1930s.

In 1980 the book was described by the writer Paul Fussell as 'British in its insouciant class condescension (Moscow was like a 'servant's quarters') and offhand anti-Semitism (the Soviet Union is run by Jews), the tone is imperially comic and the judgments quick, though always focused on the author. When Fleming gets to China, the reader is rewarded with acid portraits of Chiang Kai-shek, pronouncements on 'Red China' and the prospects of Communism (it could never take hold in China), life on the war fronts, and the nature of the Japanese empire.'

Fleming's journey through Chinese bandit country inspired Jones' choice of route from Hong Kong to Manchukuo, where he intended to stay for four weeks. A week after leaving San Francisco, the ship docked in Honolulu, where he was shown round by a local family. He wrote back to Wales:

> 'Here I am on the famous Waikiki Beach, but *entre nous* Barry Island is a thousand times better for bathing because of the coral here which sometimes cuts the feet.'

Jones saw the Pearl Harbour naval base, whose bombing by the Japanese in December 1941 precipitated the entry of the United States into the Second World War and, in an article written for the *Western Mail*, Jones displayed both his geopolitical insight and his occasional lack of prescience:

> 'What is the important strategic point in the Pacific for the defence of the United States? Hawaii. No enemy could land in California unless they first captured Hawaii. Thus the Americans are pouring millions of dollars into this vital naval base in order to dominate more than ever that half of the Pacific which lies towards America.

> ... Hawaii contains more Japanese – the potential enemy – than any other nationality. There are 140,000 Japanese, nearly one half of the population. Are they loyal to the Stars and Stripes, or do they still worship the Son of Heaven? Have they among their number a percentage of spies who report the secrets of America to Tokyo? Will they be able to blow up parts of the naval base in a time of war? Will they be able to ignite the petrol tanks?

> Those are the questions which trouble the navy men and which make the problem of Hawaii. To me it is an academic problem, because I see no reason why Japan should ever fight America, and I regard

prophecy of a United States versus Japan war as pure sensation mongering. Nevertheless, for the military and naval mind this is a grave problem.'

After a few days in Hawaii, Jones boarded a ship to Japan, where he met Günther Stein, a German journalist with whom he was already acquainted. He wrote to his family:

'I am having a great time and am most happy. I found a journalist friend, Guenther [sic] Stein, whom I knew in London, Jew, formerly of the *Berliner Tageblatt*, and we are living in the same apartment house. He's good company.'

In her book *More Than a Grain of Truth*, Jones' niece Margaret Siriol Colley describes the intrigue her uncle may have found himself inadvertently involved in as a result of his association with Stein: 'Stein was now a newspaper correspondent for the *London News Chronicle* (a known hotbed of NKVD spies, including David Crook, who was later involved in the kidnapping of POUM Trotskyist leaders during the Spanish Civil War, and also admitted to spying on Orwell in Spain). Gareth may have first met Stein in Moscow in March 1933, as he was then working for the *Berliner Tageblatt*. Stein, a German by birth, who had become a naturalised British citizen, arrived in Tokyo very shortly before Gareth in early 1935. In Tokyo, the frugal Gareth gladly accepted the invitation to share his Bunka [a Japanese era, 1804-1818] apartment – the same apartment which, from early 1936, was used by Richard Sorge, arguably the 20th Century's greatest spy, for secret radio communications with Moscow. According to FW Deakin and GR Storry, Sorge asked his Moscow paymasters to accredit Stein as a member of his spy ring, but was refused, which they attributed to Stein being on other unknown work for the Soviet secret police.'

In Tokyo Jones regularly attended the news conferences of Eiji Amau, the Japanese Foreign Office press officer. After the first press conference Jones discussed Outer Mongolia with the Russian correspondent for Tass [the Soviet news agency] and "then a man of about 45 who introduced himself as Mr Cox" [Jimmy Cox], the Reuters correspondent. Either through his acquaintance with Cox or because he had previously worked for Lloyd George, Jones had an *entree* to interviews with Japanese politicians who were making world news. Jones was instrumental in introducing Stein to several eminent Japanese figures. He would have readily related accounts of these interviews to Stein and may unwittingly have been a most valuable colleague to Stein in his role as an undercover Soviet agent.

Unaware of the intrigue he was being drawn into, Jones wrote a letter home on 20 February 1935 in which he stated:

> 'By the way I think that it is going to be a terribly quiet summer in the Far East. Japan is making friends with Russia. So a war is practically unthinkable. I'm afraid I'm in for a calm time. It looks as if Japan and China will be out of the news.'

Six months later, after venturing into what he believed was a quiet zone, he was dead.

Jones' passport. (© The Gareth Vaughan Jones Estate)

13

Mongolia

Death and Intrigue

'It is, by the way, a very safe country – no bandits.'

While the bare facts of Jones' death are known, uncertainty remains over why he was killed.

Was he eliminated in retaliation for the critical articles he had written about the Soviet regime? Was he shot because the Japanese regarded him as a spy? Or was he simply in the wrong place at the wrong time, a victim of irritated, trigger-happy bandits who had no political motivation?

When he embarked on a trip to Inner Mongolia and the Japanese-occupied area of northern China that had been renamed Manchukuo, we know from his correspondence that Jones believed himself to be in safe territory.

Before leaving Japan, he interviewed four leading politicians who had played major roles in developing the country: Yosuke Matsuoka, a diplomat and future Foreign Minister who had delivered a defiant speech withdrawing Japan from the League of Nations; General Sadao Araki, a former 'firebrand' Minister of War; Army Minister and future Prime Minister Senjuro Hayashi; and Navy Minister Mineo Osumi.

The Japanese authorities, as well as the Europeans he knew in Tokyo, were aware of Jones' onward travel plans, which took in the Philippines, Java (now part of Indonesia), Singapore, Siam (now

Thailand), French Indo-China (Vietnam and Cambodia) and Hong Kong before hitting mainland China.

During his travels, he discussed with expatriates their views about Japan's aspirations for territorial expansion. For example, while travelling by steamer between Singapore and Bangkok, Jones spoke to the ship's First Officer, who was convinced there would be war between Japan and Britain. Jones noted what the first officer told him:

> 'That's what the "Japs" want: it is oil. The Japanese fishermen come here with diesel vessels and capture the fishing trade. They are spies, they know the country inside out and they have taken soundings. They even have rubber plantations opposite the naval base. Take it from me they know as much about the naval base as the British and on their fishing vessels they have naval officers. It won't be so quiet here in two years time. Japan is sure to fight; she has to fight. She could blow up that naval base to smithereens ... the Japanese are doing just what we did. They are overpopulated and they have to expand.'

Jones disagreed, believing there was no reason why Japan and Britain could not come to an understanding. He arrived in Peking (now Beijing) on 4 July 1935 and soon after called on AJ Timperley, the Peking correspondent of the *Manchester Guardian* who shared accommodation with a *Times* correspondent called Macdonald. They both proposed Jones for membership of the Peking Club.

Jones also called on Dr Herbert Mueller, an enigmatic figure who was to play a crucial role in the Welshman's final days, and to whom he had an introduction from Wolf von Dewall, the London correspondent of *Die Berliner Zeitung*. Baron Leopold von Plessen, a diplomat working

Visiting the Borobudur Buddhist temple, Java. (© The Gareth Vaughan Jones Estate)

in the German Embassy, was another figure introduced to Jones by von Dewall.

He also went to see Sir Alexander Cadogan, the British Ambassador, noting in his diary that he found Cadogan's replies to questions about the military situation in northern China 'confused and contradictory in content'. On Sunday 7 July, Jones wrote to his family:

'Here's a grand stroke of luck. I heard that there is next Sunday a great meeting of Mongolian Princes in Inner Mongolia about 160–180 miles beyond Kalgan [now known as Zhangjiakou, 125 miles from Beijing]. I had been puzzling all day as to how to get there because the railway does not penetrate into Inner Mongolia and it is hard and expensive to get a car. It would be a wonderful opportunity but difficult to carry out.

Then suddenly, as I am drinking tea near the swimming pool of the club (where I am a temporary member), Baron von Plessen comes up and says: "Would you like to join Dr Mueller and me on an excursion into Inner Mongolia to visit Prince Teh Wong and the meeting of Princes. There will be a car at our disposal." So I jumped at the offer. I shall be away about a week. Absolutely safe country. No bandits.'

On Wednesday 10 July Jones wrote a further letter saying he would be departing for Inner Mongolia the next day, again making the point:

'It is by the way a very safe country – no bandits.'

By the following Sunday he and his companions were staying in 'a magnificent yurt, coloured inside red and gold in the palace of Prince Teh Wang – direct descendent of Genghis Khan – and leader of the Free Mongols!' In his letter home Jones commented:

'I have written my Sunday letter home from lots of strange places – from a rubber plantation in Java, from Siam, from the ruins of Angkor, from a horrible Chinese inn – but this is the strangest of the lot. I am the guest of His Highness Prince Teh Wang, the greatest man among all the Mongols whose forefather, Genghis Khan, formed the huge Mongol Empire which reached to Hungary and nearly overran Europe and whose other forefather, Kubla Khan, Dada used to read about in school (Coleridge).'

He wrote of the colours, the silks and gorgeous headdresses and fine horses, the tents, spirit worship, riders, lamas and archers whom he asserted had been magnificent.

The evening before they left Peking, a Chinese Foreign Office official had asked Jones and his fellow travellers to sign a declaration which read: 'We the undersigned herewith certify that we are going to visit Inner Mongolia at our own risk for any eventualities which may happen during our travelling. We carefully considered all warnings of the local Chinese officials who will take no responsibilities should anything happen to the undersigned.' It was signed by Jones, von Plessen and Mueller. In fact, von Plessen was not with the other two for the whole trip, although it is unclear exactly when he left them.

The reason the men were asked to sign the disclaimers was simple. They were heading into an unstable region where three powers – China, Japan and the Soviet Union – were jockeying for position and each one distrusted the others.

Japan had invaded north east China in 1931, establishing the puppet state of Manchukuo in February 1932, with Pu Yi – the last Emperor of China who had been forced to abdicate in 1912 – as its supposed ruler. In fact, Manchukuo was controlled totally by the Japanese military.

Jones with a Geisha in Tokyo. (© The Gareth Vaughan Jones Estate)

Jones and Mueller wanted to visit an area close both to Manchukuo and Soviet-dominated Outer Mongolia. Describing his and Mueller's journey, Jones wrote:

'It was uncharted land. No map contains the features or the roads. The roads were terrible, just ruts here and there ... The lorry-car nearly tumbled over. It was like being in a tank during the War. We went on for hours and hours. How we stuck it I don't know and how the car kept together I also don't know. We crossed the southern fringe of the Gobi Desert. (Did you think a year ago I would be crossing part of the Gobi Desert?) It was very sandy. We saw very few yurts. We came to some temples where we grinned at a Tibetan monk. Saw eagles, antelopes, etc.

Midnight came. We seemed to have lost our way. Luckily it was the night of the full moon. "I'm afraid," said Anatoli, the Russian chauffeur. "Are we staying anywhere near the Soviet frontier? If so, we'll be shot." We had earlier been within 30-40 miles of Soviet Outer Mongolia, but now we were 100 miles ... All day long we had passed skeletons of cows and horses killed by desert wolves.'

After 21 hours of travelling, they saw a town of mud walls beyond a ford. 'We went to some Mongol yurts half a mile away.' Jones noted. 'The Mongols just grunted from inside.'

Jones with his chauffeur, Anatoli (left), and Dr. Müeller (right). (© The Gareth Vaughan Jones Estate)

They had to stay in the car until dawn. Despite camels later pulling at the front, and then oxen, the car had to be abandoned. At 9 o'clock Jones was given a room in a temple occupied by the Japanese. 'After 29 hours I lay down on the floor in the room and slept!', he commented.

Having reached the town of Dolonor, on 23 July Jones noted:

'We were stuck in the mud for three hours; got stuck again later. Now we are lost in bandit country; very sandy. I don't think there is any danger, because 35 bandits were seen on this road yesterday and they were driven off into the mountains. Dolonor is on the map. But the other places are not.' The following day he wrote: 'We drifted onto the wrong road into the mountains, lost our way again, came down on tracks very deep and bumpy to the plain...'

At 3.30pm on Wednesday 24 July, Jones wrote:

'We have been stuck in the mud for many hours and it has been pouring. I have no idea how we shall get out. We have been pushing and pulling and digging for hours. Perhaps we'll have to wait until the land dries which might be a long time. No more bread or biscuits. We had hoped to have a Chinese meal at Dolonor last night. Peking seems a very long way indeed. There is a Mongol village a few miles away and we have sent there for men to push.'

It took five hours to free themselves from the mud in a hail storm, 'some almost as big as marbles', but then they got stuck again. It took 20 villagers to free them. 'Dr M thinks there are bandits,' he wrote on Thursday 25 July, 'but here bandits are just horse and cattle thieves and do not kill.' A later diary entry on the same day stated:

'Dr M has gone off to talk with the villagers. In Mongolia, he always wears cufflinks with the letters A.O.F.B – Ancient Order of Froth Blowers [a humorous British charitable organisation 'to foster the noble Art and gentle and healthy pastime of froth blowing amongst Gentlemen of leisure and ex-Soldiers'].'

'We are waiting in a rough inn for supper,' he noted at 10pm when they'd arrived back at Dolonor. 'In this room a man is boiling opium in a deep frying pan on a wood stove and is fanning the wood stove with a Chinese fan.'

The outside world became aware that Jones and Mueller had been abducted by bandits on their way back to Kalgan from Dolonor on 29 July when Anatoli, their driver, appeared with a message asking for a ransom of £8,000 and 200 Mauser rifles. Anatoli said the bandits had held up their vehicle with rifles and a machine gun at a range of 40 yards. Two shots had hit their vehicle's engine and the bandits, who were dressed in uniforms of the Peace Preservation Corps – the local police – looted the vehicle and carried off Jones and Mueller.

The following day, 30 July, Mueller was released. He subsequently gave a lengthy statement in which he set out his version of what had happened. He said that Herr Adam Purpis, director of Wostwag in Kalgan – a Soviet company – had provided him with a car for the trip he was undertaking with Jones: 'We were still about 100 li [30 miles] from the place when we fell in with an ox-cart carrying, to my surprise, the flags of Manchukuo and Japan. The Chinese in charge of the cart explained to me that these flags had been presented to him by Japanese in the village of Huang Ch'i Ta-Ying-Tze, and that this place now belonged to Manchukuo. That was for me the first indication that the situation in Dolonor had changed since my last visit in 1934.'

Japanese flags were all over the town and there were large numbers of Japanese officials in evidence. Mueller claimed that he and Jones were questioned by the Japanese military who said that their repeatedly standing around in the street had aroused suspicion. They were then advised on a particular route to Kaglan. It was on that road that around 1pm on 28 July they were attacked by bandits: 'They said they had been ordered to protect this road against robbers and to prevent the passage of Japanese motor-cars along it,' stated Mueller. 'They said they had taken our car for a Japanese one and invited me into a neighbouring farmhouse to drink tea and to receive the apologies of their leader. While I was accepting, Mr Jones had also got out of the car. He was immediately surrounded by a number of the people who had fired on us, bound, and led into another house where he sat on the K'ang [an interior brick platform warmed by a fire beneath and used for sleeping]. The cord with which his hands were tied behind his back was thrown over a rafter in the roof, and behind him came a man with a noose. Mr Jones thought, as he told me later, that they intended to hang him. But after a few minutes they let him step down off the K'ang and brought him to the house where I was.'

Describing in a later despatch how Jones had coped with captivity, Mueller wrote: 'When we were captured, the bandits were surprisingly harsh with Jones as he cried: "Do not touch me, I am British!" The bandits thereupon bound and gagged him. Later, however, Jones charmed his captors by singing songs in German, English and Welsh in the evenings, which saved his life. The bandits were particularly impressed when he sang David of the White Rock [*Dafydd y Garreg Wen*] in Welsh. Repeatedly they begged him to sing more and more and while their pickets watched the surrounding country, the valley resounded with the Welshman's hymns.'

Jones' personality so impressed the bandits that they abandoned their harshness. One evening when there was only one chicken for 30 men, the bandits cooked the bird and laid it before Jones, whom they described as 'the singing Welshman' while they ate cornmeal porridge. From this, Mueller said he was certain that no harm would come to Jones and reported them as saying, 'We are poor and our only chance of riches is to obtain ransom for you foreign devils.' According to Mueller, the bandits told them of their cruel destiny and that they could not quit without endangering their relatives in Manchukuo. Also that their captives should not think ill of them and should believe they were not only just good men at heart, but good Chinese as well. Subsequently, though, it seems Jones was handed on to another group of bandits.

Mueller added that the abductors were avoiding contact with the Japanese patrols, forcing Jones to ride horseback 50 miles a day and, wearing shorts – Jones and Mueller had only the clothes they were wearing – his knees were badly cut by the saddle. Nevertheless, Jones was very cheerful, regarding the experience as stimulating. Ransom notes had, by now, been written and, according to Mueller, he and Jones had decided the only thing to do was to be submissive.

Also, according to Mueller, the bandits decided to let him go on the evening of their second day of captivity on condition that he returned with the ransom, which he asserted had been set originally at $100,000. Mueller considered that the reason they let him go and not Jones was that he had a better command of the Mandarin language in order to negotiate the release of Jones for ransom. Another possible factor was that Jones was the better horseman and if they had to move quickly, Mueller held them back. Above all, Mueller believed he had been released rather than Jones because he was German.

Various complex negotiations went on. When they turned out to be unsuccessful, Mueller claimed to be suspicious that the Japanese were behind it all, stating: 'The manner of our capture makes it appear indubitable that our visit to Dolonor, coinciding as it did with preparations for important military action in Chahar [province], was most unwelcome to the Japanese.'

From notes exchanged between British Embassy officials that were disclosed later, we learn that the bandits inexplicably lowered their demands and moved into territory controlled by the Japanese.

On 1 August Jones' family received a telegram from Kalgan in his name which read: 'Well treated. Expect release soon, Love Gareth.' There was also a false report that he had been released by his captors, which undoubtedly caused extra torment for his family and friends when it turned out not to be true.

The worst possible news was conveyed to Jones' father Edgar in an early morning phone call on 16 August from a Press Association reporter: 'Oh! How terrible', he whispered after a long pause. 'Thank you for letting me know.'

Margaret Siriol Colley suggested that an unfortunate misunderstanding between two Chinese magistrates during a critical period may have had something to do with the tragedy: 'While one of them was conducting the negotiations for handing over the ransom, the bandits moved into the jurisdiction of his neighbour. The neighbour had not been warned of the negotiations and had sent troops to intercept the band. This, it was felt, may have destroyed the bandits' belief in the sincerity of the negotiations and may explain why the bandits never got the ransom money that had been sent.' Colley, though, eventually came to believe there was potentially a more sinister explanation for her uncle's death.

An officer called Lieutenant Miller from the British Embassy in Peking was sent to Inner Mongolia to look into the circumstances of Jones' death. In a report sent to the Ambassador, Sir Alexander Cadogan, following an inquiry held by Miller on 18 and 19 August, the lieutenant wrote:

'A cowherd named Li Hsiang stated that about 12 noon on or about August 12 he was looking after his cows when 60 or 70 armed mounted men not in uniform arrived from the north. They dismounted and formed a circle. The cowherd was afraid and lay down. Three shots were fired, after which the men rode off. The cowherd then noticed a body on the ground face upwards and found that it was that of a foreigner with dark hair and blue eyes wearing Chinese clothing. The foreigner appeared to be dead.

A commander of a Cavalry Unit with 100 mounted Paoantui [the Peace Preservation Corps] arrived and found the body. He went after the bandits and overtook them about 40 li [13 miles] south near Tungstmiao. Four bandits were killed and one was injured. The injured man said later that the foreigner had refused to eat for three or four days and had been unable to keep up with the bandits. He had refused to mount his horse and was shot.

A farmer who had been asked to take a written message by the Commander handed a message to General Chia about 5pm on August 13. He arrived at the village where the body was ... He noted the body had three bullet wounds. General Chia telephoned the

Provincial Government at about 9pm on August 15 stating that a body matching Jones' description had been found.'

One bullet had entered the back of Jones' head and passed out near his mouth, while two others had been fired into his back and come out through his chest. Both Miller and Mueller identified the body.

Lloyd George thought von Plessen had responsibility for Jones' death when the journalist's parents sent him a copy of the letter in which their son told how he had been assured by the diplomat that there was no danger from bandits in the area to which he travelled with Mueller. The former Prime Minister also wanted to know more about Mueller.

In a letter to CW Orde at the Foreign Office, Lloyd George wrote:

'Gareth Jones is known to have kept a very careful diary and it might easily have been possible that he knew much more than his German colleagues or colleague would like him to know, and it would not have been a very difficult thing to have arranged for the bandits to have intercepted them. Why was it, for instance, that Dr Mueller was taken to a certain house to consult with the brigands and that Gareth Jones was brought in only some considerable time afterwards? Why ... was it that Dr Mueller does not seem to have gone back to his friend Gareth Jones as it was understood that he was to have done, because he was allowed to go on parole for 10 days? Why also was it that the body is alleged to have been found 200 miles away from the place where it was supposed to have been? It is reported that Dr Mueller is the man who identified the body.

Meantime, it has been suggested that Dr Mueller may be something more than a journalist and that he may, in fact, be a secret agent, it is understood from reports which have appeared in the press in Berlin. Would you be so kind as to communicate with our Ambassador in Berlin and ask him to make private enquiries of Dr Mueller? ... I want to emphasise ... that Dr Mueller, the so-called friend and colleague of Gareth Jones on this great mission has, at any rate up to the moment, not even endeavoured to communicate a line to the parents – not even to express his condolence.

A suggestion has been made that if any significance attaches to the foregoing, a British lawyer might be asked to interview Dr Mueller for the purpose of examining him.'

Writing to a Foreign Office colleague, Mr Orde stated: 'I cannot help fearing that Mr Lloyd George is looking for something out of which he can make political capital and perhaps the best thing to do will be to ask the Embassy to get hold of Mueller if they can and to take his story; we could tell Mr Sylvester [Lloyd George's secretary] that we are doing this.' An internal memo between two Foreign Office officials, lodged at the National Archives, stated: 'We need not perhaps tell Mr Sylvester that this is the first kidnapping case which has occurred in this area in recent years, for he may take this as tending to confirm the suspicion of Japanese foul play.'

Basil Newton, of the British Embassy in Berlin, wrote to Mr Orde on 26 September 1935, stating:

'Enquiries have been made of Dr Mueller who is still in China but they do not bear out the theory that he was guilty of foul play in connection with the murder of Gareth Jones. We do not attach much significance to the fact that Mueller has not endeavoured to communicate with the parents of Gareth Jones. We have found that international journalists are journalists first and humanitarians afterwards. The story is the thing, for the story means money, kudos, and everything else and we have known them forget they had wives and children in the pursuit of knowledge. Even in this respect there is something to be said for Dr Mueller. Instead of following the regular practice of wiring his agency and then blaring a story to the world press, he gave his first version to Reuters' agency in China!! His own people will have a word to say to him when they see him. He has since made up for this lapse by contributing a fairly detailed account of the whole tragic episode.

It is hardly necessary for us to ridicule the suggestion that Mueller helped to put Gareth Jones out of the way because he happened to be in possession of some knowledge about a German-Japanese plot or secret alliance ... What is more, in view of Hitler's peculiar views on racial questions – which are no joke as any German Jew can testify – it will take a good deal to persuade him to join with Japan or any other exotic race against the chosen Aryan stock.'

An official named Howe at the British Embassy in Peking concluded in a report that, 'while certain Japanese elements may have been connected with the bandits and while the Japanese military authorities may have been responsible for their original presence in the area in question, the Japanese authorities must be acquitted of direct connivance in the affair and the actual kidnapping was the work of the bandits themselves'.

That was not, however, the view of Jones' niece Margaret Siriol Colley, who became convinced that her uncle was murdered at the behest of the Japanese for political reasons. In her book about Jones' death, *A Manchukuo Incident*, she wrote:

'The secrets that he knew died with him. The countries involved have much to answer for and none can be given any credit for trying to save him. He was merely a pawn in an international game of chess. Each had its own selfish motive not to save him and laid blame upon each other.

Why was the British Government so secretive and why did they make no attempt to raise the ransom to aid the impoverished Chahar [Provincial] Government? Was it from fear of the rise of National Socialism, Hitler and German rearmament that it did not wish to offend the Japanese for fear of a confrontation in the East? What bearing did Japan's insidious territorial expansion in China have on his death? Did the Japanese think that Gareth had access to secret information? Would the Chinese have been able to pay his ransom, which was quite a considerable sum at that time?

Gareth was an embarrassment to the Japanese. He was an inquisitive journalist who wanted to know what the Japanese were up to and made it widely known that he intended to write a book to expose the nation's intentions in the Far East; a man whom the Japanese secret police had possibly followed since his departure from Tokyo.'

Colley discounted the possibility that her uncle was a secret agent, even though from newspaper reports at the time it was clear the Japanese thought he was.

'[There] is no evidence in any document, letter or even in his diaries to give even the slightest indication of such a possibility ... Duncan Stewart, the British Special Operations Executive archivist wrote to [me] in 1998 stating that he had looked up Gareth's name in "some archival indexes which would have been quite likely to contain some reference to Gareth had he have been involved in intelligence gathering on behalf of the British Government". No such reference was located ... It would, however, have been natural for the Foreign Office, War Office or even Lloyd George himself to ask Gareth to "keep his eyes and his ears open and let us know what you think when you come back".'

On the question of attributing blame for her uncle's death, Colley concluded:

'Gareth was a young man who asked too many embarrassing questions, knew too much and would not have been afraid to expose to the world Japan's ambition to dominate China by writing leading articles in the national newspapers of Europe and America. It is the author's opinion that Gareth's capture was an act of banditry orchestrated by the Kwantung [Japanese] Army and intended to be a political incident with the excuse of invading the Province of Chahar – the province which the Japanese had recently forced the Chinese Government to demilitarise. Though Manchukuo was Japanese territory, the army and its officers were a law unto themselves.

Gareth's death may not have been part of their plan, but as he was too weak to remount his horse and because the Paoantui [Peace Preservation Corps] was in hot pursuit of the bandits, his captors shot him.'

However, further research carried out by Colley's son Nigel Colley, who created and maintained the invaluable *garethjones.org* website until his own untimely death in 2018, introduced another even more sinister possibility. Colley established that the vehicle in which Jones and Mueller were travelling when they were abducted by bandits had been supplied by a company owned by the NKVD, as the Soviet secret service was known at the time. He also discovered that Mueller himself was a Soviet agent.

The New KGB by William R Corson and Robert T Crowley, published in 1985, stated:

'Soviet intelligence has had a long and profitable experience in the world of commerce. It started in Berlin in 1921, when the Fourth Department of the Red Army sent the brothers Aaron and Abraham Ehrenlieb to Berlin, with GRU money, to organize the Eastern Trading Company, or Wostwag (West-Osteuropaeische Warenaustausch Aktiengesellschaft) at 19, Schiffbauerdamm, Berlin NW 6. The Ehrenlieb brothers were Poles who had become Soviet citizens. Both were GRU [military intelligence espionage] staff officers.

Wostwag was supposed to handle the sale of Soviet products in Germany, but in 1921, not only were there few if any Soviet products to sell, there was very little money in Germany to be spent on imports of any kind. Yet, if you pretend that you are in business, it is necessary to look and act as if you know one end of a cash register from the other. To give the firm a few props and a small inventory, the Soviet trade mission in Berlin transferred its meagre accounts to Wostwag.

By arrangement with Moscow, the firm's income was to be used in the development of espionage nets. In 1925, the brothers were recalled to Moscow and replaced by another GRU officer named Uscher Zloczower. In 1926, Abraham Ehrenlieb was dispatched to the Far East, where he set up a new company at 49 Taku Road, Tientsin, called the Far Eastern Fur Trading Company. His brother Aaron was sent to Urga [now Ulaanbaatar], Mongolia, to open a branch of Wostwag. In 1935 Aaron was ordered to New York to open the American branch of Wostwag, but he was unable to secure a visa to enter the United States.'

In a despatch sent to a German news agency, Mueller confirmed that the car in which he and Jones travelled into Inner Mongolia had been provided free of charge by Adam Purpis, a Latvian who was the director of Wostwag in Kalgan. Corson and Crowley also revealed, in their book, that five years later Purpis was in New York, running the Oriental Trading and Engineering Corporation.

The author Nigel West (Rupert Allason) has written that, based on information provided in 1940 by Soviet defector Walter Krivitsky, an assistant of Purpis' at one time had been Arnold Deutsch, the NKVD agent who recruited Kim Philby, the high ranking British intelligence officer who became a spy for the Soviet Union. Deutsch ran the Cambridge Spy Ring, of which Philby was a member, in the mid-1930s.

In 2005 the Public Record Office – now The National Archives – released a file which showed that the British Secret Services commenced their surveillance of Wostwag in 1925. The surveillance was still ongoing when Jones was murdered in 1935. However, Nigel Colley pointed out that there was no reference to the Wostwag investigation in the 500-page investigation into Jones' murder carried out by the Foreign Office, apart from one passing reference where Kitson of the Foreign Office wrote: 'According to 'Oriental Affairs' for Sept [1935] 'Wostwag' is believed to have good Soviet connections otherwise they would not be able to get the necessary trading permits for Mongolia, which no other foreign firm can get.'

A file at The National Archives accessed by Nigel Colley states:

'Purpis was general manager of Wostwag in the Far East and of the Oriental Trading and Engineering Company, when the latter was a subsidiary of Wostwag, while he was general manager of OTEC Far East following its purchase by the New York company of the same name.

The Chase National Bank of Shanghai quoted local reports in 1937 to the effect that Purpis was at one time associated with the Cheka [another iteration of the Soviet secret service] and with the Third International [a Soviet-backed organisation that advocated world communism]. According to one report mentioned by Chase, he was a former High Commissioner for the Soviet province of Outer Mongolia. The ban also stated that there was a certain amount of mystery concerning Purpis' past connections. In April 1937 Purpis ran a private import-export company at Kalgan, near Peking, under his own name.'

An MI5 file on Mueller released in 2002 identified him as a German and Soviet agent who had been in operation between 1917 and 1951. He was described as being a journalist for the *Frankfurter Zeitung*, a known Communist, and a Soviet Third International representative in China. Again, no one in MI5 passed this information onto the Foreign Office when it was carrying out its inquiry into Jones' death.

For Nigel Colley, the intrigue led him to what he saw as an obvious conclusion:

'(For) Gareth to have been kindly invited by the alleged Comintern representative, Mueller, to go on an extended trip in the vehicle provided free of charge by a trading front of the NKVD, with their own 'beefy' employee Anatoli, a supposed White Russian, as driver (read possible local military attaché?), and whose area manager, Adam Purpis, was suspected by Chase Manhattan in Shanghai of acting as banker to the Chinese communists as well as supplying them with arms, then to my suspicious mind, this scenario leaves little to doubt that together they led Gareth to his murder or in some way were indirectly responsible.'

There is, of course, no certainty about whether Jones was the victim of a politically motivated plot, but taking into account his strident attacks on the Soviet Union, Stalin's known propensity for ordering the death of his perceived enemies, as well as the strong Soviet connections that surrounded his final journey, it seems more likely than not that such was his fate.

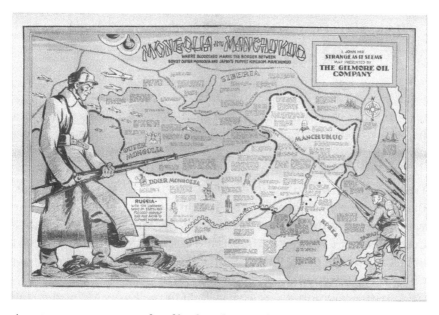

A contemporary map – produced by the Gilmore Oil Company – of Inner Mongolia, Outer Mongolia and Manchukuo.

14

Barry

A Town in Mourning

'He was Gareth: Gareth to everyone young and old – the Gareth to whom life was a joyful adventure, filled with laughter and good humour and friendliness.'

Gareth Jones was murdered on the day before his 30th birthday, and his loss was felt not just by his family and friends, but by many people across the world.

His body was cremated in China and the ashes returned to Wales, where they were interred in Merthyr Dyfan Cemetery in Barry. Memorial services had been held both in Kalgan, where the words quoted at the start of this chapter were uttered by the Chahar Commissioner for Foreign Affairs, and in the British Embassy Chapel in Peking, where many floral tributes were displayed, especially from Chinese organisations.

A further memorial service was held in the Barry Memorial Hall on Sunday 25 August 1935 – 13 days after his death – at which Councillor John Ireland, the chairman of Barry Council, presided and said that everyone present was there to 'pay their tribute of respect and affection to the memory of a Barry boy.' He felt sure he had interpreted the wish and desire of the whole of Barry in arranging the service in the Memorial Hall so that, as a town, they could have an opportunity of showing their pride in one whose career was so distinguished and whose life was such a remarkable example of character and ability.

The eulogy was given by Rev Gwilym Davies, and is worth quoting extensively, because it gives an insight into how Jones was seen by those in the community from which he came. Davies said:

'He was a Barry boy. How much of a Barry boy he was I realised one evening about two years ago outside this Memorial Hall. It was at the close of an Armistice service at which he was present and where I had to speak. After the service we were outside, waiting for his father and mother. We had been looking at the names of the men of Barry who fell in the War. He was only nine when the war broke out, so that he could have taken no part or lot in it, but there he was – I can see him now – taking off his hat and standing bare-headed in the cold of a November night beside the Memorial to the men from his town who never came back.

There was a pride about it, a pride in Barry. One could see that, and there was something else – so true of him – there was a reverence in the presence of a mystery he could not understand. Indeed, if I were asked to name, straight off, one of the deep things in him, I should say it was reverence; the reverence whose flower was that humility which made of him the friend of everybody he met.

We here, tonight, have no need to be told anything about his career. We know the steps from school to college with the prizes and the honours, then to the various posts which brought him into living contact with famous men of three continents, Europe, Asia and America; and we know of that additional endowment of a gift of tongues which was almost a miracle in itself. But you and I rarely thought of all this when he was with us. To us, as it was put in a delightful tribute – "he was Gareth: Gareth to everyone young and old" – the Gareth to whom life was a joyful adventure, filled with laughter and good humour and friendliness.

249

And with all this boyishness and love of fun, the spirit of youth personified, there was seriousness on the grave, moral issues of life that made him every inch a man. I suppose if we were to ask his colleagues in the great and exacting profession to which he belonged, they would all say of him that he was "steel true and blade straight". Like every born journalist – like every man with ink in his blood – he loved best to work at high pressure. I remember him one day coming round to my room at the office. He wanted to write a two- or three-columned article for the paper next day – it had to be next day, May 18, on the reception all over the world of the "Welsh Children's Message" [facilitated by the youth movement Urdd Gobaith Cymru, founded in 1922; the message continues annually to this day] Here was a task which made a compelling appeal to him if only for his love of children. It was 12.30pm when he came. He told me he was leaving Cardiff by train before three o'clock. He had before him on the table scores of replies in various languages; he quickly picked out those he needed. "But surely, Gareth," I said, "you cannot do the article now – it's one o'clock." "Certainly," he replied, "you go to lunch. I will get it done." And done it was, there and then, and a first rate article appeared next morning. He worked like that – 60 seconds to the minute. He lived like that – intensely in the present. But if he lived in the minute, he did not live for it.

He could forget the things that were left behind, no one better, but he did strive for the things that are before, no one harder. There was a "something" about him that it would be presumption on the part of any of us to say that we fully understood. There was an atmosphere about him which I can best describe to myself as the consciousness of a "call". That he would devote himself to public service went without saying. He owed that to the tradition of public duty of his home – a tradition which is a household word not only in Barry but all over Wales. He would not be the son of his father and mother if public spirit did not find in him a ready and an unselfish response.

BARRY

But it was more than that. It was more than that because he brought to it his own, his original contribution – a conviction best expressed, perhaps, in the words of Browning's Paracelsus – "I can devote myself, I have a life to live." I am convinced, knowing him as I did, that years ago he had heard distinctly the call – "Whom shall I send?" He answered very firmly – "Here I am, send me." And what was it – this call – this task – to which he became a "dedicated spirit"?

Well, this world is a rapidly changing world – continents are being dwarfed into countries, and countries into counties. And one of our greatest needs presently will be men and women – not with a command of languages, that is a small part of the equipment – but with powers of intellectual and spiritual interpretation – the interpretation of nation after nation, of people after people in this strange new world in which we are living.

He had this gift of international understanding; he had this genius of becoming the interpreter of nations to one another. To him was given, for example, the power, the rare power of an instinctive reaction to an international dispute not as a quarrel, which it seldom or never is, between "a right and a wrong" but between "two rights."

I am not exaggerating when I say there are very few men in the whole world equipped with the knowledge and endowed with the sympathy for this new vocation of international interpretation on a world scale. I asked a high authority last year how many men living had it – "Twenty". "Twenty," he replied. "There are not 10, there are not five. I can only think," he went on, "of three living men who have got it." And he named them – one was an American, the second was an Englishman, and the third a Spaniard. But there was a fourth – a fourth at about half their age – nearly ready for it. That, my friend, is the measure of the world's loss.

And with all this passion for internationalism he was no internationalist in the narrow sense of the term – the internationalist who is like a cut flower in a vase; the internationalist with no roots, who belongs to all countries and to none. Not at all – his internationalism was rooted in the rich soil of a healthy and a vigorous nationalism. He was British and a democrat, a lover of political freedom in every fibre of his being and Welsh to the very core – "*Cymro i'r carn*" [A Welshman to the core].

In article after article – those sketches, often unfinished, which he tossed off rapidly like an artist getting ready to paint on a big canvas – in whatever foreign land the article was written – you can see Wales peeping out, Wales constantly peeping through.

If he was writing of hospitality offered him in Java, he was thinking of the hospitality in a Welsh farmhouse. If he was writing in the Philippines and of the Philippines, his mind instantly went back to Barry and to Mr Ifor Powell of the County School, an authority on the subject. Or if he was in the Saar Valley on the eve of Plebiscite – to him it became the valley of the Taff, with the industrial importance of east Glamorgan.[After World War One, Saarland was made a protectorate of the League of Nations for 15 years, allowing France to operate its coal mines. In January 1935, at the end of the mandate, 90% of those voting in a referendum opted to return to Germany – a result hailed by Hitler as a great victory.]

I cannot trust myself to speak about something which is in all our minds – something which will become a legend all over the East: the singing of the songs of Wales in the Babylon of his captivity. But there is a problem about his death that we ought to face bravely and honestly. It is this – this murmuring in our hearts – and we have all done it, we have said: "Why should a life like this, pure and precious and fearless, why should it have been poured out like water?" Could it not have been stored up for other and greater things?

So it is here. A sacrifice like this is of the very savour of life, enriching it, ennobling it. It is deeds of daring, with no hope of material gain, that keep our civilisation from becoming stagnant and selfish. What would this world be without the pioneers, in age after age, who make a magnificent venture of themselves, in scaling heights that life may become richer for us who dwell in the valleys?

In our hearts we know that the world owes most to those who said, as Gareth Jones said in deeds not words – "not for me any calling that is easy, uneventful, safe – that I may be free to quest the horizon, and to push further back the boundaries of knowledge".'

At this distance, when Jones is best known for exposing a famine that killed millions of people, it seems odd that no reference was made to that in what was otherwise an eloquent eulogy. What this indicates is that the significance of his disclosures had not been fully appreciated by his contemporaries. The fate of large numbers of people in what to most in the west – preoccupied as they were with events in western Europe – must have seemed *terra incognita*, did not register highly in the hierarchy of concern.

Other tributes captured the sense of loss – and Jones' sense of mission. Referring to the location of his death, his former employer David Lloyd George said:

'That part of the world is a cauldron of conflicting intrigue, and one or other interests concerned probably knew that Mr Gareth Jones knew too much of what was going on. He had a passion for finding out what was happening in foreign lands wherever there was trouble, and in pursuit of his investigations he shrank from no risk. I had always been afraid that he would take one risk too many. Nothing escaped his observation, and he allowed no obstacle to turn him from his course when he thought there was some fact which he could obtain. He had the almost unfailing knack of getting at things that mattered.'

A letter published in *The Times* from Dr HF Stewart, a Fellow of Trinity College, Cambridge, Jones' alma mater, stated:

HF Stewart.

'I desire to add a pebble to the cairn of my friend and pupil, Gareth Jones. He was an extraordinary linguist; he had literary ability of no mean order; he had, to my knowledge, the makings of a good teacher. An academic or official career lay open to him, yet he preferred a life of independent activity, with its attached perils. Nevertheless, through all his adventures, he kept in touch with those who live less dangerously and I had a cheerful postcard from him at Nanking a few days before his capture.

His wit, his irrepressible sense of humour, his stories and shrewd and penetrating comments on men and things in America, Germany and Russia were to his friends an unfailing source of delight ... It is bitter to think of all that brilliance, vigour and promise brutally wiped out by the bullet of a miscreant.'

Sir Robert Webber, the proprietor of the *Western Mail* added his tribute, writing:

'The news of the tragic death of Gareth Jones has brought a feeling of deep personal loss to all his colleagues on the *Western Mail* and the *South Wales Echo* and *Evening Express*. It is like the death of a brother. He had the rare quality, which on the instant endeared him to all that met him. When we read last week that the bandits were charmed by his personality and his singing of Welsh airs, we said how like Gareth Jones. He was Gareth to everyone, young and old and nobody thought of addressing him formally. He was a delightful, lovable boy. His youthful, jubilant spirits made us forget that he was grown up and that we were talking to a most brilliant scholar. In Wales his loss will be felt in every home.'

In Germany, Jones' friend Paul Scheffer, now editor-in-chief of the still-independent *Berliner Tagblatt*, wrote a front-page tribute to his Welsh journalistic colleague:

'He was a born journalist, an ornament of his much maligned and, in its essence and obligations, much misunderstood, profession. He was modest, clever, indefatigable and above all, honourable. He was, without saying too much thereon, an enthusiastic English [sic] patriot. He was a journalist because he was always receptive to new ideas, never failed in their analyses and in the urge to report on them in the light of his own direct impressions, fully and truthfully. Through his articles on the Soviet Union in *The Times*, which did not appear under his own name, he immediately, though quite a young man, made a name for himself. He did not succumb to routine. He worked indefatigably in order to widen his outlook. He knew that without a wide outlook it is impossible to segregate and analyse impressions and to display them in all their dimensions. He regarded himself as one in the making, and never abandoned this view. He had that flair which makes the journalist.

He developed himself on a definite system - by accepting promotion and then, after securing the gain, undertaking travels which he financed by writing articles for newspapers in different countries. During the last world tour for instance (for which he had worked for two years) he wrote for the *Berliner Tageblatt*. Jones then did editorial work for a provincial newspaper in his native Wales, thence accepting a new appointment in London. He thus was learning and simultaneously working as a journalist without binding himself too early.

The number of journalists with his initiative and style is nowadays, throughout the world, quickly falling, and for this reason the tragic death of this splendid man is a particularly big loss. The International Press is abandoning its colours - in some countries more quickly than in others - but it is a fact. Instead of independent minds inspired by genuine feeling, there appear more and more men of routine, crippled journalists of widely different stamp who shoot from behind safe cover, and thereby sacrifice their consciences. The causes of this tendency are many. Today is not the time to speak of them.'

A tribute to Jones in Berliner Tagblatt, written by its editor-in-chief, and his friend, Paul Scheffer. (© The Gareth Vaughan Jones Estate)

Part Two

Gareth Jones

In memory of Gareth Richard Vaughan Jones, born 1905, who graduated from the University of Wales, Aberystwyth and the University of Cambridge. One of the first journalists to report on the *Holodomor*, the Great Famine of 1932–1933 in Soviet Ukraine.

Er cof am Gareth Richard Vaughan Jones, ganed 1905, a raddiodd o Brifysgol Cymru, Aberystwyth a Phrifysgol Caergrawnt. Un o'r newyddiadurwyr cyntaf i adrodd ar y Newyn Mawr yn yr Wcrain, 1932–1933.

Пам'яті випускника Валійського університету в м. Аберствит і Кембриджського університету Герета Ричарда Воена Джоунза (нар. 1905 р.) – одного з перших журналістів, які повідомили про Голодомор у радянській Україні 1932–1933 рр.

Placed in his honour by the Ukrainian Canadian Civil Liberties Foundation, with the assistance of the Ukrainian Autocephalous Orthodox Church in Great Britain, the Ukrainian Orthodox Church of Canada, the Ukrainian American Civil Liberties Association, and the Association of Ukrainians in Great Britain.

2 May 2006

The trilingual memorial to Jones at Aberystwyth University. (© The Gareth Vaughan Jones Estate)

'There was a knock and one of my audience entered, a slim 20-year-old with an intelligent mind and a bright look in his eye. In fluent, almost accent-free German he said: "I hear you come from Leipzig. I was also once there during the time of inflation" … In this way, and without meaning to, we became very close, so that we became friends, and this bond was sealed on joint hiking trips in the Welsh mountains.' A excerpt from Reinhard Haferkorn's tribute to Jones in Heimat und Welt, 25 August 1935.

15

A Flawed Hero?

Anti-Semitism and Allegations of Nazi Sympathies

'He has awful manners, eats like a horse, is a Jew, bangs his plate with his knife, snorts, has a bullet wound in his face, cannot stop smoking between courses, the most unpolished man you could ever imagine.'

This biography of Gareth Jones is presented in a traditional chronological order, yet there are two important, and controversial, aspects of his life that are essentially thematic in nature and require specific investigation in a dedicated section of the book. One of those themes, allegations of Jones harbouring Nazi sympathies, has been raised in recent years, while the other, his use of anti-Semitic language, has previously been overlooked. Both will be considered here.

Anti-Semitism

Admirable though Gareth Jones was in so many respects, in his private correspondence – this phraseology does not appear in any of his notebooks, published articles or speeches – he made comments which raise concerns about anti-Semitism.

It is not suggested that Jones was a conscious anti-Semite or supported, in any way, the persecution of Jews. His published articles, notebooks and private letters provide no evidence of this.

However, on a few occasions, in his private correspondence between the ages of 17 and 25, he used pejorative language when describing Jews. It is also the case that Jones had friends who were Jews, criticised the anti-Semitism he witnessed in others, and did not repeat that language during the last five years of his life, but this doesn't absolve him from the phraseology he used in the passages that follow. The comments illustrate that he was, for several years, unable to recognise a sub-conscious anti-Semitism that had developed during his student days, in particular from his German acquaintances.

On 15 July 1923, when he was weeks short of turning 18, Jones wrote to his family from Hamburg, saying:

> 'Prices are jumping up here! Monday everything was cheap. Now they have gone up 50%. In a few weeks it will not be much cheaper than England. How the Germans will live, I don't know, although they seem to be doing very well at present. The cafes are full & there seems to be quite a lot of money about. I am told that the Jews are tremendously wealthy and that they have done their best to lower the mark. The lowering of the mark seems to be a game kept up by the German Jews & bankers. Bank buildings are going up everywhere, while the real Germans are poor.'

Such was the classic Nazi view of Jews: greedily manipulating the monetary system for their own profit. The phrases 'I am told', 'seems to be', and 'real Germans', clearly indicate that the naive 17-year-old Jones kept the company of anti-Semites and, by credulously repeating their tropes without criticism, was susceptible to their influence.

To put the matter into historical context, a year before Jones wrote in these terms to his family, Hitler had given an interview in which the future Führer was unequivocal about his future intentions with regard to the Jews:

> 'If I am ever really in power, the destruction of the Jews will be my first and most important job. As soon as I have power, I shall have gallows

after gallows erected, for example, in Munich on the Marienplatz – as many of them as traffic allows. Then the Jews will be hanged one after another, and they will stay hanging until they stink. They will stay hanging as long as hygienically possible. As soon as they are untied, then the next group will follow and that will continue until the last Jew in Munich is exterminated. Exactly the same procedure will be followed in other cities until Germany is cleansed of the last Jew!'

In January 1925 Jones was studying at the University of Strasbourg in eastern France – part of Alsace-Lorraine which had been occupied by Germany for nearly 50 years until the Treaty of Versailles in 1919 returned it to France as part of the settlement terms for the First World War. In a letter home, Jones described spending time with a fellow student:

'Yesterday I went for a walk with Mons[ieur] Netter. I was surprised to learn that he was a Jew; he seemed to me typical in character of the better type of educated German, is deep in feeling, a little sentimental in regard to nature and very philosophical. He spoke in German most of the time and I found I had not forgotten so much as I thought I had.'

Jones' surprise that a Jew could share characteristics with educated Germans provides evidence of his sub-conscious acknowledgement of what were widespread negative characterisations of Jews, as amplified by his German acquaintances. It also reveals a certain naivety about the 19-year-old Welshman: as opposed to Polish Jews, for example, Jews in Germany were fully assimilated into German society. One would like to think that Jones' surprise in discovering that a young Jew could be as civilised as any other educated German helped him towards a revision of the negative perception he had become accustomed to.

This was an important period in the young man's personal development as can be seen when, in the same month, Jones wrote to his parents concerning his future career and life ambitions. As noted in Chapter 1, Jones stated:

'I would a thousand times prefer to use my knowledge of languages with an aim to obtaining a position where I could meet interesting people of all nationalities and where I could really find out the characteristics of the nations of today; why there are wars, and how they could be prevented; how national, Semitic and religious prejudices can be destroyed, and why they exist.'

Later in the same letter, Jones stated:

'I can judge men much better now than before I came to Strasbourg; and I think I can observe now their traits – national or political – more thoroughly ... Strasbourg has been an excellent experience for me in this respect.'

It would appear that the impressionable young man was developing his self-awareness, and his growing maturity was beginning to improve his ability to make judgements of the people he met and to intellectually process what they were telling him. However, he still had a way to go.

Months later, on 1 April 1925, shortly before graduating from Aberystwyth, Jones wrote about an event he witnessed in Heidelburg on the 110th anniversary of the birth of the Iron Chancellor, Otto von Bismarck, and acknowledged the anti-Semitic connotation of the swastika:

'Torch procession. Nationalist demonstration. Then we heard a band approaching and soon we saw rows of torches carried by young people in different uniforms. There were different political societies, especially *Politische Jugend* [political youth] bands and students' corporations. They all passed by us. The student corporations had their caps and their banners, with ribbons across their shoulders. Then some youth societies carried the nationalistic and monarchistic colours (red, white, black). I noticed especially a large number of 'Hackenkreuger' i.e. Monarchists, followers of Ludendorff & Hitler.

Most of them were boys between 12-18. It is a pity that Monarchists & Extremists have made use of the Youth Movement in Germany for political ends. There are Communist youth groups, Democratic, Socialist, Nationalistic and Monarchists. Then I noticed the Swastika, which in Germany signifies Monarchism and Anti-Semitism ... Rival factions shouted and torches were thrown. All sang *Deutschland Uber Alles* – not necessarily a reactionary song.'

While Jones noted his unease at the use of youth organisations for political purposes and his letter highlights the anti-Semitic connotation of the swastika, the sinister implications of the ideology it symbolised is not mentioned.

In August 1927, and now a student at Cambridge, Jones was in Riga, the capital of Latvia, learning Russian. One morning, the landlady of his lodgings, Madame Krzyzanovski, spoke to him for an hour about Russia:

'She is terribly prejudiced against Jews. She calls the present Soviet fleet not a Russian fleet but a Jewish fleet. She used to be very friendly with the last Russian Naval Minister and yesterday she was cut up because she lost a brooch which the Naval Minister gave her ... She is very bright, optimistic, always cheerful; although I believe she is worrying about her son, who is a student in Belgium. He hasn't written home for over three months. He had an exam in July & they are afraid that he has failed. He usually writes home once a month or once every two months.'

Using the intensifier 'terribly' as a synonym for 'very', as middle class people were wont to do at the time, Jones can clearly recognise virulent anti-Semitism in others, which he clearly disliked. However, by not appearing to challenge her views or voice an opinion he, like others in similar circumstances, could be criticised for being complicit in her anti-Semitism as silence is often interpreted by perpetrators as indicating tacit approval.

In October 1927, Jones wrote about a fellow student at Trinity College in these unflattering terms:

> 'The other man taking Russian is a Jew, a small little fellow, very submissive. I can't say I like him. He makes me feel very superior and very Trinity! He is not doing the History of the Slavonic Nations as I am. I talked Russian with him this morning. He knows very little; I think my Russian is better.'

In this example, Jones once again appears to be using the word 'Jew' in a pejorative sense along with other negative characteristics. A year later, however, in May 1928 and now aged 22, he decided against staying in the east Prussian town of Schneidermuhl. Writing to his parents, he believed the inhabitants to be:

> 'probably the Prussian Junker [landed nobility] type; militaristic, anti-Jewish and snobbish'.

Indicating his dislike for the reactionary nature of Junkers, who remained powerful in German society at the time, the fact that Jones chose to highlight their anti-Semitism alongside other objectionable characteristic is noteworthy of his conscious acknowledgement that it was a negative trait.

However, two months later, while studying in Leipzig, Jones wrote to his Aunt Winnie:

> 'Last night I had dinner with a student I did not like very much. I believe he was a Jew. We spoke French. He was a keen Republican, but I did not like his manners and he was too subservient, and at the same time ambitious.'

As with the earlier letter describing his fellow student at Cambridge, Jones again includes the term 'Jew' within a negative context and illustrates a recurring theme in these letters: his rejection of anti-Semitism in others is contrasted by a sub-conscious anti-Semitism of his own.

This occurs again, for the final time, in August 1930. Now working for Lloyd George as a speech writer and researcher, as well as writing articles as a freelance reporter, Jones was travelling by train from Germany into Poland. In a letter to his parents he wrote:

'When the train left Berlin, I went along to the restaurant car, and who was sat opposite me but Saul Bron, the Soviet Trade Representative for Great Britain! We had a chat on Soviet Business etc. He has awful manners, eats like a horse, is a Jew, bangs his plate with his knife, snorts, has a bullet wound in his face, cannot stop smoking between courses, the most unpolished man you could ever imagine.

Once again, the fact that Bron was Jewish was listed as one of the many objectionable aspects of his character. Jones' personal dichotomy continues, however:

'We crossed the Polish border at about 11 o'clock at night. I noticed how strict and rude the Customers Officers were with the Jews. One of them was bundled out of the train with a lot of ladies' clothing. He had to confiscate them, I believe. Whether he came back onto the train, I don't know.'

While commenting on the unsympathetic attitude of the customs officials towards Jewish passengers, Jones again noted the prejudices of others while being unaware of his own – manifested on this occasion in his description of Bron.

In contrast to the negative comments about Jews highlighted above, on other occasions Jones wrote positively about Jews he met on his travels, as when, on 11 September 1930, he wrote to his family from Warsaw, describing a conversation with a young Jewish boy. It appears that Jones enjoyed the company of the boy, a feeling that was apparently reciprocated, and was fascinated to learn, first-hand, of the fear in which the Jewish community lived:

'I had a very interesting conversation with a Jewish boy in the train. He told me that most Jews carried a small iron whip as a weapon against attacks. He showed me his and said that he often had to use it against boys who attacked him. He was very kind. He asked me where I was staying in Warsaw and when I said I did not know for sure he asked me to come and stay with him.'

Jones liked Warsaw and found the people kind. However, he wrote:

'My guide and a friend of his took me round Warsaw in a *droschke* [a horse-drawn or electric- powered carriage for up to five passengers] and wouldn't let me pay anything. The national hatreds are very strong here, especially against the Jews and against the Germans and also against the Russians. The beautiful Russian Church is being demolished and the mosques have disappeared.'

The extracts cited here from Jones' personal correspondence from July 1923 to August 1930 are the only known examples of such pejorative language and attitudes in Jones' large literary archive. All but one were penned while he was a student and none of the anti-Semitic tropes or disparaging remarks were repeated in his journalism, speeches or notebooks before his death in August 1935. Was that because he knew his views were unacceptable so kept them private, or because his views matured and he had no reason to repeat the prejudicial comments of his youth? We are not privy to any letters he received from his liberal-minded parents, or any conversations they had with their son. All we can say is that there is a total absence of such phraseology in any other family letters for the remaining five years of his life.

Jones came from a well-educated family with progressive views. As also noted in Chapter 1, his father, the respected Headmaster at Barry Grammar School, had been praised by a former pupil, Barnett

Janner, who had gone on to become an MP and President of the Board of Deputies of British Jews. Speaking in 1948, when Edgar Jones was 80 years of age, Janner said:

> 'He is a great Welshman and a man who understands what tolerance really means. He imparted to the students an understanding, which enabled us to live in harmony with each other.'

Like his parents, Jones was an enthusiastic supporter of the League of Nations and internationalism. All the available evidence shows that they were a strong and positive influence on him. However, the anti-Semitism Jones was undoubtedly exposed to during his student days – through his close friendship with German lecturer and future leading Nazi propagandist, Reinhard Haferkorn – along with the anti-Jewish prejudice that was rife amongst the higher echelons of British society within which Jones found himself in the 1920s and 1930s, meant even people of his enlightened background were sometimes susceptible to it, even sub-consciously.

The novel *My Mothers' House* (1931) by the Welsh Jewish writer Lily Tobias provides a powerful insight into the extent and nature of anti-Semitism in Britain at the time Gareth Jones was living and writing. Simon Black, the central male character, develops a sense of self-loathing as a result of being treated as a double outsider: he is Welsh and Jewish. His way of coping is to shed both identities and seek to become a model English civil servant. Early in the novel Tobias describes Black's experience of anti-Semitism at school:

> 'The children of Blaemawe [the fictional village in the Swansea valley where he was brought up] had, on the whole, accepted him as one of themselves; the constant sense of familiarity prevailing over the occasional sense of difference. But the County [school] scholars came to judgement from strange and less charitable courts.
>
> Mostly the offspring of prosperous shopkeepers, they thought it an offence to their gentility to have a 'dirty Jew' among them. The

phrase was oftenest on the lips of the captain of the cricket team, the anglicised son of a country vicar, who was doubly scandalised by the Semitic intrusion on his field of "sport".'

Explaining the resolution that Tobias' character finally reaches, Professor Jasmine Donahaye of Swansea University, wrote in her introduction to the 2015 edition of *My Mother's House*:

'Simon cannot be whole until he accepts his Jewishness, and he does eventually find a middle ground in which he sees the value of his parents' quiet faithful traditions, can take pride in his people and the Jewish past, and can repudiate the shame of otherness that he has internalised from a hostile and suspicious dominant culture.'

Prof Donahaye herself recently discovered that Jones introduced her grandparents to each other when he was a student in Strasbourg, that her grandfather – a Jew from Riga – taught him to play the balalaika, and that he was very upset over Jones' death in 1935.

The Nazi rally in Frankfurt attended by Jones in February 1933. (© The Gareth Vaughan Jones Estate)

A FLAWED HERO?

The extremes of anti-Semitism, in Nazi Germany and elsewhere, were obvious for all to see, including Gareth Jones, but the 'othering' of Jews in British culture and society was so heavily engrained in attitudes and phraseology that most didn't recognise it in themselves.

Jones was killed the day before his 30th birthday and never had the opportunity, in later years, to revisit and reflect on the language and terminology he'd used as a young man. He would never enjoy the benefit of hindsight. One would hope that an older Gareth Jones would recoil in horror and embarrassment at the language he had used when writing to his parents as a teenager and in his early 20s. We are only left with his extensive writings, the relationships he had with people of many backgrounds, and the context of the period with which to draw conclusions and make judgements.

Jones is admired because of his courage in exposing the *Holodomor* – an endeavour in which as a journalist he surpassed his contemporaries, fearlessly breaking new ground. That, for a period of his life, he didn't live up to the same high standards is disappointing. However, if Jones' apparent self-realisation enabled his conscious distain for anti-Semitism to confront his own sub-conscious prejudices, this may suggest his acknowledgement of the moral journey he needed to take.

Nazi Sympathies

Since Jones' notebooks and correspondence were re-discovered, and particularly since he was posthumously made a Hero of Ukraine in 2008, there have been renewed and concerted attempts from Communists, Russian nationalists, and assorted fellow travellers to undermine Jones' reputation specifically in order to deny the *Holodomor*. The tactic of choice has been to claim that he was a Nazi sympathiser, an obvious smear tactic the world now recognises following Russia's President Putin's spurious and globally condemned claim in February 2022 of wanting to 'de-Nazify' Ukraine.

The available evidence clearly shows that Jones was not a supporter of Hitler and the murderous brutality of the Nazis. However, his attitude towards the regime that came to power in January 1933 was inconsistent, sometimes naive and on occasions ambiguous, which can be illustrated by comments he made in speeches and in his published and private writing.

On 2 July 1931, while giving a talk to Economic Associates in Wall Street, New York, he predicted problems in Germany the following year due to elections that were due to take place and unresolved questions relating to reparations from the First World War, but added:

> 'Politically, however, I do not think that National Socialists in power would be so extreme as their programme indicates.'

Why would Jones make such a comment? He was on friendly terms with individual Nazis, some low-ranking, others further up the hierarchy. Had his personal friendships with individuals who were already or would soon be members of the Nazi party blinded him to the true purpose of their organisation?

In September 1932, for example, he received a letter from a Nazi called Carl, who told him: 'I have just returned from a Storm Attachment meeting and am just in the right mood to write to you on the political situation.' While we can assume that Jones had befriended or at least developed a friendly link with Carl, we don't have any indication as to the true nature or longevity of his relationship with Carl, who Carl was, or the complete contents of the letter.

Had Jones' understanding of the potential actions of a Nazi-led government been distorted by briefings and interviews he'd been party to with official Nazi representatives he met in London and Germany in the course of his work for Lloyd George and as a journalist? In October 1932, for example, Jones wrote to his parents, stating:

> 'On Thursday the head of the Nazis in London came and lunched with me in a small restaurant near the office. Ralph Arnold and Lawrence of the RIIA [Royal Institute of International Affairs – Chatham House] also came and we had a good discussion.'

Is it the case that Jones and his colleagues from the RIIA, along with many others in senior positions at the time, been persuaded that the extreme writings and speeches of Hitler and the other Nazi leaders were not to be taken at face value and that the Nazis would be a responsible, acceptable government?

There was ample evidence of the Nazis' thuggish behaviour before they came to power and, being fluent in German, Jones would have read Goebbels' newspaper *Der Angriff*, which proclaimed the Nazis' vile, uncompromising ideology. Yet he still sought, and described how he'd enjoyed, the company of Hitler's propaganda chief and arch anti-Semite in 1933.

Goebbels - the Nazis' arch anti-Semite.

Jones was not alone in initially being naive about the coming to power of the Nazis. In his great work *Final Solution: The Fate of the Jews 1933-39*, the Jewish historian David Cesarani described the conflicting views of diplomats about a Hitler Chancellorship:

> 'Without any caveat Sir Horace Rumbold [the British Ambassador to Germany] transmitted to the Foreign Office Papen's [former Chancellor Franz von Papen] belief that "a government under Hitler including a proportion of ministers who were not Nazis would be unable to embark on dangerous experiments." ... When he met Hitler for the first time, Rumbold found him "simple and unaffected" although his words and actions were "more calculated to appeal to the mob than to the critical faculty".'

Yet, wrote Cesarani, the American James G McDonald, chairman of the Foreign Policy Association (FPA), which encouraged public engagement with international affairs, had a wholly different view:

'It was as a representative of the FPA that he travelled to Germany in autumn 1932 and met with Ernst 'Putzi' Hanfstaengl, Hitler's American-educated publicist. Hanfstaengl got McDonald into a key rally at the Berlin Sportspalast on September 1 1932 at which Hitler steadied the nerve of his followers. The next day he lunched with Hanfstaengl and asked him about Hitler and the Jewish question.

In a report to the FPA he wrote: "Immediately his eyes lighted up, took on a fanatical look, and he launched into a tirade against the Jews. He would not admit that any Jew could be a good patriot in Germany. It was clear that he and, I presume, many of the Nazis really believe all these charges against the Jews".'

It is certainly the case that Jones wrote articles in which he made disparaging comments about Hitler and the Nazis, sometimes trenchantly so, but on occasion his reporting of Nazi parades and displays he attended – as evidenced in earlier chapters – focused more on his enjoyment of the spectacle itself than the sinister and deadly intentions of the new fascist regime. Furthermore, his assessment of German political developments as they unfolded were sometimes naively flawed. The most obvious example was an article he had published in the *South Wales News* on 25 January 1933. In it, Jones claimed that General Kurt von Schleicher, the Chancellor of the time, was a master tactician able to outsmart Hitler. He wrote:

Much to Jones' surprise, President Hindenburg appointed Hitler as Chancellor.

'The greatest triumph of [von Schleicher's] political cunning has been his complete outwitting of Hitler. In the whole of history, there are few examples of such a perfect bamboozling of any leader as Schleicher's tactics towards Hitler. The miserable Nazi leader has been hindered and deceived at every step by Schleicher's superior manipulative skill. It is the capitulation of the loud-mouthed demagogue by the silent schemer.'

Five days after Jones' article appeared, Schleicher was removed as Chancellor by President Hindenburg and replaced by Hitler. Less than 18 months later Schleicher was assassinated on Hitler's orders during the so-called Night of the Long Knives.

Holodomor-deniers who claim a close link between Jones and the Nazis point to the fact that, for example, after returning from Ukraine and Moscow with his eyewitness account of the famine, he chose to give his press conference in Berlin, which by March 1933 was the capital of Nazi Germany. The point has also been made that, according to his own diary, he had been 'treated kindly' by officials

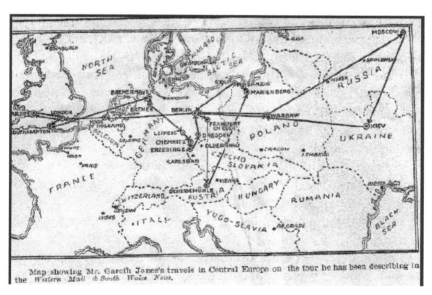

Map showing Mr. Gareth Jones's travels in Central Europe on the tour he has been describing in the *Western Mail* & *South Wales News*.

Jones' travels to central and eastern Europe in February and March 1933. The decision to return to Wales via Berlin had been made prior to his departure. (© The Gareth Vaughan Jones Estate)

of the German consulate in Kharkov and had dined with the German Ambassador to the Soviet Union on his return to Moscow.

What is overlooked, however, is that his journey to Ukraine had started and finished in London, with stop-offs in Berlin on the outward and return journeys, and he had always planned to travel to Berlin after leaving the Soviet Union. Furthermore, having uncovered such a huge story, a cataclysmic famine that the Soviets were denying, his natural journalistic instincts would be to tell the world at the earliest opportunity. Berlin had a ready supply of senior journalists from around the globe posted there, all available to help him spread the news he'd just uncovered. Jones' career in journalism had only just begun and he wouldn't have wanted to delay the release of his findings in case another journalist broke the story first.

Moreover, Jones' visit to the German consulate in Kharkiv was primarily due to his friendship with Eric Schuler, who had helped him improve his Russian while in New York in 1931. The two had become friends and by February 1933 Eric and his wife Melitta were living in Berlin. They had welcomed Jones to their home and helped him prepare for his imminent visit to the Soviet Union including ensuring he had the correct vaccinations. Eric Schuler was the nephew of the German Consul in the then Ukrainian capital, so Jones' comment that Schuler's uncle had been 'remarkably kind to me' in Kharkiv has no sinister, pro-Nazi, connotations. It merely emphasises Jones' wide network of friends who were prepared to assist him. Also, there was no British diplomatic presence in the city at that time, with the only official British Embassy or consulate in the Soviet Union being located in Moscow which Jones visited days later, along with his visit with the German Ambassador.

In August and September 1933, the Welsh language weekly newspaper *Y Cymro* published a series of letters written by Jones and leading Welsh Communist Ithel Davies. Following Jones' speech at that summer's National Eisteddfod when he had likened the authoritarian regime in the Soviet Union to the fascist dictatorships in Germany and Italy, Davies launched a furious attack on Jones for 'a distortion of the facts', claiming that because of the system of

Soviets there was no dictatorship from Moscow. 'The only dictator present is the dictatorship of the people ... The people of Russia are masters of their own house' wrote Davies. In the 2 September issue of *Y Cymro*, Jones replied to the point raised by Davies and further clarified his personal views:

'Er fy mod fel Rhyddfrydwr yn casáu llywodraeth Hitler, rhaid i mi gyfaddef bod 42 y cant o'r Almaenwyr wedi pleidleisio drosto yn yr etholiad diwethaf.'

'Even though as a Liberal I detest Hitler's government, I have to admit that 42 per cent of Germans voted for him in the last election.'

However, it is undeniable that Jones enjoyed the friendship, from his student days at Aberystwyth, with the academic Reinhard Haferkorn, with whom he stayed in Danzig after returning from Moscow, and who was to join the Nazi Party weeks later on 1 May 1933. Furthermore, in November of that year Haferkorn was one of around 900 German academics who signed a public declaration of support for Hitler, despite a programme of dismissing Jewish university and college lecturers having already begun. In 1934 he joined the SA and was classified by the Nazis as an 'absolutely reliable' National Socialist. During the Second World War Haferkorn headed up the English language unit of Germany's Foreign Office and was responsible for coordinating propaganda radio broadcasts, including those of the notorious Lord Haw-Haw (William Joyce). Captured in 1945 by the British, Haferkorn spent some time in custody, giving evidence against British collaborators who were put on trial (Joyce was hanged as a traitor). He later resumed his academic career and lived until 1983.

Jones' critics have also referred to the exuberance expressed by Jones at getting a seat on Hitler's plane as he flew to a Nazi rally in Frankfurt as another signal of where his true sympathies lay. However, it's fair to say that at the start of a young journalist's career, securing such an assignment would be seen as a personal triumph.

A major part of being a political journalist is to get access to those in power in order to report, with authority, on the globally important

Jones with Eric Schuler in New York, 1932. Schuler's uncle worked at the German consulate in Kharkiv. (© The Gareth Vaughan Jones Estate)

news of the period. Jones was no different as can be seen when he also attempted to gain access to Stalin on the next leg of his trip in early 1933. Jones also noted his exhilaration when meeting President Hoover and expressed his pleasure at securing an interview with de Valera in Ireland. Was his invitation to be one of just two journalists on that plane due to a belief among some Nazis that Jones was a man they could trust, or manipulate, or was is simply because he had a letter of introduction from Lloyd George and was one of the few correspondents who could speak fluent German and had a long-standing knowledge of German politics and culture?

As an advisor to Lloyd George, in his role as a political journalist, his friendship with Haferkorn, and during his frequent visits to Germany, Jones clearly met and nurtured close relations with many current and future Nazis. He may also have been savvy enough to realise that the recently installed Nazi regime would not seek to hamper his efforts to tell the truth about the *Holodomor* and that they would naturally be interested in his discoveries and insight into Soviet politics.

In their attempts to deny the *Holodomor*, it is obvious that Jones' connections to the Nazis would be highlighted by those sympathetic to the Soviet regime. Denigrating the name of the primary source of the incriminating evidence is a very familiar tactic, but it does not detract from the authenticity of Jones' revelations about the *Holodomor*, which have since been validated by numerous historians and documentary evidence.

These connections, events and naivety will certainly raise eyebrows, but they do not indicate any sympathies for Nazi ideology. There are no comments indicating support for Nazism in his personal notebooks, diaries, letters, speeches or newspaper articles. The opposite is, in fact, the case. There is much written evidence, particularly the published articles from his three final visits to Nazi Germany – in June 1933, October 1933 and August 1934, when his reporting clearly indicates the atrocities that were taking place, the targeting of the Jewish community and his revulsion at Nazi ideology – to disprove the accusations.

TAIR GWLAD DAN ORFOD

"Y WLADWRIAETH HOLLALLUOG"

MR. GARETH JONES A'R UNBENNAU

NID yw Mr. Gareth Jones, y newyddiadurwr, Barri, Morgannwg, yn gweld llawer o ddaioni mewn unbennaeth, ac y mae'n ofni nad ydym ni ym Mhrydain yn pwysleisio digon ar 'endithion rhyddid y person unigol, yr hyn o geir dan ddull Prydain o lywodraethu.

Bu Mr. Jones yn annerch cyfarfod o Undeb Prifysgol Cymru yn Wrecsam brynhawn dydd Mawrth ar "Gytyng-tad Rhyddid yn Ewrob," a rhyfeiriodd at y sefyllfa bresennol yn Germani, yr Eidal a Rwsia dan gynllunian o unbennaeth.

'Gareth Jones and the dictators' - A report in Y Cymro of Jones' speech at the 1933 Eisteddfod.

Had he lived longer, I have no doubt that witnessing the full extent of Nazi evil would have led him to regret that there were any ambiguities in his writings about Hitler and the regime he led.

Those who seek to exploit those aspects of Jones' reporting in an attempt to smear him as a Nazi-sympathiser in order undermine his integrity, and therefore to deny the *Holodomor*, will no doubt continue their quest to subvert history. They will never succeed, however, as the facts are very clear: in his own words, and in his native language, Jones clearly stated that he detested Hitler and his government. Furthermore, the validity of Jones' reporting of the mass starvation he witnessed while in Ukraine, purposely inflicted by Stalin's genocidal tyranny, is indisputable and globally acknowledged.

16

Jones' Journalistic Legacy

The Ongoing Battle for Truth

It is not an exaggeration to suggest that the cause for which Gareth Jones is best known – standing up for truth and against those who deny it – represents the central battleground of our time.

Many decades have passed since he defied the attempts of more established journalists to play down the man-made famine that killed millions of people in Ukraine and other parts of the Soviet Union. In doing so, he did not take an easy option. He faced vilification from others in his profession and there is a fair chance that he lost his life as a consequence of his revelations.

On one level, Jones performed a role that was very specific to his own time. He was both an eyewitness and a reporter who brought to his readers' attention the plight of people who were destroyed by cruel changes to their living conditions that they had no power to resist.

It has to be said that the immediate impact of his reporting was limited: his articles did not lead to a change of policy within the Soviet Union; farms continued to be collectivised; kulaks continued to be persecuted; and grain that could have saved lives continued to be sold for foreign currency. The blame for that must lie partly with those journalists who took it upon themselves to discredit Jones' work unjustly.

It wasn't until many years later, as the Soviet Union finally imploded because of its more general economic unsustainability, that Jones' work in exposing the famine contributed to a narrative that made an independent Ukraine plausible and necessary, but the

Welsh journalist's struggle for the truth has a significance that goes way beyond his own time and the particular circumstances he was reporting on, important as they were.

The nature of communications has, of course, changed hugely since the 1930s. Gareth Jones was one of a tiny number of individuals who had the opportunity to report on the plight of those millions who were dying in the Soviet Union from lack of food. The Soviet authorities controlled who could function as a journalist within the territory they controlled. Domestic reporters had no choice but to toe the Communist Party line – a fact that led to all manner of deceptions. Foreign journalists were also strictly controlled, and were tolerated so long as they didn't deviate from the rules they were expected to follow, which included not reporting matters that would show the regime in a bad light.

Gareth Jones broke the rules by leaving Moscow, getting off a train where he chose, and talking to peasants in an unsupervised manner that provided him with the truth the Soviet authorities were intent on concealing. He compounded his disobedience by not submitting the results of his endeavours to the censors, but by leaving for the West, where he captured the world's attention about what he had seen and heard. Throughout the process he was a solitary operator, without whose efforts what he saw would have remained unreported.

Today one would like to think that things would be different, with the vast advances in communications technology making it possible for many more reports to emerge from such tragic situations via a multitude of sources. Nevertheless, there remain constraints over what can be produced, depending where in the world a crisis is occurring. In poor areas, where conflict is likely to happen, the availability of smartphones to capture scenes of injustice is likely to be more limited. Equally, the degree of repression in a society will inhibit those who may be inclined to create footage. The brutality of the so-called Islamic State was conveyed more by shocking videos released by the organisation itself than by covert filming made by dissidents, which for obvious reasons was in very short supply.

In May 2020 the worldwide outrage over the murder of George Floyd in Minneapolis was prompted by footage of a police officer choking him to death. Sadly, such murderous acts take place every day at the behest of repressive regimes in different parts of the world, but go unnoticed because no witness is willing or able to report on them.

There is still a role, then, for the maverick reporter – professional or otherwise – who is able to provide testimony about unjust things that happen in all sorts of locations.

Gareth Jones' experience of having his famine revelations denied has a strong resonance in our era, where those who report the truth are accused of purveying 'fake news', and those who tell lies portray themselves as the authentic truth tellers. When such behaviour is displayed by the supposed leader of the free world – I refer, of course, to Donald Trump – we know we are in the midst of a communications war with no end in sight.

Optimists once believed that the huge expansion of communications would lead to greater understanding and more clarity about what news is correct and what news isn't. Few such optimists remain, and it is now accepted that malign individuals or organisations are able to manipulate millions of people using lies and distortions.

The trend towards the official sanctioning of fake news reached a shameful apogee after the invasion of Ukraine by Russia in February 2022, when news outlets who were exposing the truth about Russian atrocities were branded purveyors of fake news by the Russian state. A law was passed that brought in jail terms of up to 15 years for publishing 'knowingly false information' about the military.

As a result, many independent news organisations in Russia ceased broadcasting and many Western outlets pulled out of Russia in order to protect their journalists. The BBC halted its Russian-based reporting for a number of days before recommencing operations with a revised set of terms and descriptions of events that kept reporters within the Russian Government's stipulations while being as faithful to the truth as possible. A modern Gareth Jones who tried to report independently from areas in Russia or occupied by it would be unlikely to survive long.

The assault on press freedom in Putin's Russia was not new. In August 2021 the BBC's highly respected Moscow correspondent Sarah Rainsford had to leave the country after having her visa withdrawn, supposedly in retaliation for the expulsion of a Russian journalist from the UK two years before and threats by the British authorities to crack down on the state broadcaster RT (formerly Russia Today), widely seen as a Putin mouthpiece.

Michelle Stanistreet, general secretary of the National Union of Journalists, joined her counterpart Vladimir Solovyov, president of the Russian Union of Journalists, in condemning Ms Rainsford's expulsion, saying: 'It is vital that journalists are allowed to operate in the public interest, without undue interference or bureaucratic impediments designed to stop them doing their job. Journalists should not be used as pawns in power struggles and our unions will continue to defend the common professional interests of our members.'

For Russian journalists themselves, reporting the truth about what was happening in Putin's Russia could be literally a matter of life and death. Since Putin came to power in 1999, 25 journalists have been murdered, according to a tally kept by the US-based Committee to Protect Journalists.

Meanwhile, since the invasion of Ukraine, independent news outlets in Russia have been shut down, forcing citizens of Russia to rely more on state media, which is strongly supportive of the invasion.

The Kremlin's stranglehold over the dissemination of traditional news broadcasting had an impact. It seemed that the majority of Russians supported the invasion of Ukraine, with a series of polls indicating that up to 68% did so. Many Russian citizens appeared to have no idea about what was happening in their name, basing their judgements entirely on pictures from Russian state TV. State propaganda and fake news about Ukraine 'shooting its own citizens in the Donbas region' had in fact started back in 2014 at the time hostilities in the east of Ukraine began and since then had been increasing in its pace and volume.

The advent of social media – hailed as a democratisation of communications in which everyone is able to have a platform – has turned into a morass in which all manner of falsehoods can be spread across the world instantaneously – or more pertinently to a targeted audience – by simply pressing on a keyboard.

Those who control social media channels are reluctant to remove material that can influence the thought processes of readers even when it is demonstrably false. It is unsurprising that this should be the case when elements of the traditional media have been happy to mislead for years while paying lip-service to a commitment to accurate reporting.

How can such mendacious activities be countered? In theory at least, there was a time when editorial judgements could be made that would deprive untrue stories from gaining currency in newspapers or on broadcast channels. We know that such measures didn't always work, and that media proprietors with a political agenda could subvert any proclaimed commitment to accuracy, but at least there was, in states like the UK, a mechanism for holding those who transgressed to account.

The Internet has made that immeasurably more difficult, not least because in the United States, where social media channels are based, there is no formal regulation of the media. The First Amendment to the US Constitution protects freedom of speech and of the press – and this is interpreted by some as meaning that social media channels or the press have a legally enforceable right to distribute information that is not true. As a result of impediments like this, it is difficult to see how 'fake news' can be eliminated easily.

In the UK there is an unsustainably anomalous position where traditional media are regulated and voluntarily agree to abide by a code of conduct that aims to deliver accurate and fair reporting, while social media postings are not regulated for accuracy or fairness, but may be taken down for 'offensiveness' if enough people complain.

Today many people have become disillusioned by what is increasingly referred to disparagingly as the 'mainstream media', choosing instead to access their view on current events via their favourite social media channel, where they can be at the mercy of those with a vested interest to deceive. It's a recipe for disaster, and at its worst has become a grooming mechanism for terrorists.

The memorial plaque outside the old family home in Romilly Road, Barry.

This tendency needs to be rolled back, with news organisations recommitting themselves to their original purpose. The pendulum has swung too far in the direction of entertainment and needs to pivot once again towards serious journalism, for which our societies have a crying need.

Recognition of Jones' contribution to journalism, as well as to Ukraine, was illustrated in 2019 when – in addition to his Hero of Ukraine award of 2008 – he was further honoured when a street in the Shevchenlivskyi district of the Ukrainian capital, Kyiv, was named after him – провулок Гарета Джонса (Gareth Jones Lane) – by the city council.

The street's location, close to the city's TV tower and the Journalism Institute of the Taras Shevchenko National University, was clearly symbolic and a reminder that adhering to journalistic standards founded on truth are as important today as they were in the 1930s.

We have no alternative but to rely on intrepid journalists of principle in the Gareth Jones mould, backed up by news organisations whose brands have built up a reputation for integrity and honest reporting.

Eryl – purchased by his parents at the suggestion of Gareth Jones.

Part Three

The Jones family grave in Merthyr Dyfan cemetery, Barry.

The 'Bitter Memory of Childhood' sculpture at the monument to the victims of the Holodomor in Kyiv. (© Shutterstock)

Appendix I

The *Holodomor*

Did Stalin Specifically Target Ukraine?

A bitter controversy that has continued until today hinges on whether the Soviet Union purposefully inflicted genocide upon Ukraine during the 1933 famine. That such a famine occurred is now generally accepted, but the situation is complicated because it wasn't confined to Ukraine.

When Gareth Jones wrote his eye-witness accounts of what he saw on his walk – and when he discussed the implications of the famine with others – he tended not to specify Ukraine as the location affected. Instead he referred to the Soviet Union as a whole.

It should be remembered too that when he jumped off the train for his unauthorised walk through the famine-devastated countryside, he began in Russia and crossed the border into Ukraine. He also made no distinction between the two territories in his descriptions of the encounters he had with peasants in the villages he passed through.

There is no doubt that famine occurred in many parts of the Soviet Union in 1933. Yet the people of Ukraine believe their compatriots suffered to a disproportionate degree, and that the Soviet state – and especially its leader Stalin – was intent on inflicting an extreme form of punishment on them.

There are those, almost invariably supportive of Russia and the former Soviet Union, who take a vehemently different view. For them, the Ukrainians have been seeking to distort history in order to underpin an unjustified narrative of a nation oppressed and punished by Russia. The deaths of those who died in what Ukraine came to designate as the *Holodomor* are, according to this counterview, exploited for political purposes. Needless to say, such a view is seen as grossly offensive in Ukraine.

This is not a simple matter to unravel. Assessing the facts relating to the famine is not enough. It's necessary to look at the historical relationship between Russia and Ukraine and the political background to that relationship in the Soviet era.

For the historian Anne Applebaum, whose book *Red Famine: Stalin's War on Ukraine* argues that Ukraine was singled out for harsh treatment, the story began in 1917 when Ukraine's peasants came into conflict with the new Bolshevik regime.

For Applebaum, the famine in Ukraine was part of a larger famine that affected many parts of the Soviet Union, and which was prompted by Stalin's decision in 1929 to collectivise all farms. The decision led to an enormous amount of chaos, food shortages and hardship all across the Soviet Union.

The idea of collectivising the farms stemmed from Stalin's visceral hatred of kulaks, the peasants who owned more than eight acres of land. During the 1920s, despite the Revolution, peasants lived much as they had in the past – farming the land, running small businesses, trading and bartering. Stalin believed this should change, as Applebaum notes:

> 'Loose organisation was to be replaced by strict control ... Entrepreneurial farmers would become paid labourers. Independence was to be replaced with strict regulation. Above all, in the name of efficiency, collective farms, owned jointly by the commune or the state, were to replace all private farms. As Stalin had said in Siberia, the "unification of small and tiny peasant household farms into large collective farms ... for us is the only path". Eventually, there would be different types of collective farm with different degrees of communal ownership. But most would require their members to give up their private property – their land as well as horses, cattle, other livestock and tools – and to turn all of it over to the collective.'

THE *HOLODOMOR*

Officially, the Soviet state expected the reform to be welcomed joyfully in the villages, but in practice the changes had to be imposed from above because of the strong opposition from peasants who resented losing their land.

Collectivisation was, Applebaum notes, a disaster:

'Threatened by violence and afraid of hunger, hundreds of thousands of peasants finally relinquished their land, animals and machines to the collective farms. But just because they had been forced to move, they did not become enthusiastic collective farmers overnight. The fruits of their labour no longer belonged to them; the grain they sowed and harvested was now requisitioned by the authorities.'

Convinced by statistics likely to have been falsified that grain production was rising, the Kremlin made the disastrous and callous decision to increase the export of grain, as well as of other food products, out of the Soviet Union in exchange for hard currency. This led to food, that should have sustained members of the collective, being seized and sold overseas, inevitably creating famine conditions in the villages. The height of chaos occurred in autumn 1932, when Stalin made a series of policy decisions and orders that increased the intensity of the famine very specifically in Ukraine, as Applebaum notes:

'Stalin's policies that autumn led inexorably to famine all across the grain-growing regions of the USSR. But in November and December 1932 he twisted the knife further in Ukraine, deliberately creating a deeper crisis. Step by step, using bureaucratic language and dull legal terminology, the Soviet leadership, aided by their cowed Ukrainian counterparts, launched a famine within the famine, a disaster specifically targeted at Ukraine and the Ukrainians.

Several sets of directives that autumn, on requisitions, blacklisted farms and villages, border controls and the end of Ukrainization – along with an information blockade and extraordinary searches, designed to remove everything edible from the homes of millions of peasants – created the famine now remembered as the *Holodomor*.

The *Holodomor*, in turn, delivered the predictable result: the Ukrainian national movement disappeared completely from Soviet politics and public life. The "cruel lesson of 1919" had been learned, and Stalin intended never to repeat it.'

The details and significance of these decisions have only become apparent quite recently, when historians have had the opportunity to go through newly released Soviet archives. For a very long time – before the opening of the archives – Ukrainians had taken the view that the famine had been directed against their country by a Soviet leader who hated them. They had remembered collectively how it had unfolded. It wasn't a famine that happened because of bad weather, because of insects or because of a natural catastrophe. It happened because Stalin took decisions which had very concrete effects in Ukraine.

The famine was implemented and exacerbated by teams of activists who went from house to house and village to village confiscating food from the local population. A cordon was drawn around Ukraine that not only prevented people from leaving the territory, it also stopped peasants from travelling from the villages into the cities. It was these decisions, taken in the autumn and winter of 1932 that prevented people getting food, and by the spring of 1933 people began to die in very large numbers.

While ordinary Ukrainians remembered what happened because of their lived experience, these events were not recorded officially. While the famine was taking place, people were not allowed to write or speak about it. As we know, Western journalists based in Moscow had some inkling that a famine was going on, but they were explicitly instructed, by Communist Party officials, not to report it. Those who did so, like Gareth Jones, were shouted down by other journalists who wanted to keep their prestigious positions in Moscow. They kept up the the myth that there was a little bit of hunger but no starvation.

THE *HOLODOMOR*

In the aftermath, Soviet officials went to enormous lengths to cover up the famine, even to the extent of suppressing a census in 1937 which showed that there had been a significant drop in the population of Ukraine.

In recent years a team of Ukrainian demographers have looked again at the numbers that were tabulated at the district and provincial level before being passed on to Kharkiv and Moscow. As Applebaum notes:

> 'Thanks to their work agreement is now coalescing around two numbers: 3.9 million excess deaths, or direct losses, and 0.6 million lost births or indirect losses [the lack of natural population growth because of the famine]. That brings the total number of missing Ukrainians to 4.5 million. These figures include all victims, wherever they died – by the roadside, in prison, in orphanages. The total population of the republic at that time was about 31 million people. The direct losses amounted to about 13% of that number.'

The next census, in 1939, was falsified to give the impression there had been no fall in numbers. An academic paper by Mark Tolts of the Hebrew University of Jerusalem, presented at a conference in Toronto in 1995, demonstrated how, among other irregularities, census forms for 383,563 people residing elsewhere were falsely assigned to Ukraine for inclusion in its population total.

According to Applebaum, the cover-up was maintained for decades, but there was always what she describes as a counter-narrative that disputed the Soviet narrative. This certainly occurred inside Ukraine, but perhaps more importantly among the Ukrainian diaspora in western Europe and the United States, who maintained the collective memory of the famine. A number of low-budget, self-published oral histories – collections of memories and stories about the famine – were published, which kept the issue alive, but many outside the Ukrainian community found it difficult to believe that a state and its ruler would deliberately deprive people of food and knowingly starve them to death.

It wasn't until the 1980s, when the grip of Soviet power and censorship eased under Mikhail Gorbachev, that it became possible to speak about the famine openly. The first two books referencing the *Holodomor* were published at that time, most notably Robert Conquest's *The Harvest of Sorrow: Soviet Collectivisation and the Terror-Famine*, in 1986. Conquest's book was based largely on the numerous amateur memoirs that were available, and newspaper reports from the time of the famine, at the time regarded as controversial. The Soviet regime launched an attack on the book, publishing what purported to be their detailed refutation of its evidence and conclusions. This counter-book was titled *Fraud, Famine and Fascism*, and sought to undermine Conquest, accusing him of being a CIA agent and alleging that all the material in his book came from Nazi sources.

Ever since, when the famine has been mentioned as a specific account or a chapter in a wider history, both the Soviet government and subsequently the Russian government have done what they could to undermine the Ukrainian narrative. This continued denial of the famine is still a cause of controversy and animosity.

Once Ukraine became an independent state in 1991, the Ukrainians themselves began to work on the history of the famine by examining the archives and establishing the legitimacy of their perspective. At the same time, the Russian government has done what it could to reject or underplay the narrative. In many parts of Ukraine memorials have been erected to those who starved to death, but in areas now run by Russian-backed separatists, following the unresolved armed conflict that began in 2014, such memorials have been defaced or removed.

Stalin's motivations are clearer now, according to Applebaum, who argues that it is impossible to explain the famine without going back to 1917, which was the year not only of the Bolshevik Revolution, but also of the Ukrainian National Revolution. As authority fell apart across the collapsing Russian Empire, a group of Ukrainian intellectuals came to power in Ukraine who, for a brief period, tried to create a Ukrainian state. They declared independence from Russia and aimed to establish a separate polity, the forerunner of what eventually occurred more than 70 years later.

At that time a lot of new countries were being established from the ashes of collapsed empires: Poland was being recreated and Bulgaria, Yugoslavia and Czechoslovakia came into being, for example. Ukraine also wanted to be a beneficiary but was ultimately unsuccessful, partly because the White Army did not want to see an independent Ukraine and fought against Ukrainian forces, but more importantly because of the Bolsheviks.

One of the Bolsheviks' primary military goals during the civil war that lasted from 1917 until 1921 was to reoccupy Ukraine, and three attempts were made. Two of them failed – the second spectacularly when, in 1918, the Bolsheviks seized Kyiv. They ran the country for a short time, using the *Cheka* (the Soviet Secret Police) to challenge opposition and nationalised industry to create a Communist state but were met with a massive peasant rebellion that, according to Applebaum, hasn't been seen in Europe before or since. Eventually, following a third invasion, the Bolsheviks prevailed.

The Bolsheviks did not forget this rebellion, which was anarchic and chaotic, left-wing and anti-Bolshevik at the same time. The Ukrainian peasants were in favour of land redistribution, they had radical revolutionary slogans, but were extremely anti-Bolshevik as well. The memory of this uprising, which led to the city of Kyiv changing hands around a dozen times in 1919 and which saw the White Army and the Polish Army participating in the conflict, was something which stayed with the Bolsheviks for a long time. Trotsky wrote about the 'terrible lesson' of 1918 and 1919, and years later Stalin would refer to this period.

The Bolsheviks were very wary of the Ukrainian national movement, with its aspiration for Ukrainian sovereignty and a desire to create their own state that the Soviets believed would challenge their political model by providing a successful alternative. They were also afraid of the Ukrainian peasantry, who they rightly suspected of being anti-Bolshevik. The constant fear that such a revolt could happen again remained with the Bolsheviks, and is apparent in memoirs and archives. Even before Stalin introduced collectivisation in 1929, there was significant fear of how the Ukrainians would react and an acknowledgement that the Soviet leadership needed to pay special attention to Ukraine.

As expected, the Ukrainians rejected collectivisation and rose again in an armed rebellion. Thousands went to their barns and got the guns they had stored there since the civil war and, when the Bolsheviks arrived, started shooting at the Commissars. The spectre of a Ukrainian revolt was at the forefront of Stalin's mind, and imagination, and this was what he wanted to prevent. At the height of the food crisis in 1929, he undoubtedly saw this as his opportunity to do just that.

Stalin's desire to eliminate the kulaks did pave the way for what happened in the Ukraine and it was part of the anger and animus he deployed to convince people that what he had set in train was right. For Stalin, the peasants were the enemies of the people – enemies of the state who wanted to unravel the Revolution.

At the same time as the confiscation of food, in 1933 and 1934 Stalin also carried out a series of purges and mass arrests of members of the Ukrainian nationalist intelligentsia, including artists, writers, curators and professors, designed to eliminate Ukraine as a threat to the Bolsheviks.

Archive material makes it clear that the Ukrainian Communist Party knew what was happening. They read the reports from the regions about the shortage of food, and by 1931 and 1932 they were requesting that Stalin lower the rate of grain requisition in Ukraine, and for additional supplies to be sent. In the spring of 1932 many of the leaders of the Ukrainian Communist Party began writing to Stalin, saying disaster was looming and asking him to take immediate action. Stalin's reaction was to treat them with suspicion, writing letters to allies saying the Ukrainian Communists weren't up to the job and speculating about whether they could be trusted. He had serious suspicions that the Ukrainian Communist Party was disloyal and, in 1933 and 1934, along with the Ukrainian intelligentsia, Stalin also purged the Ukrainian Communist Party leaders.

THE *HOLODOMOR*

By now, the remaining Communist officials in Ukraine lived in fear and knew nothing could be done to halt the impending disaster. Some committed suicide, most notably the Commissar for Education Mykola Skrypnyk, an early champion of 'Ukrainian Bolshevism', later referred to as 'national communism', the belief that communism could take separate forms in different countries and was not incompatible with national sentiment in Ukraine. Skrypnyk had established Ukrainian history and language courses in the country's universities, an initiative abolished by the now loyally pro-Soviet Union Ukrainian Communist Party in January 1933. A month later Skrypnyk was forced to defend himself against the charge that he had tried to 'Ukrainise' Russian children by force. In March, as famine raged in the countryside, the Bolskeviks issued a decree eliminating Ukrainian language textbooks as well as school lessons tailored to teaching Ukrainian children their own history.

Soviet writers joined the onslaught and published articles attacking Skrypnyk's language and linguistic policies, including the development of a new Ukrainian orthography, compiled over many years with the input of scholars from Ukraine and its diaspora. At a Politburo meeting on 7 July 1933, Skrypnyk protested against the charges levelled against him, to no avail. He walked out of the meeting, returned home and shot himself. Most of the Ukrainian Communist Party leaders who weren't arrested in 1934 were arrested in 1937, and by the end of the decade the whole party had been purged so that it was now unquestioningly loyal to Stalin.

The Soviet secret police were not all ethnic Ukrainians, and the activists who went from house to house to seize food supplies were also mixed. Some were police, some secret police, some activists from Russia, others were activists from the cities and some were local. There were also local brigades that carried out the measures that led to the famine.

Considering whether what occurred amounted to genocide, Applebaum makes the point that the person who invented the term – Raphael Lemkin – was from a part of Ukraine that is now in Poland. Lemkin made it clear that his understanding of the concept, where nations sought to destroy other nations, stemmed from the European region where he was born. Genocide was a term that wasn't used widely until the 1940s, and it only came to have a legal definition after the Second World War. People felt that the Nuremberg trials hadn't answered all the questions arising out of the war's horrors, and some were left to the UN Convention on Genocide to determine.

Lemkin's definition of genocide was, argues Applebaum, exactly what Stalin did in the Ukraine: the attempt to destroy a nation, its culture, its identity, its educational system, its religion and churches. At one point Lemkin wrote a paper in which he asserted that Stalin's actions amounted to a classic definition of genocide but, during the process when the concept of genocide was being inserted into international law, an intervention ensured the *Holodomor* would not be included. As the UN Convention debated the definition of genocide in the late 1940s, a major participant in the discussion was the Soviet Union, which made it clear that the definition arrived at should not be applicable to anything that it had done. At this key international level Ukraine, as a subservient region of the USSR, had no voice at the global top table.

During the UN negotiations, the Soviet Union insisted that murders committed for political reasons should not be captured by the definition of genocide, in the way murders committed for religious, ethnic and cultural reasons could be. Accepting political murders within the definition would have meant that the deaths in the Gulag as well as other mass murders committed by the Soviet Union could have been considered as acts of genocide. The Soviets were also very keen that the word should be attached specifically to what the Germans had done – essentially that genocide was the equivalent of the Holocaust. As a consequence, it has become very difficult, internationally, to use the term in the way Lemkin intended.

Applebaum concludes that what the Soviets perpetrated in Ukraine did amount to genocide in the way Lemkin perceived it – and in the way, for her, that ordinary people imagined it. We think of genocide as murdering people not for what they've done, but for who they are. Ukrainians were murdered because they were

Ukrainians, and because of Stalin's perception of them as a threat to the implementation of his plans for collectivisation: without a doubt, they were an ethnic and political group regarded as a problem by the Bolsheviks.

Timothy Snyder, another leading historian of the period, devoted a chapter of his book, *Bloodlands: Europe Between Hitler and Stalin*, to the famine in Ukraine. As evidence of the particularly harsh treatment meted out to Ukraine by the Soviet authorities, Snyder highlights seven crucial policies that were applied there only, or primarily, in late 1932 and early 1933:

1. 18 November 1932 – peasants in Ukraine were required to return grain advances they had previously earned by meeting grain requisition targets. This meant that the few localities where peasants had had good yields were deprived of what little surplus they had earned. The party brigades and the state police were unleashed in a feverish hunt for whatever food could be found, and because they were not given receipts for the grain they did hand over, they were subject to endless searches and abuse.
2. 20 November 1932 – a meat penalty was introduced, forcing peasants unable to make grain quotas to pay a special tax in meat. Peasants who still had livestock were now forced to surrender it to the state. Cattle and pigs had been a last resort against starvation. A cow gives milk, and as a last resort could be slaughtered.
3. 28 November 1932 – a 'black list' was introduced by the Soviet authorities, according to which collective farms that failed to meet grain targets were required immediately to surrender 15 times the amount of grain that was normally due in a whole month. In practice this meant the arrival of hordes of party activists and police with the mission and the legal right to seize everything.
4. 5 December 1932 – Stalin's security chief for Ukraine, Vsevolod Balytski, who had spoken personally with Stalin, said the famine was to be understood as the result of a plot by Ukrainian

nationalists – in particular of exiles with connections to Poland. Ukrainian communists were deported to concentration camps on the basis that they had abused Soviet policies in order to spread Ukrainian nationalism. The mass arrests sent a message that anyone who defended the peasants would be condemned as an enemy. As the death toll rose into the hundreds of thousands, Ukrainian administrators knew better than to resist the party line: if they did not carry out requisitions, they would find themselves – in the best case – in the Gulag.

5. 21 December 1932 - Stalin affirmed the annual grain requisition quota for Soviet Ukraine, to be reached by January 1933. Stalin sent Lazar Kaganovich as an emissary of the Central Committee of the Communist Party to Ukraine, forcing the Ukrainian politburo to convene and confirm the requisition targets would be met. This, says Snyder, was tantamount to a death sentence for three million people. As every member of the politburo knew, grain could not be collected from an already starving population without horrific consequences.

6. 1 January 1933 - Stalin instructed that all farmers hiding grain should be prosecuted for 'theft of state property'. Ukrainian farmers were forced to decide between handing over all their grain and dying of starvation, or hiding some grain and face execution. Even if they escaped execution, their grain would be confiscated leading to death by starvation. The collective farms were left with nothing to plant for the coming autumn. Seed grain for the spring sowing could have been drawn from the trainloads bound for export or taken from the three million tonnes the Soviet Union had stored as a reserve. Instead it was seized from what little the peasants in Soviet Ukraine had. It was often the very last bit of food they had to survive until the spring harvest.

7. 14 January 1933 – Internal passports for Soviet citizens were introduced to allow them to reside in cities legally. As starvation raged throughout Ukraine in the first weeks of 1933, Stalin had sealed the borders of the republic so peasants could not flee and closed the cities so that peasants could not migrate to them in

order to beg. The sale of long-distance rail tickets to peasants was banned. Stalin's justification was that peasants were not begging for bread but engaging in a 'counter-revolutionary plot' by serving as living propaganda for Poland and other capitalist states that wished to discredit the collective farm. By the end of February 1933 some 190,000 peasants had been caught and sent back to their home villages to starve.

'Each of them may seem like an anodyne administrative measure,' wrote Synder, 'and each of them was certainly presented as such at the time, and yet each of them had to kill.' Yet the views of Applebaum and Snyder, founded as they were on a wealth of documentary evidence, continue to this day to be resisted bitterly by those who find them ideologically inconvenient.

In late 2019 a row erupted after a lecturer at the University of Alberta in Canada posted comments on Facebook to the effect that the Soviet Union had not deliberately created a famine in Ukraine and that any suggestion that it had derived from Nazi propaganda.

In his post, Dougal MacDonald, an assistant lecturer in elementary education at the university, called the *Holodomor* a 'myth'. He said the genocide was a lie perpetuated with fake photographs and news stories and spread by former Nazi collaborators. '[Canadian Prime Minister Justin] Trudeau's support for the anti-communist, pro-Nazi *Holodomor* myth is no accident,' MacDonald wrote. 'The Trudeau government's promotion of the *Holodomor* myth is more of its self-serving agenda to attempt to rewrite history, while falsely claiming to support freedom, democracy, human rights and the rule of law.'

MacDonald's comments stirred outrage among the Canadian-Ukrainian community, with the university's Ukrainian Student Society (USS) calling his post 'hate speech' and saying it demonstrated that he was not fit to teach: 'Students have a lot of respect for their professors ... and typically take what they say as truth because we assume that they know what they're talking about,' said Ivanka Soletsky, a student and USS member.

'In this case, Mr MacDonald is making claims against historical facts recognised by the government of Canada for over a decade.'

Dr. MacDonald received support from the Communist Party of Canada (Marxist-Leninist), of which he is a member. The party issued a statement which said: 'In the matter of the defamatory accusations gratuitously leveled against Dr. Dougal MacDonald insinuating he is a holocaust denier, we state categorically that Dr. MacDonald is not now and never has been a holocaust denier. Dr. MacDonald has researched and, along with others, argues against the narrative of a genocide committed in Ukraine by the Soviet state. To equate this stand with denial of the holocaust is socially irresponsible.'

The statement went on to claim that one of the fields in which Dr MacDonald had developed specific knowledge dealt with 'the workings of the Nazi propaganda machine both prior to and after World War Two directed against the Soviet Union and the anti-fascist resistance fighters led by the communists.' It added: 'He shows how those directing the Anglo-American Cold War against the peoples of the world as far back as the 1930s appropriated and spread Nazi propaganda.' MacDonald, who kept his job in the university's faculty of education and continued lecturing students on how to teach elementary school children about science and 'design and make' technology, did not name Gareth Jones, but the reference to such 'propaganda' as dating back to the 1930s was clearly intended to implicate him.

Another anti-*Holodomor* writer was even less subtle. In a series of tweets made on 31 July 2020, Jareth Copus stated: 'The film @ Mr_JonesFilm shows Gareth Jones as a hero, a warrior of truth and justice, but his real history is far darker.' Copus then linked to an article by Jones he said was 'lauding Hitler's Germany'. He continued: 'He was also an admirer of Hitler, his benefactors included secret society leaders, one of the inventors of PR and William Randolph Hearst. I needn't say more but there is plenty. Jones was at best a tool and at worst a willing propagandist.'

Responding to the news that a street in Kyiv had been named after Jones, Copus tweeted: 'Ukraine likes to name things after Nazis, their collaborators and sympathisers. Gareth Jones was no hero and not only flew on Hitler's personal plane with him but also wrote articles lauding the Nazis.' Copus tweets under the name @RodionPress, a blog which opposes the current government in Ukraine and is supportive of the Russian-backed separatists in the eastern part of the country, centred on the city of Donetsk (formerly Hughesovka). Rodion appears to be named after the Second World War General Rodion Malinovsky, a hero of Stalingrad and later – from 1957 until his death in 1967 – the Soviet Union's Minister of Defence.

Clearly the testimony of Gareth Jones that exposed the *Holodomor* still rankled greatly with those who wanted to defend the Soviet denials. Even now – more than 30 years after the Soviet Union collapsed and 90 years after the *Holodomor* – they will go out of their way to discredit a journalist who reported faithfully what he witnessed.

Yet in the most tragic way conceivable, Jones' revelations about the *Holodomor* were validated by the brutal nature of the invasion Putin launched against Ukraine in February 2022.

As the weeks went by, with Ukraine showing greater resilience than most thought possible, appalling details emerged about the war crimes committed by Russian forces as they advanced, occupied and retreated.

The gratuitous massacres of civilians, the demonisation of Ukraine's leaders in a wholly unjustified way as Nazis, and the determination to destroy whole cities that wouldn't surrender demonstrated a degree of vindictiveness towards the country that resonated down the years from the 1930s when Gareth Jones reported so vividly on Stalin's man-made famine.

In July 2021 Vladimir Putin published a 5,000-word, rambling self-penned article on the Kremlin's website which drew on centuries of history to prove that Russia and Ukraine were one people. The article was titled 'On the Historical Unity of Russians and Ukrainians', and at its very outset he suggested it was malign outside forces that sought to destroy that unity:

'First of all, I would like to emphasise that the wall that has emerged in recent years between Russia and Ukraine, between the parts of what is essentially the same historical and spiritual space, to my mind is our great common misfortune and tragedy. These are, first and foremost, the consequences of our own mistakes made at different periods of time. But these are also the result of deliberate efforts by those forces that have always sought to undermine our unity. The formula they apply has been known from time immemorial – divide and rule. There is nothing new here. Hence the attempts to play on the 'national question' and sow discord among people, the overarching goal being to divide and then to pit the parts of a single people against one another.'

In what was described by the US think tank, the Atlantic Council, as a 'particularly ominous passage', Putin questioned the legitimacy of Ukraine's borders and argued that much of modern-day Ukraine occupies historically Russian lands. He went so far as to state: 'Russia was robbed.' Elsewhere in the article, he hinted at a fresh annexation of Ukrainian territory, claiming: 'I am becoming more and more convinced of this: Kyiv simply does not need Donbas.'

In a passage of direct relevance to the quest for truth of Gareth Jones in relation to the *Holodomor*, Putin stated:

'In essence, Ukraine's ruling circles decided to justify their country's independence through the denial of its past … They began to mythologise and rewrite history, edit out everything that united us, and refer to the period when Ukraine was part of the Russian Empire and the Soviet Union as an occupation. The common tragedy of collectivisation and famine of the early 1930s was portrayed as the genocide of the Ukrainian people.'

He ended the article by appearing to suggest that Ukrainian statehood itself ultimately depended on Moscow's consent, stating, 'I am confident that true sovereignty of Ukraine is possible only in partnership with Russia.'

THE *HOLODOMOR*

In a televised speech delivered on the day in February 2022 when his military forces invaded Ukraine, Putin said:

'Today's events are not connected with the desire to infringe on the interests of Ukraine and the Ukrainian people. They are connected with the protection of Russia itself from those who took Ukraine hostage and are trying to use it against our country and its people.'

Turning the true situation on its head, the Russian leader stated, in order to justify his invasion:

'The leading Nato countries, in order to achieve their own goals, support extreme nationalists and neo-Nazis in Ukraine in everything, who, in turn, will never forgive the Crimeans and Sevastopol residents for their free choice: reunification with Russia.'

Removing the Kyiv regime – which had, of course, been elected – was therefore seen as a patriotic duty, but if in his article and his speech Putin stopped short of calling for the eradication of Ukrainian culture, events that followed the invasion suggested that may have been the true aim.

In April 2022, for example, one of Russia's largest textbook publishers, Prosveshcheniye, ordered editors to minimise or remove references to Ukraine as a country, Kyiv as a capital city, and even the Ukrainian national flag from schoolbooks on history, literature and geography: 'The task before us is to make it look like Ukraine simply does not exist,' the editors were told.

Appendix 2

Walter Duranty

The Betrayal of Journalism

Walter Duranty, who did his best to discredit Gareth Jones' reports of the famine, may have been the *New York Times*' Moscow Bureau Chief, but his roots were firmly in Liverpool where he was born on 25 May 1884.

His grandfather had moved to nearby Birkenhead from the West Indies in 1842, setting up a successful merchant business in which his father worked. But tragedy struck when Duranty was 10: both his parents were killed in a train crash. In his 1981 book *Angels in Stalin's Paradise: Western Reporters in Soviet Russia, 1917-37 – Case Study of Louis Fischer and Walter Duranty*, James William Crowl wrote:

> 'Duranty was sent to live with his father's ageing bachelor uncle who largely turned him over to a succession of English public schools. It was the beginning of his study of the classics ... Smaller than his classmates and still trying to adjust to the loss of his family, he had to endure the taunts of fellow students because of his middle-class background. His unhappiness in these years left a lasting imprint, and much of his determination to excel and prove himself apparently stemmed from these early school experiences.'

He completed his education at Emmanuel College, Cambridge, from which he graduated with a first in Classics. After leaving university, Duranty spent his time enjoying himself in London, New York and mostly Paris, financed by a trust fund his wealthy grandfather had provided.

In a revelation that may confirm the worst suspicions of Duranty's detractors, his biographer Sally J Taylor has claimed that during his time in Paris, he met the infamous Satanist Aleister Crowley and engaged in magic rituals with him. Duranty then embarked on a relationship with Crowley's mistress Jane Cheron, eventually marrying her.

Crowley called Duranty 'my old friend' and quoted from the latter's book *I Write as I Please* in his book *Magick Without Tears*. Their friendship was said to have been 'cemented by the pair's common interest in smoking opium and in a woman, said to be a former artist's model.'

In December 1913, Duranty joined the European service of the *New York Times*, and during the final phase of the First World War he was an embedded reporter with the French army. When the US government, in October 1919, appointed a high commissioner to the Baltic states, Duranty was sent by the *New York Times* to Riga to report on his activities. While he didn't go into Soviet territory at that time, he was close enough to find out more about the implications of the 1917 Revolution.

At the beginning of March 1920, he returned to Paris taking over as Bureau Chief for the *New York Times*, and remained in the city until April 1922 when he was sent by his employers to Moscow, from where he filed stories about all the important news events relating to the Soviet Union over the next 12 years.

In 1924, while on holiday in France, Duranty's left leg was badly damaged in a train crash. Gangrene was found in the wound and his leg had to be amputated. After his recovery he returned to Moscow, but his disability inevitably made him less mobile than he had been previously. He could not have undertaken the walking tour in Ukraine that provided Jones with the devastating eyewitness evidence of famine conditions, for example, and it was Duranty's reaction to Jones' revelations about the famine that in due course led to the destruction of the *New York Times*' man's reputation.

Decades later, in the wake of the collapse of the Soviet Union and the creation of an independent state of Ukraine, there were calls for

Duranty to be stripped of the Pulitzer prize he had been awarded for a series of articles written in 1931, two years before Jones' exposé of the famine. Duranty's articles have been dismissed as straightforward propaganda designed to promote the cause of Stalin and his version of Soviet Communism. As Duranty plays such a major role in the career of Gareth Jones, it's very appropriate that closer attention is given to those articles, and Duranty's public denigration of Jones.

Nigel Colley, a great nephew of Jones' who together with his mother, Margaret Siriol Colley, did so much to keep knowledge of their relative alive, was in no doubt. In a note on the website he constructed to host a huge amount of written material relating to Gareth Jones, including Duranty's Pulitzer-winning articles, he wrote unapologetically:

'The executive editor of the *New York Times*, Bill Keller, told *The Washington Post* on October 23 2003, that the newspaper would have no objection if the Pulitzer Prize Board wanted to revoke Mr. Duranty's award. Mr. Keller called Mr. Duranty's work "pretty dreadful ... It was a parroting of propaganda."

It will be taken as read that no royalties are due on this unauthorised reproduction of this article. As such they are also perceived as having no truthful value whatsoever, are only reproduced for academic and educational purposes, not intended to defraud the *New York Times* of any morally legitimate royalty revenue and are published without financial gain.

In any event, the copyright for the above may well only reside, 70 years after its publication, with the heirs of Walter Duranty, and with whom we have no personal animosity whatsoever. Nevertheless, any contention of copyright violation may be taken up under the jurisdiction of English law.'

Colley then gave his home address as the premises at which any financial claims could be served, concluding with the defiant assertion: 'Any prosecution will, you can be assured, be defended in the public domain.' The message was repeated under all 13 of Duranty's articles.

It's important to be aware that at the time Duranty was writing, few people in the West had more than a cursory understanding of how the Soviet Union operated. The articles were introduced as being a series 'on present conditions in Russia', but they could in no sense be described as conventional reportage. In the main they were analytical 'think pieces' that purported to explain the way Stalin was running the country, and how things had changed since Lenin's day. There can be a fine line between explanation and propaganda.

The first article was headlined 'Red Russia of today ruled by Stalinism not by Communism', and from its first two sentences the controversial nature of Duranty's polemic is immediately apparent:

'Russia today cannot be judged by Western standards or interpreted in Western terms. Western Marxists and Socialists go nearly as far wrong about it as the 'bourgeois' critics because they fail to understand that the dominant principle of the Soviet Union, though called Marxism or Communism, is now a very different thing from the theoretical conception advanced by Karl Marx.

In 13 years Russia has transformed Marxism – which was only a theory anyway – to suit its racial needs and characteristics, which are strange and peculiar, and fundamentally more Asiatic than European.'

From the outset, then, we are being told that Russia is a special and unique case, and that the way its system has developed is explicable on racial grounds. Duranty continued:

'The dominant principle in Russia today is not Marxism or even Leninism, although the latter is its official title, but Stalinism – to use a word which Joseph Stalin deprecates and rejects.

307

I mean that, just as Leninism meant Marxian theory plus practical application, plus Russia, so Stalinism denotes a further development from Leninism and bears witness to the prodigious influence of the Russian character and folkways upon what seemed the rigid theory of Marx. Stalinism is a tree that has grown from the alien seed of Marxism planted in Russian soil, and whether Western Socialists like it or not it is a Russian tree.'

Seeking to justify this view, Duranty described what he saw as the relationship between ruler and people during the centuries when Russia was ruled by the Tsars – and the circumstances that led eventually to the Revolution:

'Old Russia was an amorphous mass, held together by a mystic, half Asian idea of an imperial régime wherein the emperor was exalted to the position of God's vice regent, with limitless power over the bodies, souls, property and even thoughts of his subjects. That, at least, was the theory, and it was only when the Czars themselves began to question it and 'act human' that a spirit of doubt and eventual rebellion became manifest,'

Duranty went on to argue that the ideas outlined by Marx in *The Communist Manifesto*:

'suited the Russian masses much better than the Western theory of individualism and private enterprise imported by Peter the Great and his successors.

Lenin took and shaped Marxism to fit the Russian foot, and although circumstances compelled him to abandon it temporarily for the New Economic Policy, he always maintained that this political manoeuvre was not a basic change of policy. Sure enough, Stalin, his successor and devout disciple, first emasculated the NEP and then set about abolishing it.'

308

WALTER DURANTY

The definition of New Economic Policy on Wikipedia is accurate, and includes reference to an important change to farming taxation that was introduced by Lenin and scrapped by Stalin:

'The New Economic Policy (NEP) was an economic policy of the Soviet Union proposed by Vladimir Lenin in 1921 as a temporary expedient. Lenin characterised the NEP in 1922 as an economic system that would include "a free market and capitalism, both subject to state control," while socialised state enterprises would operate on "a profit basis".

The NEP represented a more market-oriented economic policy (deemed necessary after the Russian Civil War of 1918 to 1922) to foster the economy of the country, which had suffered severely since 1914. The Soviet authorities partially revoked the complete nationalisation of industry (established during the period of War Communism of 1918 to 1921) and introduced a system of mixed economy which allowed private individuals to own small enterprises, while the state continued to control banks, foreign trade, and large industries.

In addition, the NEP abolished *prodrazvyorstka* (forced grain-requisition) and introduced *prodnalog*: a tax on farmers, payable in the form of raw agricultural product.

The Bolshevik government adopted the NEP in the course of the 10th Congress of the All-Russian Communist Party (March 1921) and promulgated it by a decree on March 21 1921: 'On the Replacement of *Prodrazvyorstka* by *Prodnalog*. Further decrees refined the policy. Other policies included monetary reform (1922–1924) and the attraction of foreign capital.

The NEP policy created a new category of people called NEPmen.

Joseph Stalin abandoned the NEP in 1928.'

309

If the first section of Duranty's opening article in the series that went on to win the Pulitzer prize can be defended as unaligned reporting, he then switches tone to become openly supportive of Stalin, writing:

> 'That is what Stalin did and is doing to our boasted Western individualism and spirit of personal initiative – which was what the NEP meant – not because Stalin is so powerful or cruel and full of hate for the capitalist system as such, but because he has a flair for political management unrivalled since Charles Murphy died.'

Charles Murphy, better known as 'Boss Murphy' controlled Tammany Hall from 1902 until his death in 1924. Tammany Hall was a New York City political organisation founded in 1786 and incorporated on May 12, 1789, as the Tammany Society. It was the Democratic Party political machine that played a major role in controlling New York City and New York State politics, and helping immigrants, most notably the Irish, rise in American politics from the 1790s to the 1960s. Duranty continued:

> 'Stalin is giving the Russian people – the Russian masses, not Westernized landlords, industrialists bankers and intellectuals, but Russia's 150 million peasants and workers – what they really want namely, joint effort, communal effort. And communal life is as acceptable to them as it is repugnant to a Westerner. It is one of the reasons why Russian Bolshevism will never succeed in the United States, Great Britain, France or other parts west of the Rhine.'

According to Duranty – who had interviewed Stalin the previous year – the Soviet leader did not think of himself 'as a dictator or an autocrat', but as the guardian of the sacred flame, or 'party line' as the Bolsheviks term it, which for want of a better name must be labelled Stalinism: 'Its authority is as absolute as any emperor's – it is an inflexible rule of thought, ethics, conduct and purpose that none may transgress.'

Its practical form was in the Five Year Plan, intended to transform the Soviet Union into an industrial economy far more quickly than had happened in the West.

In another article, headlined 'Socialism First Aim in Soviet's Programme: Trade Gains Second', Duranty stated that agriculture would be the most important element of the plan in its early years. In view of the famine that destroyed so many lives, Duranty was right, although not necessarily for the reason he expected. A crucial part of the plan would, he wrote, entail 'the political socialization of peasant holdings, or collective farming as it is called'.

So far as industrial production was concerned, Duranty was clear that 'in any and all cases one may say the supply produced is far inferior to the home demand'. According to the Kremlin, it nevertheless had no choice but to export goods despite the West's 'credit blockade', which forced the Soviet Union to sell in order to buy the equipment and advice it needed from abroad. Demonstrating that he was capable of being more than a mere Soviet mouthpiece, Duranty noted that while the Soviet Union was capable of building great tractor or steel plants, electric power stations and paper mills, it was likely not to be able to run them properly:

'Almost without exception new Soviet plants, coal mines, railroads and other enterprises, clumsily and wastefully managed, produce goods of indifferent quality and in amounts below the schedule. But - and it is a most important 'but' – the Russians are learning and improving every day.

In the writer's opinion, based on the advice of scores of foreign specialists of all nationalities, it will be twice or thrice five years before Soviet Russia gets her industry going on scale and with efficiency to compare with America or Germany now.'

Given the intervention of the Second World War, Duranty's prediction of how long it would take for the Soviet economy to catch up with those of America and Germany wasn't tested directly, but given those countries' relative economic performances after the war, it seems wildly optimistic. In the short term, of course, the policy of exporting grain for foreign currency so industrial capacity could be increased was pursued, with devastating human consequences. As Duranty went on to state:

> '... nothing short of a world embargo will prevent Soviet Russia from selling her goods – at a lower price than any capitalist country can meet – in order to buy the equipment she requires.'

In a further article, headlined 'Trade Equilibrium is New Soviet Goal', Duranty alluded to the suffering caused by what the Russians saw as trade inequilibrium. Quoting 'the Bolsheviks', he wrote:

> 'It is clearly less to our interest, who have an avid, clamorous demand at home for everything we export, to sell goods abroad at bankrupt prices than - for the capitalist countries whose surplus stocks far exceed the capacity of home consumption.
>
> What the capitalist countries sell abroad is a real surplus, whereas our sales inflict a hardship on our people and are a painful necessity in order to buy the equipment and technical knowledge we cannot yet produce at home.'
>
> ... Here the world Depression pinches the Soviet hard, not only because of the odium involved in the charge of dumping goods at almost any terms upon an already saturated market but from the material loss in the depreciated prices.'

Yet he was able to derive a positive from the way the Depression signalled major problems for the capitalist system:

> 'Despite the assertions abroad to the contrary, this correspondent can state positively that the Russians derive no pleasure from tightening their own belts to pay for imports and they would be delighted

to retain for home consumption much of what they are now exporting if a loan or long-term credits enabled them to buy without immediate payment. On the other hand, the world Depression has been an important encouragement to the Soviet because it appears to demonstrate a grave flaw in the capitalist system.'

Meanwhile, real hardship was growing for Soviet citizens.

Headlined 'Soviet Fixes Opinion By Wider Control', Duranty's next article concentrated on the regime's control of the media:

'It may be said without fear of contradiction that the Stalinist machine is better organized for the formation and control of public opinion in a great country than anything history has hitherto known.'

In what must have seemed an extraordinary statement even at the time, Duranty claimed that Soviet censorship was not harmful to a free press:

'It cannot be said ... that the Kremlin abuses the terrific power of the press, the radio and Communist party effort. Stalin may not be one of the world's great men in the sense that Lenin was, but he certainly 'knows his politics' and has been careful to correct the dangers of unchallenged authoritative and unified control of public opinion by what is known as 'self-criticism', which is not the least interesting feature or the Stalinist system.'

At the end of the article, Duranty rather flippantly – and with the self-assurance of someone who knew he was safe – turned the spotlight on himself:

'To a foreign correspondent self-criticism is a potent though double edged weapon. As a skate for thin ice it has unrivalled usefulness – and peril. To employ it brings the rhythmic charm of perfect balance; to misuse it means disaster. And the uncertain chance of one or the other makes the difficult and often dreary life of the American reporter in Russia so infinitely worth living.'

Giving an example of how the Soviet regime was made to look bad because of an act of censorship, Duranty referred to an incident at a Moscow open-air market in which a smoke bomb was let off, and goods and money stolen in the panic, which resulted in seven children and two adults being trampled to death. He wrote:

'On the same afternoon a foreign diplomat asked the writer about it. Between 3 and 4pm the writer received two telephone messages on the subject. At 6pm the writer's chauffeur returned from a filling station with a lurid account. By 8pm every square and street car was abuzz.

The censor said the story was barred, but that perhaps there would be a communiqué the next day. An investigation established the facts pretty exactly, but for some reason the authorities declined to release the affair. A week later the writer read in a White Russian newspaper abroad front-page stories headed, 'Starving Population Revolts in Moscow' with the subhead 'Food Riots Occur at Many Points In Soviet Capital – Bloodshed Police and Cheka Battalion Use Gas and Machine Guns'.

Who is to blame for that but the Bolsheviks themselves? There is a glaring contradiction between their all-embracing and successful formation of public opinion at home and their attitude toward news for abroad, which, if secondary, is nevertheless important.

To lean over backward against helping or 'propagandizing' foreign reporters may gratify the Soviet ego and caress the growing Soviet pride, but it makes life hard for foreign reporters.'

In this article Duranty presented himself not as a moral journalist opposing censorship as a matter of principle, but as someone who was in effect offering PR advice to the regime whose actions he was covering.

The next article – headed 'Stalinism Smashes Foes In Marx's Name' – had Duranty playing a semantic game in which liquidating the kulak class had a more benign – and more fanciful – meaning than was in fact the case. He wrote:

'It is hard and horrible, for twentieth century America to hear this, but facts are facts. Stalinism not only aims but boasts of aiming at the complete smashing of class boundaries, at the death of all distinctions save talent and State service between man and man. Rank may replace class in the Bolshevik cosmogony to satisfy human needs, but rank based on merit, not on wealth or birth.

But what, you may ask, becomes of "the former People" or the kulaks or engineers thus doomed apparently to perish? Must all of them and their families be physically abolished? Of course not – they must be "liquidated" or melted in the hot fire of exile and labor into the proletarian mass.

To illustrate – they take a kulak or other type of "former" individualism – a private business man or self-seeking engineer – and send him to the northern woods or Siberian construction camps. Sometimes his family goes, too. More generally it remains to be absorbed by poverty into the lower proletarian surroundings.

Then they tell him: "You outcast! You man that was, and now is not! You can get back your civic rights; can be reborn a proletarian; can become a free member of our ant heap by working for and with us for our communal purpose. If you don't, we won't actually kill you, but you won't eat much, won't be happy, will remain forever an outsider, as an enemy, as we consider it, even if ultimately you return from exile and rejoin your family. Because in this sub-Communist ant heap those who are not with us are against us, and the final fate of such enemies is death."

315

That, reduced to its harsh essentials, is Stalinism today.'

And what was Duranty's response to this way of operating?:

> 'It is not lovely, nor, in the outside world, of good repute, and your correspondent has no brief for or against it, nor any purpose save to try to tell the truth. But truth it is – ant-heap system, ant-heap morality – each for all and all for each, not each for self and the devil take the hindmost.

> An ugly, harsh, cruel creed this Stalinism, flattening and beating down with, so far, no more than a hope or promise of a subsequent raising up. Perhaps this hope is vain and the promise a lie. That is a secret of the future. But whatever happens later, it is the key and core of present Russia.'

Duranty's decision to absolve himself from any obligation to make a judgement about the brutality of the Stalinist regime was an indication of moral bankruptcy, and the kind of value-free approach that can give journalism a bad name.

Duranty's two final Pulitzer-winning articles were both longer pieces published in the *New York Times* magazine.

The first was headed 'The Russian Looks At The World' and sought to answer the question, 'What does the average Russian think?' Duranty suggested there was 'a deep gulf between those who reached the thinking age before and those who reached it after the revolution'. He wrote:

> 'It is a commonplace to speak of the changed outlook upon life of the "post-war generation" at Europe, as compared with its elders. Yet the war did not fundamentally alter the structure of European society, whereas the Bolshevist revolution literally stood the old order of Russia upon its head. Its most cherished ideals – the belief in God, the importance of money and property, the sanctity of family ties, the respect due to rank and birth and authority were shattered

wholesale and in many cases replaced by their exact opposites. To the "average" older Russian this destruction spelled blasphemy. To the 'average' youngster of today it means that a lot of obsolete rubbish has been swept onto the dust heap, as I have heard it said with pride.'

Duranty then contrasted the old order with the new, and speculated in a nuanced way about how Russians would compare them:

'Russians well know – nearly all of them save an incorrigibly romantic handful of the former ruling class and a larger, but still numerically insignificant section of obtusely conservative peasants – that the clock of life cannot be set backward, and that any attempt to restore the old order would be futile. Moreover – I say it with deep conviction – they do not want the old order restored, with its Czars and Popes and "Black Hundreds" and gendarmes and landlords ... They do not want it and they will not have it.

But one may venture to question whether they want, on the other hand, to work so hard, so eagerly [for] the "five-year plan in four years" as the Soviet press would like us to believe. Or whether they thrill with enthusiasm at the thought of "Socialist construction" and the slogan, "We must equal and surpass America".

Or whether the suppression of small home craft and peasant production of food and commodities – which played a far greater role in Russia's economic life than is generally realized, and is the cause of no small part of the present shortage from which they suffer greatly - is not distasteful to them like soap in the mouth instead of butter.

Or, finally, whether they really enjoy being herded into collective farms (however more productive than their wretched little individual holdings, and however more truly contributing to their ultimate good), or being forced, if they belong to the urban population, to stand in line for hours to buy the necessities of life or secure them on a niggardly ration system through 'closed distribution centres' in their factories or offices.

The "average Russian" is a meek and long-suffering creature, but it cannot be denied that he is disturbed and distressed by the present violent change of his habits and life-ways.'

Much of this analysis is perceptive and not tainted by propaganda, in contrast to many of Duranty's shorter articles published in the *New York Times* itself. Perhaps he was conscious of the fact that his magazine pieces were appearing in a series to which distinguished international writers like Andre Maurois and Emil Ludwig had also contributed.

However, Duranty seemed oblivious to the very real menace posed to farm workers and their families by the collectivisation of farms. Significantly, he went on to write in this first magazine article that the 'average Russian thinks first and foremost about food and clothing. The commodity shortage is so acute nowadays that what to eat and wear counts more than the fate of nations'.

The last sentence is particularly evocative of a time when getting the next meal could not be taken for granted. It hints at the truth Duranty could have told if he'd had the courage and integrity to do so.

He completed this article by writing about what he saw as the increasing xenophobia and political isolationism of the 'average Russian':

'It is somewhat surprising that although internationalism is one of the basic dogmas of the Bolshevist religion, the Soviet régime has thus far fostered the growth of Russian Nationalism to no small extent. It is probably neither the Bolshevist fault nor desire, but the inevitable consequence of the 'outlaw' position in which this country was placed by foreign hostility. To a primitive people the subtleties of international brotherhood of the "workers and peasants of the world" are apt to be lost in a simple human dislike of enemies, who wish to bring back their hated masters or steal their land and make them a foreign "colony" like India or an "exploited nation" like China.

Unfortunately, it cannot be denied that the average Russian, although still friendly and on the whole respectful toward the Western stranger within his gates, is becoming en masse more and more xenophobic and nationally arrogant. Which may have dire consequences in the future and already cannot be viewed without disquiet.'

Duranty's analysis comes across as an honest appraisal, again untainted by propaganda. It showed he was capable of not pulling his punches when he chose to.

The second *New York Times* magazine article – and the final in the Pulitzer series – was headlined 'Stalin's Russia Is An Echo Of Iron Ivan's'.

Duranty returned to the theme that the character of the Bolshevik regime was more 'Asiatic' than European, writing:

'[However] racially the people of Russia west of the Urals may have been European, the system under which they livid, of complete subservience to a despotic monarch, was far more akin to Asia than to Europe. They were not Asiatics, but they thought and acted like Asiatics, and thus by the Aristotelian canon indubitably acquired an Asiatic character.

As the nineteenth century progressed little waves of Western liberalism began to lap at the fortress of Oriental czardom. But its real weakness lay within the walls, which were being imperceptibly corroded by foreign ideas introduced by the court itself. At the end, the imperial family was more foreign than Russian, but Nicholas II, however well-meaning, could not emerge from the shell of autocracy he had inherited. His efforts to do so, whether voluntary or under pressure of the foreign spirit that had spread far and wide, only weakened the shell. The gulf between top and bottom, between the more than half-foreign court and the Russian masses, was too deep and wide, the bridges too few, and the time too short.

Bolshevism has given back to Russia something the Russian people have always understood - absolute authority unmellowed by the democracy or liberalism of the West. Once more the seat of power is Moscow's Kremlin, not the foreign-looking city named for St Peter. The Communist Party sits now where Ivan sat, with less pomp and luxury but no less power, and like Ivan [the Terrible] receives "wonderful great awe and obedience" that men must give not only the goods which they have been "scraping and scratching" for all their lives, but even life itself.

Under this supreme "commandment" the mass of the Russian people - only grandsons, remember, of the serfs, just two generations removed from virtual slavery - are being taught a regime of joint interest, effort and sacrifice whose roots strike deep into their history. And more than that, there is hope before them of a brilliant future when they and the power above them, which is sprung from their own loins and wielded by men like them, shall have merged to form one whole of ruled and rulers. There is education before them, denied for centuries to their "dark masses" and the training in self-government to which they never aspired. More Asiatic than European, perhaps, in its present phase, but especially more Russian than either.'

Here Duranty returned to purple prose, seeking to justify the brutality of totalitarianism by enveloping it in a pseudo-mystical miasma that was ultimately racist.

Overall, it seems beyond doubt that Duranty was a propagandist for the Soviet Union and especially for Stalin. Someone like Jones, who believed it was his duty to expose the famine, was clearly destined not to get on with Duranty.

Duranty's biographer Sally J Taylor – whose 1990 book *Stalin's Apologist, Walter Duranty: The New York Times's Man in Moscow* could in no sense be described as a panegyric – was unable to confirm allegations that he was supportive of the Soviet Union because he had been blackmailed about his private life or because he had been paid by the KGB to slant his reporting. Taylor described Duranty as the 'Dean' of Western correspondents in Moscow in the tumultuous 1920s and 1930s.

A review of Taylor's book by Michael Kirkman in the journal *British Journalism Review* stated:

'He was undeniably astute and knowledgeable, far more so than the correspondents and journalistic visitors who came and went during his long tenure.

Duranty has been accused of overlooking or soft-pedalling Stalin's remorseless persecutions, his murderous destruction of the Kulaks, the more prosperous peasants who resisted collectivisation, the depredations of the first Five Year Plan, the show trials that condemned the Old Bolsheviks who were wiped out by the dictator in the later 1930s.

Duranty's critics have bitterly criticised what they saw as the betrayal of trust that prevented him from recognising and reporting these crimes. Without conclusive proof, they accused Duranty of misleading the public about Stalin because he had been somehow corrupted.

Taylor gives us a portrait of corruption, but it is an intellectual corruption based oddly enough on a firm conviction in itself produced by chronic indecision and by a desire to avoid moral judgement.

Early on, with the help of a perceptive Cambridge instructor, Duranty recognised that he had a character flaw. This flaw, strongly resembling the ambivalence that Americans call objectivity, revealed too many sides of a question for [Duranty] to be sure which of them was quite true.'

Appendix 3

Animal Farm

Was Gareth Jones George Orwell's Mr Jones?

In recent years there has been growing currency for the view that George Orwell 'borrowed' Gareth Jones' surname in naming one of the main characters in his satirical allegory *Animal Farm*. The speculative idea was initially put forward by Jones' great nephew Nigel Colley in a 2004 article published on the garethjones.org website, which was later added to.

This suggested connection was highlighted in the 2019 feature film *Mr Jones*, about Jones' exposé of the famine in the Soviet Union, when Orwell and Jones are depicted as briefly meeting in a London restaurant – an event that didn't actually take place.

The underlying central thesis of *Animal Farm*, of course, is that the Russian Revolution was a disaster and exchanged one autocracy for another, with devastating consequences for ordinary people. Mr Jones, the farmer of Manor Farm, was an allegorical representation of Tsar Nicholas II, who was overthrown by the animals of his farm, who in turn represent Bolshevik and liberal revolutionaries.

The book provides a deservedly unflattering portrait of Mr Jones, who in keeping with the Tsar was depicted as an incompetent master and an alcoholic. There could therefore be no direct allegorical link between Mr Jones and Gareth Jones, whose revelations about the famine would have been applauded by Orwell. Instead, Colley implies that Orwell's decision to use Jones' surname was an act of homage to someone he may not have met, but had come to admire after reading about him.

In his article on the matter, Colley homes in on the fact that *Animal Farm* contains a section on the famine in which Orwell wrote:

'In January food fell short. The corn ration was drastically reduced, and it was announced that an extra potato ration would be issued to make up for it. Then it was discovered that the greater part of the potato crop had been frosted in the clamps, which had not been covered thickly enough. The potatoes had become soft and discoloured, and only a few were edible. For days at a time the animals had nothing to eat but chaff and mangels. Starvation seemed to stare them in the face.

It was vitally necessary to conceal this fact from the outside world. Emboldened by the collapse of the windmill [that had been meant to supply the farm with energy], the human beings were inventing fresh lies about Animal Farm. Once again it was being put about that all the animals were dying of famine and disease, and that they were continually fighting among themselves and had resorted to cannibalism and infanticide.'

In his 2010 book *Bloodlands: Europe Between Hitler and Stalin,* the American historian Timothy Snyder wrote:

'Survival was a moral as well as a physical struggle. A woman doctor wrote to a friend in June 1933 that she had not yet become a cannibal, but was "not sure that I shall not be one by the time my letter reaches you". The good people died first. Those who refused to steal or to prostitute themselves died. Those who gave food to others died. Those who refused to eat corpses died. Those who refused to kill their fellow man died. Parents who resisted cannibalism died before their children did.'

The Soviet regime printed posters declaring: 'To eat your own children is a barbarian act,' and more than 2,500 people were convicted of cannibalism during the *Holodomor*. Although depicted in the film *Mr*

Jones, in order to reflect the historical truth of the famine, no acts of cannibalism were actually witnessed by Jones during his walk through Russia and Ukraine as there is no mention of it in his notes, articles or speeches.

For Colley, the reference in *Animal Farm* to 'human beings' spreading lies about a famine is a direct reference to Jones, who was the main foreign eyewitness to the *Holodomor*. While he acknowledges that Orwell and Jones never met, he suggests that Orwell became aware of Jones' role in exposing the famine by reading Eugene Lyons' book *Assignment in Utopia*.

Lyons, who had been a member of the Moscow press corps in 1933, later wrote about the way in which Jones had been disparaged and traduced by other journalists who wanted to play down the famine to maintain their comfortable positions in the Soviet capital. Referring to the section in *Animal Farm* where 'human beings' were accused of telling lies about a non-existent famine, Colley quoted Lyons, who wrote: 'Poor Gareth Jones must have been the most surprised human being alive when the facts he so painstakingly garnered from our mouths were snowed under by our denials.' Colley continued:

'Now, consider what better name could Orwell have chosen for one of his actual human beings in *Animal Farm* than "Mr Jones"? However, Orwell uses the term human being 28 times in Animal Farm - 27 times are nothing to do with Gareth, unless of course you count this one occurrence: "The only good human being is a dead one".

But, if one considers that Orwell started writing and formulating his ideas for *Animal Farm* at about the same time as reviewing Lyons in 1938, and especially how important Lyons was to Orwell, then Gareth as a "human being" would have been to the fore in Orwell's mind.'

Colley ran his hypothesis past an Orwell scholar, noting:

'Following an email I sent to Jackie Jura of Orwelltoday.com, she thought it quite possible that Orwell had Gareth in mind, in his specific choice of surname, Mr Jones, the farmer.

In a 2004 email to myself, she wrote: "In the most recent biography – *Inside George Orwell* – by Gordon Bowker, he mentions on page 385 that one of the influences on Orwell in the writing of 1984 were the writings of Eugene Lyons ... I think that more or less clinches that Orwell was aware of Gareth Jones and what had been done to him." [i.e. the "damning Jones as a liar" episode].

In an earlier email dated January 15 2004, Ms Jura wrote: "... it struck me that Orwell HAD mentioned Gareth Jones after all in the character of Farmer Jones in Animal Farm!! Just like how the Communists had killed the Tsar and all his family, so too had the Communists just as ruthlessly and cruelly killed Gareth Jones. And so Orwell gave the Tsar character the name of Jones".'

While there is no documentary evidence or third party testimony that Orwell had Gareth Jones in mind when he decided to name his Tsar figure Mr Jones, the belief among some that he did, will undoubtedly persist.

Appendix 4

Mr Jones

Interview with Agnieszka Holland

At a packed Chapter Arts Centre in Cardiff on Friday 31 January 2020 – the day the UK left the EU – the author interviewed Agnieszka Holland, director of the film *Mr Jones*, which portrayed the events surrounding Jones' exposure of the famine in 1933, known in Ukraine as the *Holodomor*. The interview took place on stage after the film's Welsh premiere.

MS: A lot of your work has necessarily related to authoritarian regimes, particularly in your homeland of Poland. You were also working with some of the other great film directors from Poland in the Soviet-dominated period, and in the time of the struggle for the end of the repressive Stalinist regimes that were in those countries. How would you say that your style as a director was formed by those kinds of experiences and living in that kind of society?

AH: It's difficult for me to analyse it, but I think that life experience is something exceptionally helpful for the filmmaker and storyteller, because you know how complex and complicated reality is, how history is not something which ended, which is finished, which is over, but how it projects into the present and the future, and also how absolute and definite are humans' destiny, and also how the nature of humanity is quite bleak. I have this existential pessimism. I don't believe that humanity is good – I don't believe it! Anyway, it's much easier to serve evil than to serve good, and it's why also I am fascinated by characters who go against the flow, like Gareth Jones, for example. The biggest mystery for me is what makes you be a writer, and where the courage is coming from, if it's not stupidity and lack of imagination. Living in a totalitarian regime, my father was a victim of that. My grandparents and the whole family of my father died in the Holocaust in Poland. My mother was not Jewish, and she was saved as a teenager by a Jewish family that was fighting in the [Warsaw] Uprising. So I had quite a heavy parentage. And at the same time even living under the pressure of a Communist regime, there was so much energy and curiosity and the desire to learn and speak, that I became some kind of a communicator. It's why I tell very different stories if I feel that they are somehow important to me – important and/or beautiful or terrible, and in the first place, especially when I am touching history, relevant to our days.

MS: How did you come across the Gareth Jones story?

AH: Andrea Chalupa, who is an American journalist – a very active one and very political – is a descendant of Ukrainian parents, and her grandfather was a survivor of the Big Famine, the *Holodomor*. He was also an important witness who was reporting those stories after the Second World War to the world, and was also a witness to the US Congress. She had been a journalist herself when she found this story of Gareth Jones. I think she felt that he was of her point of view and her hero. So she wrote this screenplay, introducing also *Animal Farm* and George Orwell to the story, which I liked when I read the script, and which also had some personal meaning because it was the first book – *Animal Farm* – her grandfather read after the Second World War in a displaced persons camp. He and his fellow Ukrainians found out that it's about them, it's exactly what they went through in Ukraine. So they translated it into Ukrainian – it was the first foreign language to which Orwell's book was translated. So it was a mix of the personal and big history for both of us. She sent me the script. I receive quite a lot of scripts which speak about atrocities of the 20th Century, and after three big movies about the Holocaust I decided that I'd paid my tribute to that. Mostly when I receive [such a script] I just read five pages and put it aside. It can be whatever – the Armenian genocide, Rwanda, Kampuchea, and also Communist crimes – but I feel that the Communist crimes – Stalinist crimes, but not only – were not told in the scale and with the strength which is necessary to reach global public opinion, especially in the last 30 years after the fall of the Iron Curtain, it somehow vanished from our memory, and it's forgotten and forgiven. I think it's terribly unjust, not only to the victims who are nameless and voiceless, but also because it projects into the future that we cannot recognise some danger which is present or coming, like in Ukraine for example, in our days, in the last five years, because we forgot exactly what happened in this part of the world in the 20th Century.

MS: One of the extraordinary things I've discovered when researching the book I've been writing about Gareth is how, even to this day, there remains a serious controversy about whether Ukraine was singled out for special treatment [by Stalin]. There's a great book written by the academic Anne Applebaum [*Red Famine: Stalin's War on Ukraine*] which really to my mind nails it, because she has gone through an enormous amount of research material, including documents that were previously unavailable in Soviet times, and has demonstrated using statistical methods and other resource materials to show really without a doubt that Ukraine was singled out for special treatment. It wasn't obviously the only part of the Soviet Union affected by the famine.

AH: Yes, it wasn't the only one. In my opinion, and of course I cannot be a judge. I read Anne's book, I read also Timothy Snyder [author of *Bloodlands*], I read several other articles and studies. Of course there's a lot of controversy about it, like the number of victims, for example. It varies between four million and nine or ten million. It means that we cannot count five million people? It shows the character of this crime, and the secrecy and the manipulation of data, of documents, of everything, which makes it practically impossible to know for sure. It's true that there's not a document with Stalin's signature which gives the order to kill or to create the conditions for death, especially for the Ukrainians, but it cost Ukraine millions of lives, and it changed not only the spirit of the country because it was so crushing and humiliating, and the fact that it was impossible to talk about it made it like an unworked trauma, and this trauma is going through the generations. We were speaking to the young actors when we cast them. Immediately after reading one line they started to cry. They are the fifth generation of survivors. It's also very important to understand, politically speaking, that Ukraine in those times was divided between Poland and the Soviet Union. The western part was in Poland, and the eastern part, with Donbas, Donetsk etc was in the Soviet part. It means the victims have been there. In Poland there was no famine. The famine was in Stalin's territory. Millions of people vanished and the villages and little cities were practically emptied and then repopulated by people coming from Russia. Still today this conflict of mentality and culture rules the experience between the western and eastern part of Ukraine. It had incredibly deep consequences for this country, much deeper than for any other part of the Soviet Union.

MS: The part of the story that demonstrates the conflict, if you like, between truth and lies is the conflict between Gareth Jones and Walter Duranty. We know that people who were working in the Soviet Union, in Moscow, at the time, the press pack, if you like, the press pack as they might be called, tended very much – and Duranty was the main exponent of this, but others were doing the same – to play down the whole thing. I suppose that really feeds into the whole notion of what Mr Trump originally described as 'fake news' – but he was the exponent of fake news who invented the term. In terms of the 21st Century, now and as we go forward, what lessons do you think we can draw from the Gareth Jones story?

AH: When I read the script it was natural to me, immediately, that it's so relevant to our own days. The fake news, the propaganda, the manipulation, the corruption of the media, the polarisation of the country is very much the same and the lessons were similar. It means we can take lessons from the past, because we know the end of this kind of behaviour and mechanism. In our time societies became, because of political manipulation, extremely polarised, and they are cut in two halves. Today we have the day of Brexit officially, and Great Britain is divided into two camps as well, concerning this decision which can be incredibly important politically – I'm not talking about the economic consequences even, but about political consequences. They can be enormous. We cannot even imagine yet how deep they could be. The press, also for a monetary reason, is following one of those paths. They are supporting one or other political agenda and especially with social media supporting very much this kind of partisan approach, the space in between the platform, the *agora*, where public opinion can be trustful to have objective and non-partisan truth is shrinking, and I'm pretty sure that without free and objective media, democracy cannot survive. It's like a crucial fear, where you know this battle is going on. And it's what Gareth's message was. There's this conversation [in the film] between him and Ada. He says journalism is the most noble occupation because you have to report the truth. She says, 'Whose truth?' and he answered, 'There is only one truth'. Ada replied, 'You're so naive'. So it's the same, and we've seen in 1939, 1940 and 1941 and so on what happens when the media are corrupted, the governments are blind, public opinion is lazy and indifferent and there is no courage. So yes, we can take some lessons from this story.

AH: [In response to a member of the audience who asked whether she thought her film could act as a catalyst for other little-known stories from the Stalinist era to be told, Ms Holland said:] It's difficult for one film, especially not a big popular film to make the difference. I think it's step by step. I was never thinking about how widely I can reach some aim. I'm just trying to speak out, and to wake up empathy about things like that. With the Holocaust, actually, it was a similar story. After the Second World War, the survivors didn't talk and no one was really interested for decades. It was only in the late Eighties practically when it started to come to the global consciousness, with sometimes pretty kitschy TV series, like *Holocaust* for example with Meryl Streep, or with Spielberg's film *Schindler's List* – and a bit with my movie *Europa, Europa*. A few movies and a few TV series suddenly made an incredible change. For Americans or for Germans, I think it was a tremendous change. The Holocaust became the heritage of global history and of global humanity, let's say. It didn't happen with the Communist crimes for many reasons which are maybe too complicated to discuss now because it's a question of the history of entente and political history and so on, but I think that somehow, you know, it's waiting, and if you will not be in a hurry something really dangerous can happen. I was shocked a few years ago when I read about this survey that was carried out in Russia. One of the questions was, 'Who was the greatest leader in Russian history?' – and Josef Stalin won. He was number one. Most of the victims of Josef Stalin had been Russian, or Soviet citizens at least. So in every family, practically, was someone who was a witness or a victim of his crimes but, still, for the population of today, he is the greatest leader. To try to translate it to our imagination, I ask myself what would we think if the same survey were to be made in Germany today and Adolf Hitler wins? Then we understand that it's some kind of danger – the danger which is in silence and forgiveness and the lie. History can play an extremely important role in our days, and with the current situation we see it pretty well.

Afterwards, a great famine happened in China, and for the same reason Mao Zedong decided to make a big [economic] jump, to collectivise very quickly the countryside. And he starved about 40-50 million peasants in doing that. No one is talking about it. You know, I think we are now at the point where the Holocaust has lost its importance. And I was thinking that it – the Holocaust – was some kind of vaccination for humanity and that the European Union was some kind of result of this conscience and this vaccination. And this vaccine is evaporating now – it doesn't work any more. So we are not immune any more. We are somehow susceptible to the virus."

GC: [Graham Colley, a great-nephew of Gareth Jones, was also on stage at the Welsh premiere, and when asked what significance Gareth Jones had for his family, he said:] My great-grandmother, Gareth's mother, was devastated when he died. She was so devastated that she blocked it out, as did the rest of the family, for a generation. When Gareth's sister, who remained in the house in Barry, had to go into care, my mother went into the attic room, which was Gareth's room, and found a suitcase full of diaries. There was a feeling with her that Gareth's memory should be honoured. She wrote a book – *More Than a Grain of Truth* – and she was determined that Gareth's story should be told.'

GC: [Asked about the way Gareth Jones had been portrayed in the film, Mr Colley commented:] I know there's been some dispute in the family about the way he's been portrayed. I think my comment is, 'who criticises Shakespeare for his historical accuracy?' Not many people. Clearly when you're making a film it has to be dramatic – and the film has brought far more attention to the story of Gareth Jones than the documentaries or books that have been written in the past. GC: [When it was put to Mr Colley that it was strange that while Gareth Jones was a national hero in Ukraine, until pretty recently he was barely known in Wales, Mr Colley said:] I think that's for the reason I was saying earlier – the family, my great-grandmother – just wanted to shut out all memories because it was so bad for her when he was murdered in Manchuria that it was kept quiet. Although at the time, there was a lot of fuss: Lloyd George spoke about it, there was a book published, *In Search of News*, which had his collected articles from the *Western Mail*, and there was a University of Wales scholarship set up which many people donated to. There were things happening at the time, but I think the world moved on and it was forgotten about. GC: [Asked whether he thought Gareth would become more of a legend in the future, possibly as a result of the film, Mr Colley said:] I certainly hope so. Agnieszka spoke very passionately about the way that news is treated and the way that truth is treated. Yesterday, and the day before, I was over in Brussels at the European Parliament and a lot of what they feel there [about the UK's departure from the EU], and a lot of what has happened, is because of the fake news that was spread before the referendum.

Index

INDEX

335

INDEX

INDEX

INDEX

Nazi Party xiv-xv, 99
'Nepmen' 110, 309
Netter, Monsieur 261
Newark (USA) 68
New Deal 222
New Economic Policy (NEP, Soviet
    Union) 51, 110, 151, 308-10
New York (USA) xiv, 19, 46, 53-7, 59,
    64-5, 67, 70, 79, 83, 134, 173,
    203, 215-7, 226, 245-6, 270, 304,
    310
New Yorker 57
New York American 223
New York Evening Post 135
New York Herald Tribune 102, 107
New York Post 134
New York Times xvi, 126, 168, 170,
    173-5, 304-22
News Chronicle 136, 228
Newton, Basil 241
Nicaragua, Minister for (USA) 58
Night of the Long Knives 192, 273
Nizhny Novgorod (Russia) 175
NKVD 228, 244-6
Norddeutscher Lloyd (North German
    Lloyd) 71-2
Norman, Montague 'Monty' 74
North Caucasia/ North Caucasus (see
    Caucasus)
North River, New York 67
Nuremberg (Germany) 296

O'Brien, Terence 54
O'Connell Street, Dublin 205-6
O'Donnells, The 208
O'Duffy, Eoin 205
OGPU 45, 103, 106-8, 112, 123-4,
    133, 144, 153, 156, 163, 212
Omsk (Russia) 17
One's Company: A Journey to China 226
Orde, CW 240-1
Oriental Trading and Engineering
    Corporation 245
Orwell, George 228, 322-5, 327

Orwelltoday.com 325
Oslo (Norway) 28
Osumi, Mineo 230
Oswestry (England) 3
OTEC Far East 245
Outer Mongolia (see Mongolia)
Ovey, Sir Esmond 130, 132, 157
Owen, Rev Hugh 220

Pacific Ocean 227
Paddington, London 53
Palace of the Soviets, Moscow 105
Palestine 39
Pankhurst, Christabel 10
Paracelsus 251
Pares, Sir Bernard ix, 15-8, 21, 38, 46,
    77, 81, 214, 217
Paris (France) 10, 27, 61, 304-5
Paslovsky, Mr 56
Passportisation 106, 110, 149-50
Peace Preservation Corps 236, 239,
    243
Pearl Harbour naval base, Hawaii 227
Peking (now Beijing, China) 215, 231,
    235, 239, 242, 246, 248
Peking Club, China 231
People's Commissariat for Agriculture
    (see Narkomzen)
People's Commissariat for Education
    (see Narkompros)
People's Commissariat for Foreign
    Affairs (see Narkomindel)
People's Commissariat for State Farms
    (see Narkomsovkhoz)
Peter the Great 308
Petrewschtchew, Anatoli 234, 236,
    246
Petroushka 29
Philby, Kim 18, 245
Philippines 215, 230, 252
Pilsudski, Jozef 35
Pittsburgh, Pennsylvania (USA) 72
Plaid Genedlaethol Cymru (now Plaid
    Cymru) 201-2

341

INDEX

343

INDEX

345

Bibliography

Apart from an extensive archive held by the National Library of Wales at Aberystwyth and the contents of a website created by two members of Jones' family, there is not an enormous amount of literature relating specifically to Gareth Jones. However, the following sources were invaluable:

Books

Gareth Jones: A Manchukuo Incident, Margaret Siriol Colley (Nigel Colley, 1999)

Gareth Jones: Eyewitness to the Holodomor, Ray Gamache (Welsh Academic Press, 2018)

Gareth Jones: On Assignment in Nazi Germany 1933-34, Ray Gamache (Welsh Academic Press, 2021)

More Than a Grain of Truth: The Official Biography of Gareth Jones, Margaret Siriol Colley (Lume Books, 2021)

Angels in Stalin's Paradise: Western Reporters in Soviet Russia 1917-37 - Case Study of Louis Fischer and Walter Duranty, James William Crowle (Rowman & Littlefield, 1981)

Animal Farm, George Orwell (Penguin Modern Classics, 2000)

Assignment in Utopia, Eugene Lyons (Transaction Publishers, 1991)

Bloodlands: Europe Between Hitler and Stalin, Timothy Snyder (Bodley Head, 2010)

Hitler 1889-1936: Hubris, Ian Kershaw (Penguin, 2001)

My Mother's House, Lily Tobias (Honno, 2015)

Plaid Cymru: The Emergence of a Political Party, Laura McAllister (Seren, 2001)

Red Famine: Stalin's War on Ukraine, Anne Applebaum (Allen Lane, 2017)

Stalin's Apologist: Walter Duranty - The New York Times' Man in Moscow, S. J. Taylor (Oxford University Press, 2020)

The Harvest of Sorrow: Soviet Collectivisation and the Terror-Famine, Robert Conquest (Bodley Head, 2018)

Websites

garethjones.org - contains most of Jones' published articles and other useful material

library.wales/garethvaughanjones - a significant proportion of the Gareth Jones archive held by the National Library of Wales has now been digitised and can be accessed on the National Library's website

welsh academic press

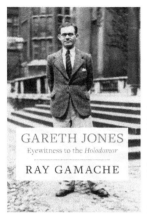

GARETH JONES
Eyewitness to the *Holodomor*

Ray Gamache

'Excellent ... serves as a warning to journalists not to be taken in by official sources and political ideology but to report what they actually learn through their own efforts.'
Prof. Maurine H. Beasley, Univ. of Maryland

'...meticulously researched book [that] returns Gareth Jones to his rightful status, as one of the most outstanding journalists of his generation'
Nigel Linsan Colley, www.garethjones.org

'Extraordinary ... Jones' articles ... caused a sensation ... Because [his] notebooks record immediate impressions and describe events as they were happening, they have an unusual freshness ... Jones' reputation has revived thanks to the Ukrainian government's broader efforts to tell the history of the famine.'
Anne Applebaum, The New York Review

978-1-86057-1220	256pp	£19.99	PB
978-1-86057-1466	256pp	£19.99	EBK

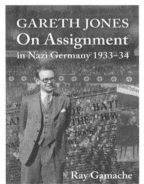

GARETH JONES
On Assignment in Nazi Germany 1933-34

Ray Gamache

'Ray Gamache dispenses with some of the myths that surround the biography of the enigmatic writer Gareth Jones, and adds substantially to the historical record of his life and times.'
Anne Applebaum

'essential reading for every student of the history of the 1930s.'
Marco Carynnyk

Since Gareth Jones's historic press conference in Berlin in 1933 when he became the first journalist to reveal the existence and extent of the *Holodomor*, his professional reputation have been the focus of a determined campaign by those who deny the famine ever happened. In this ground breaking study, Ray Gamache thoroughly examines Jones's extensive notebooks, letters, articles and speeches to provide a compelling narrative which refutes claims of Jones's Nazi sympathies, stating: 'Based on available documentation, that Jones had a deep, abiding love of Germany is obvious. However, to twist events of his life into a narrative in which his reporting of mass starvation is represented as collusion with the Nazi propaganda ministry is ultimately to deny the suffering of those Ukrainians who needlessly perished.'

978-1-86057-1480	190pp	£19.99	PB
978-1-86057-1534	190pp	£19.99	EBK

welsh academic press

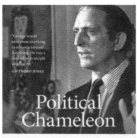

POLITICAL CHAMELEON
In Search of George Thomas

Martin Shipton

'Compelling' **Kevin McGuire**

'A brilliant book' **Guto Harri**

'I picked up this book expecting it to be a hatchet job, but it is a very fair book and a very well researched book. The problem with George Thomas is that one can write a book that is very fair and very well researched yet he still comes out of it very badly.' **Vaughan Roderick, BBC Radio Wales**

Drawing on previously unpublished material from Thomas' vast personal and political archive in the National Library of Wales, and interviews with many who knew him during his career, award-winning journalist Martin Shipton reveals the real George Thomas, the complex character behind the carefully crafted facade of the devout Christian, and discovers a number of surprising and shocking personae – including the sexual predator – of this ultimate *Political Chameleon.*

| 978-1-86057-137-4 | 304pp | £16.99 | PB |
| 978-1-86057-1381 | 304pp | £16.99 | EBK |

MORGAN JONES
Man of Conscience

Wayne David

'Wayne David deserves great credit for bringing Morgan Jones to life in this well-researched and very readable book.'
Nick Thomas-Symonds MP

'Wayne David writes of one of his predecessors as Labour MP for Caerphilly with the understanding of the political insider and the contextual knowledge of the historian.'
Professor Dai Smith

'Jones was a man of principle and pragmatism.'
Hilary Benn MP, from his Foreword

Imprisoned in Wormwood Scrubs for his pacifist beliefs during the First World War, Morgan Jones made history by becoming the first conscientious objector to be elected an MP when he won the Caerphilly by-election for Labour in 1921.

| 978-1-86057-1411 | 128pp | £16.99 | PB |
| 978-1-86057-1541 | 128pp | £16.99 | EBK |

welsh academic press

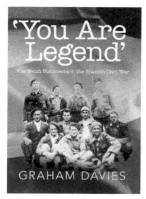

'YOU ARE LEGEND'
The Welsh Volunteers in the Spanish Civil War

Graham Davies

'*Excellent. A paean to the working men and women of Wales who went to Spain to fight in defence of the fledgling Spanish Republic.*'
Keith Jones, son of volunteer Tom Jones from Rhosllanerchrugog

'*Well researched, and using previously unpublished sources, 'You Are Legend' is recommended reading. It is important that the contribution of the large number of Welsh volunteers continues to be recognised.*'
Mary Greening, daughter of volunteer Edwin Greening of Aberdare

'*A highly readable and comprehensively researched account of the Welsh Brigaders.*'
Alan Warren, Spanish Civil War historian

Almost 200 Welshmen and women volunteered to join the International Brigade and travelled to Spain to fight fascism alongside the Republican government during the 1936-1939 Spanish Civil War. While over 150 returned home, at least 35 died during the brutal conflict. '*You Are Legend*' is their remarkable story.

| 978-1-86057-1305 | 224pp | £19.99 | PB |
| 978-1-86057-1558 | 224pp | £19.99 | EBK |

ABERFAN
Government and Disaster
(Second Edition)

Iain McLean & Martin Johnes

'*The full truth about Aberfan*'
The Guardian

'*The research is outstanding...the investigation is substantial, balanced and authoritative...this is certainly the definitive book on the subject... Meticulous.*'
John R. Davis, *Journal of Contemporary British History*

'*Excellent...thorough and sympathetic.*'
Headway 2000 (Aberfan Community Newspaper)

'*Intelligent and moving*'
Planet

Aberfan - Government & Disaster is widely recognised as the definitive study of the disaster and, following meticulous research of previously unavailable public records - kept confidential by the UK Government's 30-year rule - the authors explain how and why the disaster happened and why nobody was held responsible.

| 978-1-86057-1336 | 224pp (+16pp photo section) | £19.99 | PB |
| 978-1-86057-1459 | 224pp (+16pp photo section) | £19.99 | EBK |

Lightning Source UK Ltd.
Milton Keynes UK
UKHW021100070722
405518UK00005B/50